Implementing
The Early Years Foundation Stage:
A Handbook

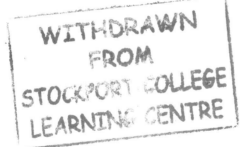

Implementing
The Early Years Foundation Stage:
A Handbook

Pat Beckley, Karen Elvidge, Helen Hendry

Open University Press

Open University Press
McGraw-Hill Education
McGraw-Hill House
Shoppenhangers Road
Maidenhead
Berkshire
England
SL6 2QL

email: enquiries@openup.co.uk
world wide web: www.openup.co.uk

and

Two Penn Plaza, New York, NY 10121-2289, USA

First published 2009

A catalogue record of this book is available from the British Library

ISBN 13: 9780335236152 (pb) 9780335236169 (hb)
ISBN 10: 0335236154 (pb) 0335236162 (hb)

Library of Congress Cataloging-in-Publication Data
CIP data has been applied for

Typeset by Aptara Inc., India
Printed in the UK by Bell and Bain Ltd., Glasgow

Fictitous names of companies, products, people, characters and/or data that may be used herein (in case studies or in examples) are not intended to represent any real individual, company, product or event.

Mixed Sources
Product group from well-managed
forests and other controlled sources
www.fsc.org Cert no. TT-COC-002769
© 1996 Forest Stewardship Council

The *McGraw·Hill* Companies

Contents

The contributors

Pat Beckley

Pat is the Academic Coordinator for the 3–7 age phase on the PGCE Primary course at Bishop Grosseteste University College, Lincoln. She has taught children in the 3–11 age range, becoming the leader in each age phase, including organizing an Early Years Unit for a number of years. As an advanced skills teacher, Pat supported colleagues and settings, leading INSET and formulating action plans. Her work used research to inform her practice in schools. This included an Advanced Diploma in Special Educational Needs with a focus on early years, an MEd based on approaches to early years literacy and participation in the Effective Early Years Project. Working with the Children's University in Hull she helped to coordinate community involvement in children's learning. She is currently completing an EdD thesis which concerns a comparison of approaches to early years literacy between Lincolnshire, England and Hedmark, Norway. Her work has included liaison with educationalists in Norway, attendance at international conferences and participation as an executive member of the national organization TACTYC (Training, Advancement and Cooperation in Teaching Young Children).

Karen Elvidge

Karen has taught children from 2.5–16 years of age in mainstream, independent and special schools including in the secure unit of a community home with education on the premises. She has a particular interest and expertise in the EYFS and has been an early years coordinator and music coordinator in a mainstream school, literacy coordinator and SENCO in independent education and an educational provider for the pre-school age group, running a private kindergarten. Karen was also the Head of the pre-preparatory department of Lincoln Cathedral School. As one of the original 12 'Letterland' advisers, Karen worked with literacy coordinators and schools to develop a multi-sensory approach to teaching phonic skills to young children. She also taught elements of the BTEC Early Years programme at Lincoln College.

The core curriculum, assessment and planning learning, and inclusion, diversity and equality formed the programmes of study for her MA in Primary Education. Karen has led in-service training in Brazil and has worked with European partners to develop a CD-Rom outlining good practice in teaching children with special educational needs.

Partnership with early years practitioners in Romania through Spurgeons has been ongoing for several years to investigate and share good practice internationally. Currently, she is the academic coordinator for the Flexi route PGCE programme at the Bishop Grosseteste University College Lincoln, and the East Midlands regional coordinator for Multiverse. She is undertaking research into the effective use of ICT in the EYFS at the University College.

Helen Hendry

Helen is an early years specialist with particular interests in communication, language and literacy, inclusion, English as an additional language (EAL) and social and emotional aspects of learning. She has taught in all age groups in the primary phase and has managed the Foundation Stage departments of three primary schools in both rural and urban locations. She has worked as a lead Foundation Stage practitioner and profile moderator in Cornwall and has most recently supported and advised early years practitioners in a range of settings including the private, voluntary and independent sector, childminders, maintained primary and nursery schools and children's centres in Slough. Now a Senior Lecturer in ITT at Bishop Grosseteste University College Lincoln, she has completed an MEd, including research into peer collaboration in 3-year-olds' play and the preparation of ITT students for responding to the needs of pupils with EAL.

Preface

This book will interest those involved in the care and education of young children aged from birth to five years. Many changes are taking place in early years provision, including the Early Years Foundation Stage framework, which became statutory in 2008. Our aim is to provide strategies to aid its implementation, with case studies of effective practice, examples of plans and formats for practical use and a rationale for the work, supported by theories of learning and research findings.

The book follows the Early Years Foundation Stage format and is based on its practical application in early years settings. It draws on the Every Child Matters agenda, with the ethos of the book reflecting the values of ensuring each child is valued and respected as a unique individual, in which positive relationships and enabling environments create an atmosphere where children can thrive. These sentiments are interconnected and form the foundation for learning and development to take place.

Significant changes are occurring for our early years provision yet the successful, creative and stimulating ways in which they are implemented emphasize the crucial nature of the roles of practitioners working in early years settings and provision.

Pat Beckley, Karen Elvidge, Helen Hendry

Acknowledgements

We would like to thank Nick Redfern, Cathryn Jones, Katrina Lyons, all the children in the EYFS at Waddington Redwood Primary School and their parents and carers for allowing us to use their photographs, giving up their time and generally supporting this publication.

We would all like to thank our families and colleagues for their support and tolerance during the writing of this book.

Definition of terms

Parent: For the purpose of this publication the terms parent, parents or parents and carers will be used interchangeably to relate to anyone who is responsible for a child in a parental role, whether this is for example another family member, step-parent, foster carer or guardian.

Family: For the purpose of this publication the term family is used to refer to the main caring network of adult(s) in the child's home, including extended and single-parent families and other carers.

Practitioners, staff members, providers, early years educators: These terms have been used interchangeably to represent any adult working to deliver the EYFS with children from birth to 5. Where a specific point is made that relates in particular to the circumstances of **childminders** or qualified **teachers** these words are used.

Setting: This term is used to refer to any organization that delivers the EYFS, including childminders, private, voluntary and independent settings and maintained schools. Where a specific point is made in relation to **home-based** or **school-based** provision these words are used.

Child: This term is used to refer to any child within the birth-5 age range. Where points are made that relate to a specific age range the age will be given or qualified with another term such as toddler or baby.

Foreword

Providing high-quality educational contexts for our youngest children is, arguably, one of the most important social priorities for governments and educationalists alike. Thankfully, I believe this has been increasingly accepted and recognized by the nation's leaders and the education profession. Supporting all children in order that they will have the best start in life and, eventually, fulfil their potential, has been strengthened through several initiatives and guidance documents for early years educators and carers.

The most recent *Statutory Framework for the Early Years Foundation Stage* builds on previous frameworks such as the *Curriculum Guidance for the Foundation Stage*, the *Birth to Three Matters* framework and the *National Standards for Under 8s Daycare and Childminding*.

However, the number and speed with which new initiatives have been introduced over recent years has made significant demands on practitioners, trainers and students alike. At this early point in the implementation of EYFS in all early years settings, a book that will support all those committed to providing the high-quality provision the framework aims to support is most welcome.

An essential for such a book is that it should be written by those with experience, commitment, and at the cutting edge of recent research in the field of child development and early years education. Between them, the three writers offer all of the above attributes. Under the careful guidance and effective team work of the authors of this book, PGCE trainees at Bishop Grosseteste University College, Lincoln receive the highest quality training and become confident, well-educated and skilled newly qualified teachers, as confirmed by feedback from head teachers who appoint them to posts in their schools.

The strength of this team work has been a key part in making this book a success and the authors have drawn on the high-quality sessions they have been teaching as part of the PGCE programme over the last twelve months. I know from my work with this team of early years tutors that readers will find the book as useful as the trainees do. It will be a major contribution to the fulfilment of the aims of EYFS and Every Child Matters.

Judith Laurie
Head of Department PGCE/GTP Primary
Bishop Grosseteste University College Lincoln

Introduction

Implementing the Early Years Foundation Stage: A Handbook has been designed to support those working with early years children and provide professional guidelines for practitioners to design and implement planning for the children in their care. The framework became statutory in September 2008 and provides a basis to develop appropriate provision for young children.

Historical perspective

A brief outline of past legislation can provide some understanding of the deliberations taken place regarding the welfare of young children. In 1870 members of the Houses of Parliament debated the compulsory school starting age. It was argued, 'Five was a tender age for compulsory attendance' or 'It was never too early to inculcate habits of decency, cleanliness and order' (Anning 1991: 3). However, the importance of earning a living was considered. Starting school early and finishing at an early age to gain employment was seen as a solution. 'In 1876 children from three years old could be taken to "babies" rooms which offered training in alphabet recitation, picture recognition and marching to music' (Anning 1991: 3). The Hadow Report (1931) marked a change in emphasis, stating that children should be given experiences and activity rather than be perceived as 'empty vessels' to store facts.

The Plowden Report (CACE 1967) noted that young children would progress further if they had access to nursery education, with beneficial effects following concerns regarding social deprivation. The Bullock Report (1975) advocated a number of measures for raising standards and highlighted the importance of home/school links. It also suggested a monitoring of standards and noted concern over aspects of continuity for children. Research focusing on children's transition from a pre-school unit to a Reception class by Cleave *et al.* (1982) revealed differences between the two settings in the main types of activity available to the children and in the organization delivered.

The 1988 Education Reform Act and the introduction of the National Curriculum influenced early years provision in some settings through the 'top-down' pressure perceived from the Key Stage 1 curriculum. The Children Act in 1989 noted the need to have joint services for young children between education and social service departments.

Starting with Quality, a report commissioned by the DES in 1990 (Rumboldt 1990) gave a strong impetus to changes for early years provision. It advocated a national frame-work for guidelines. In 1996 *Nursery Education: Desirable Outcomes for Children's Learning on Entering Compulsory Education* was published (SCAA 1996), which gave guidelines for six curriculum areas including *personal and social development, language and literacy, mathematical development, knowledge and understanding of the world, creative development* and *physical development*. In 2000 The *Curriculum Guidance for the Foundation Stage* was published (QCA/DfEE 2000), which kept six areas of learning but included 'stepping stones' for younger children's progress. In 2002 the Foundation Stage was recognized as part of the National Curriculum, and *Birth to Three Matters* was published (Sure Start 2002), which provided a framework of guidelines for those working with children aged from birth to three. This included a basis of four aspects: The Strong Child, The Skilful Communicator, The Competent Learner and The Healthy Child.

The National Strategy website states: 'The Early Years Foundation Stage brings together: *Curriculum Guidelines for the Foundation Stage* (2000), the *Birth to Three Matters* (2002) framework and the *National Standards for the Under 8s Daycare and Childminding* (2003), building a coherent and flexible approach to care and learning.'

Every Child Matters

The Every Child Matters agenda (DfES 2003) underpins the Early Years Foundation Stage framework. It states: 'The vision is to create a joined-up system of health, family support, childcare and education services so that all children get the best start possi-ble in the vital early years' (DfES 2003: 2). It followed the Lord Laming enquiry into the death of Victoria Climbie whose abuse by her carers had been missed by agen-cies. *Every Child Matters: Change for Children* was linked to five strands promoting the outcomes:

- *Be healthy;*
- *Stay safe;*
- *Enjoy and achieve;*
- *Make a positive contribution;*
- *Achieve economic well-being.*

and forms the basis of the Unique Child, which is central to the planning for EYFS provision.

The Early Years Foundation Stage

According to a government response to queries regarding the framework (December 2008), 'The Early Years Foundation Stage is designed to support all playgroups, nurseries, kindergartens and childminders, to ensure that every child in their care is able to benefit

Figure 1 The achievements of all children are celebrated.

from the advantages that good quality and consistent care provides. It offers a play-based framework to support early learning and care for all children from birth to five.'

What is in the EYFS? It is a framework that forms a foundation for children's learning and development for the future, while highlighting the importance of appreciating that each child is unique. As a statutory framework children have access to guidelines which are common to all and can be transferred from a variety of providers and settings. It provides a basis for shared dialogue between practitioners and all those involved with children aged between birth and five years.

There has been some debate regarding the introduction of the Early Years Foundation Stage, with concern over the combination of two existing age phases, birth to 3 and 3–5, the amount designated to a play-based approach in the constraints of the framework and queries regarding the notion of professionalism where practitioners receive a standard framework. However, research was used to inform the framework.

Research

Why and how has the EYFS been developed? With the growth of early years provision much research has focused on achieving quality of provision. There is debate regarding the nature of such quality, although few doubt the importance of a play-based framework for young children. *The Effective Provision of Pre-School Education* (Sylva *et al.* 2004) sought to make recommendations to promote the nature of the provision for young children. It stated:

- Good quality pre-school experiences support children's social and educational development.
- Good quality provision can be found across all types of early years settings, with integrated centres that offer combined education and childcare and nursery schools delivering the best results.
- Learning at home with parents, combined with high-quality pre-school education, makes a positive difference to children's social and intellectual development.
- Disadvantaged children in particular benefit significantly from good quality pre-school experiences.

The Minister for Sure Start, Catherine Ashton, stated:
'We are at the beginning of a radical change in the way we deliver services for children and families to ensure all children get a sure start in life.'

(Press release, March 2003)

Findings from *Key Elements of Effective Practice* (DCSF 2007d), based on research, highlighted aspects of practice including key elements of early years expertise to implement the principles for early years education and care. It stated that 'through initial and ongoing training and development, practitioners need to develop, demonstrate and continuously improve their

- relationships with both children and adults;
- understanding of the individual and diverse ways that children learn and develop;
- knowledge and understanding in order to actively support and extend children's learning in and across all areas and aspects of learning and development;
- practice in meeting all children's needs, learning styles and interests;
- work with parents, carers and the wider community;
- work with other professionals in and beyond the setting.

(DCSF 2007d)

Provision

Implementing the Early Years Foundation Stage: A Handbook provides an overview of the principles of the framework and practical strategies to support work in a range of settings. It can be used as a reference for those involved in the study of aspects of early years provision. The book aims to

- support those involved in the implementation of the new Early Years Foundation Stage guidelines;

- give an understanding of the rationale and themes in the document;
- provide practical guidelines to aid practice within the settings;
- foster further understanding of EYFS for those involved with related aspects, for example practitioners working in other key stages, HE, FE, advisory capacity;
- be a source of reference for students and trainees working in this area;
- promote good practice by helping practitioners to develop their practice and raise their standards of achievement in their work;
- provide guidelines for interested parents, carers, childminders and so on;
- make links between the EYFS curriculum and current research, theory and practice, including national initiatives and international perspectives.

The book covers the main outline of the *Early Years Foundation Stage* document, providing a discussion of the rationale for the aspects, with guidelines and suggestions of activities to support practitioners who work with the age phase. It consists of five parts. The parts cover the four themes of the Early Years Foundation Stage:

- A Unique Child
- Positive Relationships
- Enabling Environments
- Learning and Development

The final part consists of the six areas of learning and development with practical suggestions for implementation.

Part 1

A Unique Child

1 Child development

This chapter covers consideration of the multiple approaches and theories regarding child development. It provides a knowledge and understanding of some of the principles underpinning notions of child development. It recognizes a range of theoretical perspectives of child development and builds an appreciation between theory and practice. It explains how aspects of child development are interrelated and discusses the importance of the social context on individual development. Discussion is incorporated regarding the child as a competent learner and skilful communicator. Multiple approaches to child development include physical, cognitive, social and emotional, linguistic and spiritual development.

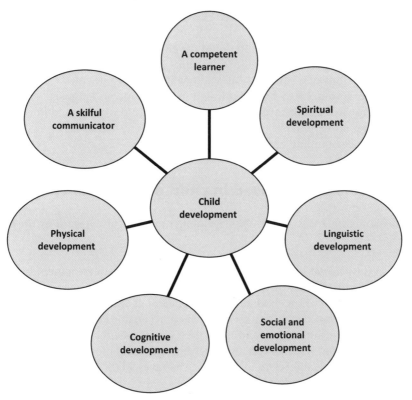

Multiple approaches to child development

Each theme in the Unique Child section is linked to the EYFS principle 'Every child is a competent learner from birth who can be resilient, capable, confident and self-assured.' The EYFS framework organizes information regarding child development into six broad phases of development although it is emphasized that each child's progress is unique to the child and developments occur at different rates. The six phases are birth to three months, eight to 20 months, 16–26 months, 22–36 months, 30–50 months and 40–60 months. Consideration is given to the overlapping nature of broad phases of development.

What does the notion of child development cover?

According to the EYFS framework, 'Babies and children develop in individual ways and at varying rates. Every area of development – physical, cognitive, linguistic, spiritual, social and emotional, is equally important.'

Child development is concerned with a number of factors including:

- awareness of differing theories and research findings regarding child development;
- consideration of ways in which the child is brought up and the rationale for it;
- thinking about how a child might develop;
- reflections on the effect of relationships with peers and adults for the child;
- evaluations of what constitutes an enabling environment;
- cultural values transmitted through such activities as language;
- a knowledge of life events of the individual child which could impact on his or her development;
- an understanding of the child as being unique.

What factors are involved in child development?

There are many influences on a child's development and theories regarding the process, including:

- *Developmental theory* – theories concerned with the development of children from birth to maturity.
- *Construction* – how children construct meanings and make sense of their world.
- *Social construction* – how social interactions enable children to develop their knowledge and understanding of their environment and their place in it.
- *Relationships* – which can affect development and motivation.
- *Growth* – usually refers to physical changves, such as increasing height or weight.
- *Childhood* – an arbitrary division in the sequence of human development.
- *Heredity* – the transmission of characteristics from parents to their children.

- *Interactions with the environment and others* – which can actively influence the developing networks of the brain.

There are differing views concerning child development. It could be viewed as a combination of genetic endowment and the environment in which the child is placed. The way in which the child constructs meanings could also influence how the world is perceived and physical development, with social interactions forming a powerful factor.

What influences could affect development?

Throughout the time spent in the early years setting there are issues that might affect a child. Parents' or key adults' views concerning how to care for children, show affection, praise, respect or neglect a child could be crucial. Other relationships the child has could also be a factor, for example the collaboration with friends, number of siblings and security in close relationships. Significant changes in family circumstances, such as birth, deaths or separation, could also have an impact on development. Other factors could include health, the support of the community and the quality of early years provision.

Child development is a complex process which involves the child acquiring the cultural rules, attitudes, values and social skills necessary for integration into a wide range of activities and organizations, such as an early years setting, the school, a place of worship or a friend's home. The socialization process involves the child in social learning, play, imitation and observation of modelled behaviour through interaction with parents, adults and other children and learning and reflecting on the experiences gained.

The transition between home and early years setting is a significant step in the young child's life. This can be promoted through a child's active learning or 'play'. There are many definitions of play and different explanations for using play. The classical theories of play include surplus energy theory, relaxation theory, practise theory and recapitulation theory. The surplus energy theory concerns the release of excess energy in the form of aimless play activity. In the relaxation theory play is perceived as a means to regain energy, for example a short break to exercise before formal work continues. The practice theory describes the way in which children practise the roles they might carry out in later life, for example through role play as participants at a hospital. The recapitulation theory regards the idea that children rehearse activities such as chasing.

In the early years children can construct their own knowledge and understanding through interactions with others and their environment through play.

Cultural development

Culture is transmitted through children's play in language used and the way the environment is organized. Special rules apply in a variety of social areas, such as at home or in the setting. A child's toy in one culture could be a serious ritual object in another.

Children create meaningful contexts to play in and construct social worlds. They create worlds of imagination and fantasy. Children can set up and direct the created worlds in which a leader and followers emerge. There are politics of play with rule setting. Children know the rules they devise themselves and those organized by adults. There could be differing systems operating as children respond to boundaries set between their peers, in a setting or at home.

Physical development

Physical development can be broken down into two types:

> Gross motor skills involve the use of large muscles through activities such as climbing, running, balancing and pulling. Children use their whole body in such activities as climbing, riding bikes, building or using pieces of equipment in a directed approach or independently.

> Fine motor skills relate to the coordination of hand and eye movements through activities such as cutting and pasting, working puzzles, table games, drawing and painting, water play and so on. Precision grows through constant experience and practice. These activities are persistent and repetitive, and they can be readily incorporated into play activities.

Appropriate opportunities and materials are necessary for different types of physical development to take place. Play of this nature helps increase self-confidence and autonomy as well as promoting physical health and feelings of well-being.

Consideration could be given to mobility and movement, such as crawling, sitting, standing, walking, climbing and the use of gross motor skills and fine motor skills. How does the child learn to walk, run, catch, climb, throw, roll, fall and swim?

Cognitive development

Cognitive development is concerned with the child as 'knower', how the child thinks, learns, acquires concepts, remembers, understands relationships and solves problems. The child is actively trying to 'make sense of the world' or construct a meaningful picture of the world through the senses of sight, touch, smell, taste and hearing. Theorists include Piaget, Vygotsky, Bruner and Kohlberg.

Piaget (1896–1980)

Birth to 2 years: Sensori-motor

The child uses extensive trial and error movements and develops bodily control and hand–eye coordination. The perceptual field is organized into objects having permanent identity under varying conditions. The child learns to differentiate him/herself from and relate to an external world of objects and events. There is a beginning of symbolic thought (mental operations), for example remembering, anticipating, pretending. Motor actions show reversibility, such as hiding and retrieving an object.

2–4 years: Pre-operational

This concerns the development of mental imagery. It is believed that, through play, a child is able to represent and organize experiences. Language gradually takes over mental operations from motor and visual imagery, especially during social play and when communicating. Language and thinking emphasizes 'egocentricity'. Thought is irrational, inconsistent and closely linked to the child's own needs and feelings. Reality is seen from the child's point of view.

4–7 years: Intuitive

The child's perceptions dominate thinking, which shows a lack of reversibility as a result. Thinking moves towards stability and reversibility and there is a transitional stage where judgements are correct in some cases.

7–11 years: Concrete operational

This stage is concerned with concrete materials, such as classifying or forming a series. These systematic, logical structures or 'operations' gradually replace global inconsistent actions of the previous stage. Concepts are organized into classificatory systems, for example dogs, cats or adults. Operations with concrete materials present can be imagined.

11–16 years: Formal operational

Operations on symbols and ideas can be carried out mentally. The child no longer needs to deal with objects directly. The child can move away from the actual and consider the possible. Formal operations involve propositions, hypotheses, logical relationships and contradictions. The child can formulate and test out hypotheses and is capable of considering variables and discovering general laws and principles.

Vygotsky (1896–1934)

Vygotsky stressed the importance of social interaction to promote children's development. Young children are encouraged to be active learners benefiting from first-hand learning. Sometime, by interacting with someone who is more skilful, the child can be encouraged to achieve at the next level. The difference between what is possible unaided and what is possible with support is called the Zone of Proximal Development (ZPD). The adult (expert) has an engineered conversation with the child (novice) in which the adult constructs easy questions that the child answers and through the process of answering the questions the child is able to make appropriate learning connections and understand the next step or steps in learning. Vygostsky claimed there was a gap between a child's actual development and their potential development. This would be followed by internalization where a child would reflect upon what was discovered.

Bruner (1915–)

Bruner suggests that humans can learn without any accompanying observable behaviour. He recognized that cognitive growth resulted from the environment and experiences, with internal action occurring to process the information.

Bruner identified three modes of representation, corresponding to these developmental stages used to make meaning:

- Enactive representation – physical amplification.
- Iconic representation – sensory amplification.
- Symbolic representation – intellectual amplification.

While some theorists believe children progress through a series of stages, others consider that they build on their experiences and interactions to develop their understandings.

Social and emotional development

Social and emotional development are inextricably linked. The word 'emotion' in psychology refers to the 'feeling' or 'affective' component of behaviour. The term incorporates such emotions as fear, anger, rage, liking, love and desire. They may be divided into two broad groups – those which are pleasant and those that are unpleasant. Emotional states involve physiological reactions such as a pounding heart, 'butterflies', muscle tension or sickness. Observed emotions include facial expressions, body posture, speech and action, for example to run away. Children can learn to construct their world through social interactions and communication, gaining knowledge and understanding of their surroundings and an awareness of their standing within it.

Linguistic development

Linguistics, or the scientific study of language, has a variety of forms and is significant for developing our understanding and making sense of the world. Through non-verbal communication, spoken language and literacy we can reflect and internalize on our learning and use communication to 'scaffold' our understanding. Linguistic activities should permeate throughout the early years environment. Bruner believed it was important for adults to 'scaffold' or help to develop children's language through interaction.

Spiritual development

This refers to the development of spiritual and ethical behaviour in the child and is linked to the child's growing awareness of what is acceptable and what is unacceptable behaviour. The way in which ethical issues are handled may have consequences for the individual's conscience. A growing understanding of complex issues can develop, for example right and wrong, injustice, or truthfulness.

Kohlberg (1927–87)

Kohlberg devised a theory of moral development where morality could be viewed in stages from 1 to 6 in sequence of higher order reasoning from Stage 1, where actions are concerned with outcomes including avoiding punishment to Stage 6, where there are complex moral principles.

A competent learner

Babies learn as an ongoing development in the growing awareness of the world in which they live, focusing on their surroundings and the people close to them. Through exploration and discovery they learn to make sense of the world and use their growing knowledge to expand their achievements based on what they can do. This play helps children to build foundations and construct their learning. Language and interactions with those around them promotes understanding and knowledge about their world, communicates values and beliefs, and encourages the thinking skills that help to foster deeper cognitive development.

Case study

In a nursery setting children and parents/carers were welcomed as they entered the provision. Discussions were shared concerning events that had happened since they last met. Individual children eagerly responded to the activities available and knew the routines of the setting, which enabled them to feel secure and ready to progress in their learning. They met their key person, practised and consolidated learning a skill in a small group, found their names, shared news with their friends, and determined their learning for the session, using photographs to plan their time. From this secure and safe beginning they were able to extend their learning through exploration and investigation, accessing resources and materials throughout the provision.

A skilful communicator

From the earliest age babies respond to others through communication such as eye contact, bodily movements and sounds made, including bubbling, cooing, gurgling and crying. They develop their understanding using their senses and learning styles. This can be encouraged by caring relationships that give individuals the confidence and self-esteem to build on their knowledge, take risks in their learning and explore, investigate and discover.

Case study

A baby cooed and smiled at her father. Father smiled and responded, laughing at the articles around them including a picture book, a flower and some fruit on the table. Baby copied father's modelled expressions, delighting in their shared communication.

Research regarding child development is ongoing and new insights into how children develop influence practice and perceptions. Bowlby's Attachment Theory (Bowlby 1953) emphasized the importance of the relationship between the child and an adult. This has implications for early years provision: it is important that children feel secure with the key adults in their lives in order that they can develop and progress happily. Recent research on babies and young children has provided evidence that very young children can recognize familiar faces and respond to stimuli around them. Our perceptions regarding child development change as further research reveals new understandings of how children develop and learn. Early years provision can have great impact on children's constructions and meanings of their world and the social interactions within them to enable them to build on their prior learning and progress. Waller argues: 'There are multiple and diverse childhoods and in order to study childhood one has to consider a range of perspectives' (2005: 59).

Reflections

- How do you ensure you are supporting the needs of each child?
- Are some children given more attention than others?
- Do you cater for different learning styles, interests and strengths?
- How can children construct their own understandings in the provision provided?

2   Inclusive Practice

This chapter enables practitioners to consider the distinctive characteristics of an inclusive setting in which the diversity of the staff team and of the children enriches the provision.

When this chapter has been studied, practitioners should reflect upon their own provision so that children who attend the setting and children who will attend the setting in the future benefit from high-quality, inclusive provision that personalizes learning experiences to meet the needs of the children.

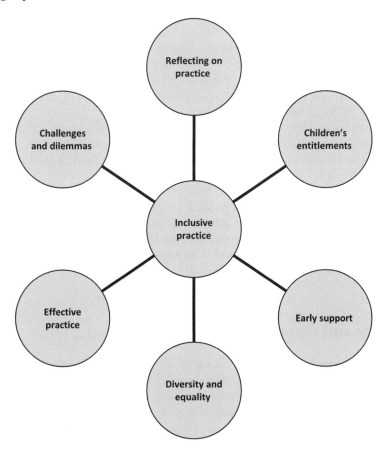

Elements of inclusion, diversity and equality

Children's Entitlements

The SEN Code of Practice (DfES 2001) brought together the key principles of support for children with special needs and support for children with disabilities. This was further enhanced by the *Every Child Matters* (DfES 2003) outcomes of staying safe, being healthy, enjoying and achieving, making a positive contribution and achieving economic well-being. Fundamentally, this legislation pivots on a principle of ensuring high standards of care and high expectations for all children outside the family home. Practitioners must ensure progress in learning by developing positive relationships with all children and their parents and carers, based on non-judgemental mutual respect with regard to ethnicity, culture or religion, home language, family background, gender and ability.

Some children attend more than one setting or have an additional carer. Effective communication systems are essential between the various practitioners, carers and parents. The recent development of common terms of reference between agencies and a common assessment framework have been designed to support multi-agency working. Through listening, as well as advising, practitioners must have high expectations of every child.

Everyone is a product of their own personal circumstances and it is important for practitioners to recognize the personal history that has shaped their own personal prejudices and stereotypical reactions. These could be described as accepting 'people like us', and rejecting 'people like them'. Practitioners must also have a statistical awareness of how children from a depressed socio-economic background need additional support to overcome potential barriers to learning.

Learning opportunities should be planned and informed from observations of what each child can do, identifying the next small steps in learning.

Policies and procedures for the safe and efficient management of settings are required by law. A list of records required is included in Appendix A.

Children have a legal entitlement to be treated fairly with regard to race, religion and ability. Parents are entitled to choose a setting that will enable their children to communicate in their first language. All settings are expected to have a sufficient grasp of English to be able to summon emergency help or read instructions such as those on administering medicines or related to food allergies. Settings should also develop the children's ability to communicate in English.

Diversity and Equality

All children are special and have a variety of needs to be met. Some children's needs are more specific. Historically, the only way to elicit help and support for children with learning difficulties and disabilities has been to categorize them by their needs. From 1921 a **medical deficit model** of excluding from schools children who were diagnosed as having disabling conditions effectively ostracized them from society. Although categories of need diminished over time, it was rare to find children with special educational needs in mainstream schools and settings before 1978 when discussions about inclusion began in earnest. Fear of integrating children into settings and class-rooms persisted, with a view that mainstream provision could not meet the needs of the children.

Research into inclusive learning initially reflected society's opinion that children with disabilities were educationally sub-normal and often that a child with a physical disability must also be mentally defective. This view was fanned by the need to label a child's needs in order to obtain a statement. The statement defined an amount of money for special equipment or human resources to meet the child's needs.

Under *Every Child Matters* (DfES 2003) and the Children Act (DfES 2004) children with special needs are entitled to be included in mainstream provision and to have their identified needs met. There remain about 2 per cent of all children with complex needs who benefit from learning in special schools and settings.

Every child is entitled to learn and make progress, even if the rate of progress is inhibited by the child's particular needs. The skill of the practitioner is to identify what each child can do and set learning opportunities based on observations of the child's prior achievement, interests and personal strengths.

Before a child with special needs enters the setting, it is important to spend time with his or her parents and carers to find out how needs are met at home. Transition points in a child's learning journey are important and should be planned for. Where a child has identified needs, the transition from home to setting and EYFS setting to mainstream education should be planned for well in advance.

Case study

James had meningitis at 2 years of age which damaged his hearing. He was given a cochlear implant which looked like a plastic disc connected to his hearing system to give him an amount of hearing in one ear. There had been a delay in picking up his hearing loss which meant that the processor needed to be adjusted gradually to introduce sounds to a child who had been deaf. His mother had learned British sign language (BSL) signing at night school to help him to learn to communicate. James was due to enter the setting with a signing assistant in September. In July, his new key worker made an appointment to visit him at home to gain an insight into changes that the family had made at home to accommodate his needs. The first innovation seen in the home was that when the doorbell was pressed, the lights in the house flashed on and off. The mother explained that James had been bemused by the fact that every time she went to the door, someone was outside waiting to come in but when he went to the door, no one was on the other side of the glass. The practitioner thought about the auditory cues in the setting. For example, a double handclap signified 'stop and look this way'. The use of the light flashing on and off could be used for all of the children as well as an auditory cue. James's mother told the practitioner that he startled easily if anyone suddenly tapped him to gain attention. The practitioner had not considered the need to stand in front of him to gain eye contact before trying to communicate with James. The practitioner asked how to sign 'Mummy', 'James', 'Good morning' and toileting signs. At home, the television was adapted to receive a signing assistant narrating the gist of the programme.

After the visit, the practitioner had a clearer understanding of James's needs and had an opportunity to meet him and his mother away from the bustle of the setting. Consideration needed to be given to how he would develop spatial awareness of other children in the outdoor area, how the social aspect of his development would be affected by having a constant signing companion and adjustments to the setting needed to meet his needs.

Notice that the practitioner's intention was to learn from the parent with the expert knowledge about her child's needs and how these could be met. The practitioner used familiar ideas from home to communicate with the child. All staff at the setting were made aware of the need to stand in front of James to communicate with him and to avoid startling him by tapping him to gain attention. The practitioner started a home/school liaison notebook so that the parents and the setting could communicate with each other when necessary. Discussions took place with the signing assistant who was inducted into the setting before James's September start. All of the children learned some basic signs so that James would feel included. James ensured that he was involved in the various activities on offer, supported by his assistant. When possible, the assistant stepped back to allow James to play and communicate independently.

It is not only children with special needs who need additional support and personalized learning. Children from diverse backgrounds enrich the setting with the variety of cultural mores and traditions from their life outside school. Traditions are not static but are constantly 'changing and fusing', merging home tradition with the regional traditions in which families live. This means that in areas where most people share a similar ethnicity, cultural links may be stronger, although 'people identify with different aspects of their heritage in different situations' (QCA 2006). While it is impossible to describe the background of every child, and it would be wrong to assume that all families from a particular culture or ethnic background subscribe to one way of living, it is important for providers to have an awareness of some cultural mores and values that may affect the behaviour of the children in their care.

Case study

Daya has very recently entered Britain with her parents who have left Zimbabwe under difficult circumstances. Cholera and lack of basic facilities have meant that Daya's parents are tired, shocked and depressed. The key worker has tried to communicate with the parents and has needed support from the Ethnic Minority Advisory Service to translate their needs and the support required for Daya such as her likes and dislikes and how she communicates her physical needs.

The key worker researched information about Bulawayo, the town where Daya was born, and displayed pictures of the mountains that were familiar to Daya in addition to the images of children from a variety of cultures displayed in the setting. With support from the Ethnic Minority Advisory Service, the key worker also displayed a welcome greeting in the family's first language with the greetings from other countries. The key worker established that Daya had no known food allergies or medical needs.

The key worker became the link between the parents and the other agencies supporting the family. The family were encouraged to continue their first language at home. The key worker chose another child to be a buddy for Daya. The children quickly learned to communicate with Daya. Within six weeks she was able to understand basic words in English. Understanding developed before she began to speak English.

Daya became tired quickly, partly due to her need to concentrate hard to understand instructions and partly due to her unfamiliar context. She made use of a quiet area, relaxing on the cushions and closing her eyes when she needed a break.

The staff team were aware of her lack of English and her lack of familiarity with local settings such as the park and the town. They used visual prompts where possible to introduce key vocabulary to the child. It was important to help the parents to mix with other parents from the setting to prevent social exclusion.

Asylum seekers have often left their home country in a hurry. The experiences and approaches to learning that are offered in the setting may not be familiar to the parents who were raised in a completely different community. The parents may be in need of counselling and support to cope with the trauma of this upheaval and an education system that is based on different values. For many, the extended family may not be in England and may still be in danger. The children will need to be encouraged to continue their first language with native speakers in order to consolidate their knowledge of grammar in one language. Research shows that it is possible for a young child to speak one language at home and a completely different language in the setting provided that visual prompts are in place and the same adults speak their different languages consistently. Language difficulties occur when parents with little knowledge of English try to speak to the child only in an incorrect form of English. However, it is easy to underestimate the task that Daya faces in the new setting. Having learned her first language, she must quickly grasp the new language in order to make the same progress as her peers. Her learning curve is very steep and is dependent on her making the huge effort to engage in the learning process. Her most significant tool for catching up, her first language, is not available to her at this critical time. She needs to become competent in English because most of the teaching in school is dialogic and based on learning using literacy skills.

The task she faces is described by South (1999):

- to progress from a radically different starting point from other children;
- to learn a new language;

- to learn the curriculum in a new language;
- to acquire the appropriate social skills;
- to accommodate the new language, values, culture and expectations alongside the existing ones she has learned at home.

It will be important to listen to the parents' cultural and religious requirements.

Case study

Ahmed is from a Muslim background and from a country in which Christians perform menial tasks. The family have no concept of a multicultural society. There is an expectation that he needs to perform a set of cleansing rituals if he breaks wind. In his previous community, he squatted to urinate, and is learning to sit on an English toilet rather than stand at a urinal. The toilets from the home tradition are not the same as the toilets in an English home. During Ramadan his parents, who are strict Muslims, do not eat or drink between sunrise and sunset although they allow their children to take sips of water and enough food to satisfy hunger. Their religious book is the Quoran, which should never be placed on the floor. It should be kept on a high shelf. Women who are menstruating and therefore considered unclean are not allowed to touch the Quoran or enter a mosque. Daily prayers are at prescribed times, facing West. Ahmed's parents require him to wear a crocheted cap at all times and to keep arms and legs covered. He is not allowed to dance or listen to music. Within his home culture, he is automatically of higher status than girls and his parents, whose marriage was arranged, have strong views about him dressing and undressing within the setting. After he is collected from the setting, Ahmed attends the mosque with his father, where he is beginning to receive additional teaching in a language that is read from right to left.

In order to make progress in the setting, practitioners need to be aware of Ahmed's personal circumstances and individual needs. His experience of food will be different and story settings from the English culture may be unfamiliar to him. The practitioner needs to listen to his parents' views about his care. When introducing a story, for example about a strawberry tart, Ahmed needs to experience a strawberry tart in order to understand what the story is about. He needs to taste its sweetness, feel its stickiness and explore its depths with his tongue while being given the key vocabulary, 'strawberry tart'. This may mean taking him to one side to enculture him into the experience before sharing the book with his group. At the mention of 'strawberry tart', he will pick up the key words with an understanding of the meaning. This positive listening experience will encourage him to persevere with the tricky job of learning an additional language.

The setting also included several children from the Gypsy Roma Traveller (GRT) community.

Children from Gypsy Roma and Traveller backgrounds sometimes find conventional settings puzzling because the provider allows the children to eat and play indoors. Some **GRT** families consider this to be dirty as their traditions are firmly based on Hindu principles. Food is prepared outside; meat and vegetables are prepared and served in separate dishes. Traditionally, the children are encouraged to play outside, keeping the interior of the house or trailer immaculately clean. Pets are not allowed indoors. Parents may seem very young as traditionally children are encouraged to marry as soon as they begin to show interest in the opposite sex. Strict ethics apply. Some parents may have had a poor experience of school and may have left with limited literacy skills with which to communicate in writing. There may even be a general aura of mistrust that will need to be overcome.

Early Support

Key points that come out of the case studies above include the early identification of the needs of each child whether these relate to learning difficulties, disabilities, ethnicity, or whether the child is gifted and talented. It is essential to meet the personalized needs of all of the children.

Where applicable, practitioners work through the steps of the SEN Code of Practice (DfES 2001) with support from the Special Educational Needs Coordinator (SENCO). Note that the rules about who is allowed to be the SENCO are in the process of change. By September 2010, SENCOs in schools will have to have qualified teacher status and have completed the NQT induction year. Special needs are identified by communicating with the parents and carers before setting up support systems for the child. Usually, parents are relieved to talk about the learning differences that they have noticed related to their child. It is important to listen to the parents' views and wishes for their child (and where possible to listen to the child's views) and to include them in reviews of the child's care that is additional or extra to the care received by other children of a similar age. Children whose needs can be accommodated by adjustments to the setting need a written individual plan of early years support reviewed at least twice a year containing SMART targets for development that state who is giving support, what that support will be, the required resources and the expected, measurable outcomes that identify progress. These children are said to be operating at an 'Early Years Action level of support'. When outside agencies are also involved in meeting the child's personal targets, this is described as 'Early Years Action plus'. A small number of children with special needs will have a statement that entitles them to a stated number of hours of one:one support. The steps to achieve this are clearly set out in the SEN toolkit.

Reviews will need to include representatives from all of the agencies involved in working with the child, the family and, at the end of the review, the child. Pragmatically, parents who become aware that their child has special needs also want to know about the support available for their child. The local authority has a duty of care to put the parents in touch with a named person who is responsible for their support. Early needs should be recorded and where necessary shared with the appropriate agencies. Records should identify children who are not making progress or who have unusual patterns of behaviour. In order to receive the support needed, the setting will need to show evidence of observations that have been carried out, comparing the target child to a control member of the group.

The focus for development should be on what a child can do and on his or her interests and preferences.

The **Multiverse** website has been set up to support and develop the personal understanding of practitioners about the variety of cultural groups and research findings about effective inclusive practice. A note of caution is important because any one family will have adapted traditions.

Ethnicity should be recorded as follows:

White-British
The EYFS document suggests that this should include: Irish, Traveller of Irish Heritage, Gypsy, Roma, and any other white background. The GRT community suggest that they are a separate category and have the right to record their ethnicity separately.
Gypsy Roma, Traveller
To include gypsies, Irish Travellers, fairground and circus people, horse traders and new age Travellers
Mixed-White and Black Caribbean
To include: white and black African, white and Asian, any other mixed background
Asian or Asian British:
To include: Indian, Pakistani, Bangladeshi, or any other Asian background
Black or black British
To include: Caribbean, African or any other black background
Chinese
Any other ethnic background

Effective Practice

Children are individuals with individual life-world experiences, approaches to learning and individual strengths and areas for development. For the young child, most experiences are fresh and new. Learning is an exciting adventure waiting to happen. Children need to be encouraged to discover what interests them and what they are good at and celebrate their findings and achievements with caring and effective practitioners in an atmosphere of mutual respect. They also need to be encouraged to question and enquire about everything and anything in the world that captures their imagination. They need time to stop and marvel at new life or the wonders of nature or to hear the story of Goldilocks yet again.

While there are different learning styles, children need a **VAK** or **visual, auditory and kinaesthetic approach to learning** to ensure that every child has an equal opportunity to learn.

All children must feel safe and valued. This can be achieved by setting consistent behavioural boundaries that are reinforced by the whole staff team. All settings need to have a diversity and equality policy that sets out the expectations of equal opportunities for all in an environment in which racial prejudice and discrimination are unacceptable. All staff should be aware of anti-discriminatory practice and all staff should expect every child to be fully included in the setting, feeling included, safe and valued. Practitioners encourage children to work cooperatively and develop positive relationships with other children, by discussing friendship and making friends, and helping children to discover what makes a good friend.

Challenges and Dilemmas

New children in any setting take time to adjust to the new routines and personalities within the setting. It is useful to stagger the induction of new children so that staff have time to settle individuals in to their new setting. Most early years practitioners achieve this by making home visits to young children before they are introduced to the setting so that the important relationship between the practitioner and the child begins on familiar territory. The child has the opportunity to introduce the practitioner to members of the family, important pet and favourite toys. The practitioner also has an opportunity to see the child's home circumstances and to begin to build a relationship with parents and carers. This helps the practitioner to meet the initial needs of every child by being a familiar face in the new environment and by being able to make reference to family members, pets and toys seen at home. Sometimes there are children who have experienced a very sheltered upbringing for whom the noise and activity of the setting is surprising. Such children often appear to attract the negative attention of children who are behaviourally challenged. It is important to protect these children from unwelcome attention and support their transition into the setting.

Where the parent has significant needs, the practitioner should focus on the needs of the child. This occasionally means informing other agencies of the child's needs if, for example, the child is malnourished or underweight or if the practitioner suspects that the parent is under the influence of alcohol or drugs.

The key worker maintains incident records as the lead practitioner in an inter-agency team, acting as a point of contact for everyone involved with the welfare of the child.

Reflections

- Does the setting have a visual timetable to support all children including children with SEN and children whose first language is not English?
- Is information shared in pictures, words and signs?
- Are personalized needs shared with all members of the staff team? Remember, a warm smile is the same in every language.

- Does the setting display named photographs of staff?
- How do children know that they are welcome in the setting?
- Is there a welcome poster in a variety of languages?
- Are there positive images of children from a variety of cultures displayed within the setting?
- Do the books reflect positive images of disability?
- Are festivals from the six major world religions shared and celebrated?
- Do displays celebrate the learning of all of the children?
- Is there a quiet space in which children can relax when necessary?

3   Keeping Safe

This chapter reflects upon the most recent definition of safeguarding children.

On completion of the chapter, practitioners should have an awareness of the legal requirements of the EYFS framework and the reasons behind these.

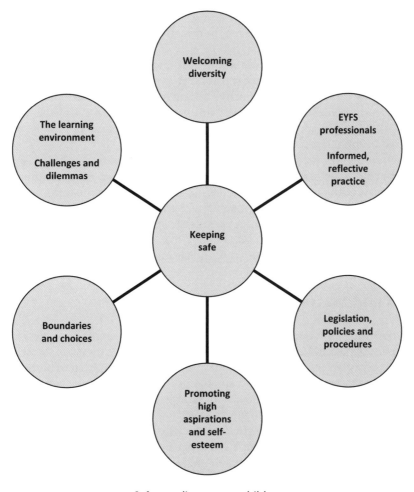

Safeguarding young children

A priority of every home and setting has to be to provide a safe, secure and inclusive environment in which the safety and welfare of every baby and young child are important issues. In this **enabling environment**, professionals develop children intellectually, creatively, physically, socially and emotionally.

According to the most recent definition, **safeguarding children** (December 2008) is:

> The process of protecting children from abuse or neglect, preventing impairment of their health and development, and ensuring they are growing up in circumstances consistent with the provision of safe and effective care that enables children to have optimum life chances and enter adulthood successfully.

To ensure that this happens, the government has introduced **multi-agency** Children's Trusts in every local authority. The Board of each Trust, which will be comprised of representatives from the local authority, health authority, police, schools and other services, has the responsibility of ensuring the safety of all children by insisting that all agencies work together, sharing information to support the well-being of all children.

At setting and childminder level, this will mean taking common-sense precautions to protect children and to report particular incidents to the Board so that multi-agency working can be effective. Effective information sharing, collaboration and understanding between everyone involved with the child are essential elements of good practice. The diagram above shows the key areas and objectives of *keeping safe* to be considered in this chapter.

Common-sense precautions include training all practitioners to fill sinks and baths with cold water before hot water and testing this with an elbow before allowing children access to the water. Taps at toddler height should have the water temperature regulated to merely warm to prevent scalding. Kettles and hot liquids (including staff drinks) should be kept out of reach. A curly kettle lead will help to prevent a dangling hazard. As babies become more mobile, cupboards can be fitted with safety fasteners to keep small fingers away from china, glass and cleaning materials for example.

Every Child Matters

Babies and young children are totally dependent on their parents and carers to introduce them responsibly to the dangers of the world in which they live. Most parents, carers and early years professionals are responsible adults, committed to nurturing children and introducing children to acceptable risk. This is acknowledged in the latest report from inspections of EYFS and school settings.

There is a shared understanding of the need to provide developmentally appropriate activities for babies and young children. Debate focuses on what 'developmentally appropriate' means when, for example, statistics from 2006 show that the increase of obesity in children aged between 2 and 10 increased from 9.6 per cent in 1995 to 16.6 per cent in 2005. This is often attributed to an increasingly sedentary lifestyle. Most young lives are influenced by a potentially hazardous range of media including te-vision, radio and unsupervised access to the internet. Adults are often naïve in their understanding of the menace of internet grooming through such sites as Facebook and YouTube and are unaware of the risks of posting images of children on these and similar sites. Learning and Teaching Scotland (2007) stress that the content of software and internet sites should be carefully vetted to ensure that these are free from violent and sexual content. All computers accessed by young children should have **firewall** settings at a safe level to protect the children.

Some potential risks are unacceptable such as those involving child protection issues. There are significant case studies including the death of Victoria Climbie and more recently Baby P. in 2008 that have highlighted the need for all agencies to work together, sharing information, using shared terms of reference in order to protect children from harm. On 12 November 2008 an urgent report was commissioned from Lord Laming on the key features of good safeguarding practice and whether good practice was being applied across the country, including the development of professional accountability, interagency effectiveness and public accountability.

The procedures to be followed are outlined in *Working Together to Safeguard Children* (DfES 2006c).

The government have produced a free leaflet, *What To Do if you are Worried a Child is Being Abused*, available at: www.dfes.gov.uk (DfES 2005), which includes five excellent flowcharts outlining what to do and who to inform of the setting's concerns.

Case study

Victoria Adjo Climbie was born on 2 November 1991 as the fifth of seven children. At age 6 she was happy, intelligent and articulate. Her father's aunt, Marie Therese Kouao, offered to take Victoria from her home on the Ivory Coast to France to further her education. Victoria was reportedly happy to be chosen. At the age of 8 she died in England of multi-organ failure and hypothermia with 128 separate injuries recorded on her body including burns and beatings. Marks on her wrists and ankles indicated that her arms and legs had been tied together. She had been lying in a black bin bag in her own urine and faeces. Although a number of professionals saw Victoria during her stay in England, a lack of communication between individuals meant that she remained in Kouao's flat and under Kouao's tyranny.

Lord Laming's report (DoH 2003), following Victoria's death, outlined the need for effective interagency working and introduced the five outcomes of *Every Child Matters*, from which *stay safe* is a priority for all childminders and settings. It is our collective and legislative responsibility to pass on information where abuse is suspected. In many cases, abusers have pre-experienced a number of personal stress factors. It is essential for all practitioners to be aware that abuse and neglect happen in every neighbourhood and in families across social boundaries even though the cases that are highlighted in the press often occur in lower socio-economic and minority ethnic groups. Every professional needs to be vigilant and aware that all human beings are capable of extreme acts of mental and physical cruelty and abuse.

All practitioners must record and report unusual bruises or marks such as round cigarette burns, strap marks, bite marks and fingerprint bruises on limbs. Note that abused children often portray personality changes, becoming either comparatively withdrawn or hyperactive.

Reflections

- Do I know to whom my concerns should be addressed if I am concerned about a child in my care?
- Have I copied the flowcharts from www.dfes.gov.uk for my quick reference?
- Have I passed on information that could be vital in preventing abuse?

Case study

News headlines in August 2002 told of the shocking murders of Jessica Chapman and Holly Wells by the school caretaker, Ian Huntley.

Sadly, this case study shows that predators such as Ian Huntley do still succeed in working in settings with children. (Huntley befriended the two girls from a position of trust as the school caretaker.) It is therefore very important to ensure that babies and children are never left unattended or in the care of volunteers or employees who do not hold CRB/List 99 clearance. Managers should insist upon seeing copies of **Criminal Records Bureau (CRB)** clearance certificates. They must obtain photocopies of certificates and qualifications for working with children before employing staff and ensure that volunteers and visitors from the wider community are never left unsupervised with babies and children. Written records should be kept to demonstrate to Ofsted that checks have been made. These records must show the date of issue and the number of the enhanced CRB disclosure.

Providers must ensure that all adults with access to the children, including other members of the family living at the premises where children are minded, are 'suitable'. Also note that a new vetting and barring scheme came into effect in Autumn 2008.

Look for the CRB Code of Practice and explanatory guide to make decisions about suitability. Always ask for references from previous employment and check any gaps in the employment history. Check all qualifications and ask for photo identity such as passports and driving licences. Also ask for a medical history. Letters of confirmation of employment should state that providers expect employees to declare all convictions, cautions and court orders which may disqualify them from working with children. Providers must notify Ofsted of:

- any change of provider or person with direct responsibility for early years provision, including name, address, date of birth, former names and aliases;
- any proposal of childminders to employ an assistant;
- any changes of persons of 16 years or over living or working on childminding premises including name, address, date of birth, former names and aliases;
- any proposal to change the hours during which childcare is provided which will entail the provision of overnight care;
- any changes to the premises that affect the space available and the quality of childcare such as structural alterations or adding an extension or changes to the external environment such as adding a pond, swimming pool or removing fencing;
- any change of name or address;
- any change in the registered number of a company or registration of a charity;
- any change of address of premises on which childcare is provided;
- any criminal offence committed by the registered provider after the time of registration.

An EYFS provider who, without reasonable excuse, fails to comply with this requirement commits an offence.

There is also a legal requirement that practitioners must not be under the influence of alcohol or any other substance that will affect their ability to care for the children. Practitioners taking prescription medicines that will affect their ability to care for children should seek medical advice and only work directly with children if their ability to look after children is unimpaired. If staff have been absent due to mental health issues, arrangements should be made for them to see Occupational Health before returning to work.

All adults should be aware of the contents of personal bags that may impact on the children's health and safety, for example matches, cigarettes and personal medicines including prescription medicines and over-the-counter medicines such as paracetamol. These should be kept in a locked cupboard at all times.

Training and Prior Experience

Managers should have at least two years of experience of working in an EYFS setting.

Childminders must have attended level 3 training within six months of registration and hold a current paediatric first aid certificate at the point of registration. A trained first aider must be on duty at all times. Assistants must hold level 2 certificates as defined by the Children's Workforce Development Council (CWDC).

All staff should undergo **induction training** in evacuation procedures, child protection and health and safety policy issues.

Regular staff **appraisals** should identify the training needs of all staff and a programme of continuing professional development should be in place to meet individual needs.

Fire evacuation procedures

Providers must take reasonable steps to ensure the safety of the children, staff and others on the premises and should record regular fire evacuation practices in a log, including any evacuation problems encountered and how these will be resolved. Fire alarms, smoke alarms, fire extinguishers and fire blankets should be checked regularly, as should obstruction-free, labelled fire exits.

All EYFS settings must be smoking-free environments.

Reflections

- Do we meet the legal requirements outlined above and in sections 3.5 to 3.9 of the EYFS framework?
- Have we kept copies of employment histories, references and CRB/List 99 disclosure evidence of all adults including staff members, committee members and volunteers?
- Have we informed Ofsted of any changes outlined above?
- Have we implemented an induction programme and a training programme to meet individual needs?
- Are volunteers or other adults on the premises allowed unsupervised access to the children?
- From an early age, children should be encouraged to understand their right to say 'No' as part of learning to stay safe. Very young children have a sense of what is acceptable and what is not. It is important for children to learn about how to express personal preferences and simple moral viewpoints.

Case study

In 1996, in the Scottish town of Dunblane, 16 children and one adult were murdered by Thomas Watt Hamilton, a former scout leader, who then committed suicide. Hamilton had gained entry to the school carrying two nine millimetre HP pistols and two Smith and Wesson revolvers. With 743 cartridges, he fired 109 shots. Hamilton killed a class of 5- and 6-year-olds.

The Cullen Inquiry (Scottish Office 1996) subsequently recommended changes to access arrangements in schools, reflecting on what could have been done to minimize the risk to children. Security in schools has been increased.

Reflections

- How secure is your perimeter? Can children open gates?
- Are your exterior access points locked while you are working?
- Do you have mobile phone access to emergency services without leaving the children unsupervised?
- Do you have a crisis contingency plan?
- What happens on visits away from your day-to-day setting?
- Staffing ratios?

Fabrication or induction of illness in a child

This rare form of abuse is defined as a child suffering or likely to suffer significant harm from a parent, carer or employee.

Managers and staff should refer to HM government guidance (2007) at www.everychildmatters.gov.uk/socialcare/safeguarding and refer to section 11, which calls for 'effective cooperation between agencies and professionals, sensitive working with parents and carers in the best interest of the child, and the careful exercise of professional judgement based on the thorough judgement and critical analysis of available information'.

Informed, Reflective Practice and Continuing Professional Development

There is an expectation that early years professionals and teachers will be able to predict the difference between an acceptable risk and a potential hazard. All early years professionals should read the safeguarding policy to be aware of local procedures for reporting their concerns about a child. In settings, this will usually be to a designated senior member of staff or a named deputy. In the home, this will be directly to the local authority. Staff are expected to develop their understanding of safeguarding children over time, by reflecting upon practice and accountability, with the benefit of hindsight. An allegation of abuse can lead to criminal proceedings. Children should be comfortable to communicate their thoughts and feelings to a trusted responsible adult. It is essential that procedures are followed and children are not asked leading questions or 'coached', which may make their evidence inadmissible in court. It is also important be honest with a child. You may be the first person to uncover alleged abuse. It is not possible to promise to keep this as a secret between yourself and the child.

Legislation, Policy and Procedures

To support best practice in all settings, managers should put in place policies for the setting including the following:

- **A policy to safeguard the children.** A named member of the management team should take responsibility for ensuring that child protection issues are recorded in ink and reported in line with current legislation. All staff share the responsibility for sharing information related to child protection issues. A quick overview of the procedures is included in appendices but the most up-to-date information will be found on the internet.
- **A health and safety policy for staff, visitors and volunteers.** Due regard must be paid to the health and safety laws related to keeping information about accidents and incidents and informing parents and carers of these, such as minor head bumps. All young children who have received a blow to the head should be carefully monitored for drowsiness, sickness or bleeding from the ears. These symptoms are significant and warrant urgent medical attention. In such instances, parents or carers should be contacted and children should be taken to hospital by ambulance, not by car. Head injuries can be serious even when the child has fallen from standing. Public play areas are accountable for health and safety assessments but childminders should check that there is no broken glass or other hazard present and that the height of the equipment and size of steps is developmentally appropriate.
- **A policy for administering medicines.** Early years practitioners should be aware of their legal responsibilities with regard to administering medicines and ensure that, where appropriate, staff are adequately trained, for example to administer epi pens.

Additionally, managers need to protect their staff by ensuring that policies and practice within the setting have regard to current legislation and best practice.

Promoting High Aspirations and Self-Esteem

Children learn best in a positive atmosphere where their small steps of achievement are acknowledged and efforts are praised. They also achieve when the expectations of adult carers are high. This is particularly important for children with special educational needs and gifted and talented children, but is also true of all children.

A thoughtless comment can damage the child's confidence in his or her own ability in an area of learning. The skilled professional engages in a dialogue with the child at play to support and extend learning.

The EYFS framework (DfES 2007b) reminds all carers of their personal responsibility with regard to diversity and inclusion, to ensure that every child feels included and not disadvantaged and values diversity in others. Hutchin (2007), reflecting upon updated (EPPE) research (Sylva *et al.* 2004), emphasizes the importance of considering a child's home background in order to provide appropriately for the child's needs. Both Hutchin and Sylva *et al.* highlight the need to plan from what is known about the child rather than from vague assumptions of what might be developmentally appropriate.

Boundaries and Choices

From birth, children begin to determine a real sense of safety and danger, right and wrong, by sensing the changes in body language, facial expression and voice tone of parents and carers. Notice the startle gesture of the young baby in response to sudden movement or loud noise. It is therefore important to set routines and consistent boundaries from the beginning in an atmosphere of mutual respect. All practitioners should have and share high expectations of all the children in their care, speaking their expectations in positive language. **Corporal punishment** is not acceptable from any member of staff, volunteer or person over 16 working on the premises. A named person should have responsibility for behaviour management in every setting and should keep records of complaints made against individual members of staff for at least three years.

Case study

Michael is running across the room, which is potentially hazardous because of corners of furniture. The practitioner reinforces with 'Walk' rather than 'Don't run.'

This is because the child holds the last word spoken in his mind. 'Run' reinforces the action he is performing. 'Walk' introduces the expected change of action.

Physical correction such as tapping or slapping is not acceptable in England or Wales. Non-verbal signals are just as powerful as raised voices.

Where there are many interactions between parents or carers and children, children determine their place within society. Where the interactions are fewer or are of lower quality, children begin to seek attention by gaining a response from the adult, either positive or negative. Lack of an expected response is very scary. Children often test their boundaries to see if the rules stay the same at home or in other caring settings. Acceptable boundaries should be made clear to the children through shared values by adults who model their expectations. It is useful to discuss behaviours and boundaries through the language of choice. That is: 'It is your choice: choose to pack away the bricks and you can join the other children having a story.' Adults should think through their behaviour plan in terms of a hierarchy of rewards and sanctions that allow the children to alter their choice of behaviour and own up to what they have done without fear of the consequences. It is vitally important for the boundaries of acceptable and unacceptable behaviour to be consistent both across the setting and from day to day.

It is very important for adults to consider whether their interactions are giving appropriate messages to the child. Children with Autistic Spectrum Disorder are less able to read facial expressions and may take what is said literally (for example, 'Pull your socks up').

Case study

Ben, aged 4, wants to play with his favourite bicycle but Stephen is riding on it. Ben walks over to Stephen and pushes him off the bicycle. The practitioner intervenes.
Adult: Did you mean to push Stephen off his bike or was it an accident?
Ben: (*Thinks about this question with his head tilted over to the left*). I did it on tortoise!
    The adult then faces a dilemma. On one hand he or she wants to praise Ben for his honesty and on the other hand he has used violence to get what he wants and should be punished.

Reflections

Do you?
- Praise Ben for owning up? What message does this give to Stephen?
- Give your attention to Stephen? What is the effect on Ben?

The Learning Environment, Challenges And Dilemmas

Activities should be planned for an indoor and outdoor learning environment. There should be a balance between child-initiated and adult-led activities. It is the responsibility of every practitioner to identify the potential risk element of every activity and plan to minimize the danger for the child or children involved. This will include regularly checking the outdoor environment for potential hazards including broken glass and animal excrement as well as hazardous plants such as those with thorns, for example roses and thistles, and poisonous plants such as deadly nightshade and laburnum (Wikipedia 2008).

Case study

Dinesh is playing in water. There is a paddling pool placed against the perimeter fence containing floating toys. Dinesh wants a toy at the furthest side of the pond that is beyond his reach. He stretches out his arm, leans forward and falls into the water. In 10 cm of water, Dinesh drowns.

Playing with water in a paddling pool, sink or bath is potentially hazardous but is also worthwhile. A practitioner with an awareness of danger would have foreseen the risk and would have positioned himself or herself where the water activity could be seen at all times. When Dinesh fell into the water, the adult would have been able to intervene in time and should have had the basic first aid skills to prolong life until medical attention could be summoned.

Reflections

- Is an adult with an awareness of the potential risk always aware of the water tray, bath or sink?
- Can children retrieve equipment from the water without leaning across the top?
- Are there other activities that need constant vigilance?

In an early years setting, all cleaning materials, glass and medicines should be kept in a locked cupboard with the exception of ventolin inhalers which should be kept with the child where possible.

Electric cables should be situated away from main thoroughfares and potential dangers such as open power sockets should be covered with blank plugs. Water and electricity must be kept apart.

Small objects may be pushed into every orifice! Valuable learning experiences involve using seeds, beads, wax crayons, counters, plastic money and so on. All of these are hazardous if swallowed. The children will explore objects with their mouths as well as their fingers.

Case study

Susan was taken to the doctor by her mother because there was a strong smell exuding from her. On close examination, the doctor traced the smell to her nose and, with tweezers, removed a small bead from her nostril.

Always report unusual smells to the parents and seek professional support from a doctor rather than trying to intervene.

Supervision is needed for all activities involving real tools such as cutting implements. It is distressing to see baby curls in a pile on the floor when children are left unsupervised with scissors! Small children can and will cut hair with plastic scissors.

Children cannot be protected from every danger. Adults need to be aware of potential hazards and learn a healthy level of caution, also teaching children to carry and use tools safely.

Conclusion

All early years professionals are committed to work with a variety of external agencies to create a safe environment for the children in their care. This role is significant in protecting children from harm and abuse. Professionals should attend training periodically to help them to recognize children who are at risk or who are suffering 'significant harm'. Professionals should reflect on their own local situation to identify areas for development. Where abuse is suspected, practitioners should not automatically assume that this is the case but should share their concerns with the designated person with responsibility for child protection and follow the flowcharts in the appendices to work with other agencies and service providers. Remember: abuse takes a variety of forms and is present across socio-economic boundaries.

Safeguarding children presents more challenges than solutions.

4 Health and well-being

This chapter covers key recommendations for healthy eating and drinking, expectations for managing medical needs and accidents as well as promoting health and well-being and balancing physical activity and risk. Ways to support children's emotional needs and their impact on learning are also considered.

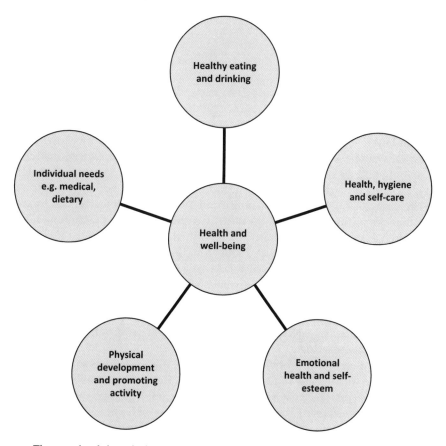

The needs of the whole child must be met before learning can take place

The Early Years Foundation Stage document (EYFS) (DFES 2007a) highlights key features that contribute to the health and well-being of birth to 5-year-olds in education and care provision. These include:

- healthy eating;
- appropriate care for medical needs, health and safety and personal hygiene;
- physical development, safe exploration, and opportunities for rest and relaxation;
- emotional security (building friendships, developing independence and experiencing routines).

This EYFS principle covers several linked expectations for children, which are essential to their ability to learn and develop. They link to the theories of Maslow (1968), who describes basic human needs first as physiological (food, drink, sleep, shelter, care). These elements must be met before children are able to learn. The EYFS takes this further by expecting these elements to be of high quality, responsive to the latest research and understanding about children and well-matched to their individual needs.

Healthy eating

What is healthy eating for birth to 5-year-olds?

The EYFS document does not specify requirements for healthy eating in the Early Years Foundation Stage and so this is open to interpretation. Healthy eating for birth to 5-year-olds can be a complex process. Media attention and guidance for adults and older school children has led to a growing awareness of the problems of childhood obesity, focusing on a diet high in sugar, salt and fat and lack of exercise (Robinson 2006; Croghan 2007; Oliver 2008; School Food Trust 2008). However, it is important to note that the recommendations for healthy eating are not the same for adults and older children as they are for children under 5 (British Nutrition Foundation 2004a). In a survey of East Sussex nurseries (PLA 2008a) four out of five of the nurseries surveyed were providing food that was potentially damaging for pre-school children as it did not contain enough calories. Some EYFS providers had created meals and snacks that were over-reliant on fruit and vegetables and lacking in the fats, carbohydrates and proteins needed for children in the birth to 5 age group to thrive. Providers must therefore make sure that they keep up to date with nutritional information specific to the age group with which they are working.

As well as offering nutritionally balanced food, EYFS providers should be encouraging children to try a variety of flavours, including fruit and vegetables, so that these healthy choices are established. Ofsted (2005) also suggest that good early years settings use fresh fruit and vegetables, 'some using organic and even home-grown produce', and do not use processed food. A more detailed breakdown of appropriate food choices for different age groups is available from the British Nutrition Foundation (BNF 2004a). Drinking water should be freely available and accessible for children (Ofsted 2005) as well as milk; sugary drinks, including diluted fruit juice, should be limited to meal times (BNF 2004b).

Case study

A Montessori nursery school keeps a jug of water and coloured beakers available for the children to access as they wish. With adult support the 3- and 4-year-old children quickly develop the independence and coordination to pour their own drinks and ask an adult to refill the jug when needed. They understand that they need to put used beakers into the empty washing up bowl to avoid spreading germs.

Timing, choice and routines

Similarly, the EYFS does not give specific guidance about how providers should offer food and drink to children. It is normal practice for early years providers to have set times for snacks and meals but in most schools and many day care environments children eat with adult supervision rather than adult participation. How adults participate in food preparation and meal times are signals to children about the importance of these times. Ideally, food times should be shared with an adult and be a relaxed social opportunity. They should not be overshadowed by the pressure of time or expectations of silence (Ofsted 2005; Pryke 2006). Equally, by expecting children to finish plates of food or even bottles of milk providers are not establishing healthy eating habits. Small children, including babies, regulate their food intake naturally over a 24-hour period. Expecting children to continue eating to please an adult may teach them to override their natural awareness of hunger, which could lead to problems with overeating later in life (Pryke 2006). Main meals have value as a social occasion and an opportunity to model eating behaviour. However, it is a good idea for providers to make snacks available at different times during the day or on a self-service basis, to encourage independence. Practitioners should monitor children's food and drink intake and work with parents and carers to ensure that each child gets a balance throughout the day rather than expecting children always to eat a set amount in one sitting.

Meals and snacks offer a great opportunity to provide food from a range of cultures and move away from the expectations of the restaurant children's menu, which often includes highly processed food. Again this helps children to be open to new tastes (Ofsted 2005; Pryke 2006). A way of making this manageable is to change a small amount of a favourite or recognized meal at a time and to allow children a choice between two new things, so they feel in control (Pryke 2006).

Case study

Members of staff in a large day care setting fill in daily food and drink diaries for all their key children throughout the age groups. They include details of quantity and timing of drinks, snacks and meals. Marie is 2 and goes to the setting every day. When Marie's mum reports that she is refusing vegetables at home, the staff members make sure that she is offered a little serving of new vegetables whenever they are available and record their success rates in the diary. Marie's key worker reassures her mum about the hidden vegetables in many of the dishes served, and suggests that she does the same at home. She talks about her favourite vegetables when having lunch with Marie and the other children in her group, offering a healthy role model.

Making it work

Much more than offering healthy choices to children, the expectations of the EYFS are to promote an understanding of healthy choices and provide the grounding for maintaining these in later life. Perhaps the most important principle of successful promotion of healthy eating is involving the children in the process. This may be by growing their own produce, selecting it in the market or shop, preparing their own dishes, or simply choosing from a range of snacks on a table (Ofsted 2005; Croghan 2007). Successful healthy eating arrangements should take into account individual dietary needs and preferences and rely on the provider communicating effectively with parents and carers in order for this to happen, whether these are a result of religion or food intolerance. Sharing menus with parents and including a variety of dishes from different cultures as part of everyday menus can ensure that everyone feels included. Children with allergies should be made known to all staff, including volunteers and those working on a temporary basis (see medical needs below). Providers can use links available to community nurses, health visitors and community dentists to get up-to-date advice and support and engage in community projects that promote awareness of healthy lifestyles for families (DCFS and NHS 2008a).

Medical needs, health and hygiene

Preventative measures are one of the important responsibilities of EYFS providers in meeting this expectation. Food hygiene standards are maintained as part of the welfare requirements and conditions of registration, as are appropriate practices for staff hygiene when changing nappies and cleaning feeding equipment. However, to move beyond this and consider ways in which providers can promote good health, children need to be involved in establishing healthy routines for their own self-care. Children in the EYFS often have their own toothbrushes, flannels and beakers in child care settings and these practices can also be adapted to include children at school. Children can initially be taught to brush their teeth at certain times and then later develop a greater understanding of why this is necessary and which food or drink may harm teeth. Providers can actively teach children to wash their hands at appropriate points

Figure 4.1   Using visual reminders for hand washing is simple but effective.

in the day and to throw away used tissues when they have blown their nose. Games, routines, visual reminders and rhymes can be used to reinforce messages about killing germs. These routines are basic aspects of self-care but play an important function in health promotion as one of the most common causes of absence from school and work is the spread of common colds and infections (Croghan 2007; DCSF and NHS 2008b) (Figure 4.1).

A further preventative challenge for schools and settings is providing sun protection for children who are spending increasing amounts of the day outside. Palmer (2006) points out that concern about the risk to health from sun damage is just one of the many reasons for the decrease in physical activity outdoors for children. Again, working with parents and carers is essential to ensure that children have hats, sun cream and sunglasses as appropriate. In some cases settings may gain permission to provide children with these as part of their care during an EYFS day. As with nappies and creams, this needs to be negotiated with the families concerned so that individual needs are met.

Case study

A childminder, who cares for three EYFS children at different times in the week, keeps an individual basket of nappies, creams and sun cream for each of the children in her care. She sends home a reminder note when anything is running low.

EYFS providers must have a system for managing medicines and dealing with accidents, injury or illness of children in their care. This will include managing the medical needs of children with long-term conditions such as **asthma, diabetes** and **epilepsy** as well as sometimes making arrangements to include children with more complex medical needs such as **tube-feeding** (DfES 2005b). Children who have a complex medical need may come under the rulings of the Disability Discrimination Act (OPSI 1995) and later amendments (OPSI 2001). This broadly means that schools and early years settings are required to make 'reasonable adjustments' (OPSI 1995, 2001) in order for them to be able to attend the setting. Often schools are particularly concerned about children with physical needs or delayed development that require arrangements for nappy changing. While this may necessitate some reorganization of space and staffing it is an expectation that must be met by law.

Each setting must have a specific policy and procedure for managing medicines. Certain staff will be asked to administer medication as an additional responsibility and this should be part of their contract, not an informal addition. A policy for managing medicines should include:

- daily procedures;
- emergency arrangements;
- procedures for trips and outings;
- information about parental responsibility and permissions;
- information about staff training, roles and responsibilities;
- storage of medicines;
- record keeping; and
- disposal of medicines.

Parents should be encouraged to administer medicines outside the time that the child is in the setting. If this is not possible parents should attempt to provide an additional supply to be kept at the setting, as providers are not allowed to administer medicine from a relabelled container (DfES 2005). With regard to unforeseen events all settings should maintain an accident book, which is completed in ink, undertake risk assessment in the setting and when travelling beyond it, and ensure that staff are trained in emergency procedures and first aid. Parents, staff and carers must be informed about any bumps to the head that individual children have sustained so they can monitor for signs of concussion. Maintaining a safe environment and regularly checking and cleaning equipment contribute to this aspect of children's welfare (see Chapter 16). Children are vulnerable to accidents and the responsibility for avoiding as many as possible is that of all adults in an EYFS setting (PLA 2008b). However, practitioners, parents and carers need to be aware that even with careful health and safety procedures children will still occasionally injure themselves. They also need opportunities to experience low-level physical risks, such as running on a hard surface or climbing on a low bench in order to develop their own judgement of situations for the future. Research suggests that children's own understanding of risk may be limited and adults can improve this through the experiences that are available to children (RoSPA 2008). Practitioners should aim to strike a balance between meeting the legislative requirements and limiting children's freedom to learn from experience.

Managing Medicines in Schools and Early Years Settings (DfES 2005b) gives very specific guidance about supporting children with long-term medical needs such as **anaphylaxis** or diabetes and possible ways to draw up a health care plan for individuals. Some key issues of good practice include ensuring that all staff are well informed about these arrangements and the individual children who need medical attention. Settings may need a specific policy or section of a policy to outline how they will make reasonable adaptations and provision for children who may need complex care arrangements such as tube-feeding. While teachers are not expected to administer medication or assist with invasive procedures as part of their normal duties they may be expected to carry out emergency procedures for particular children and receive training for this. Non-teaching staff may have responsibilities for managing specific medical needs included in their contract of employment. Further information about ways in which settings can ensure they provide for children with complex needs is available from *Including Me* (Carlin 2005).

Case study

Amrit had an epileptic seizure during the summer before her entry to the nursery class at her small local school. Her parents contacted the school and they consulted the school nurse. A joint meeting with the parents, school and nurse was held to prepare for Amrit's admission to school. Her admission had to be delayed by a week in order for teaching and non-teaching staff to be trained in emergency procedure, including administering valium. This ensured that there would always be a trained member of staff available. A health plan including staff consent, the storing and updating of medication and emergency procedure was drawn up with staff and parents.

Physical activity

As mentioned earlier in this chapter, rising obesity levels are a concern for the Department of Health and government as a whole (DoH 2006, 2008). However, physical activity contributes more to the health and well-being of children in the EYFS than simply combatting rising weight levels amongst the population. Guidance from NICE

(2007) underlines the importance of active play as underpinning all the aspects of the EYFS and emphasizes that early years providers must offer daily indoor and outdoor play experiences. This has been fundamental to good early years practice for some time but NICE moves the expectations further by suggesting that all providers should 'minimise sedentary activities during play time [and] provide regular opportunities for enjoyable active play and structured physical activity sessions' (NICE 2007).

They also stress the role that providers have to play in promoting active play with parents and carers. Palmer (2006) draws on research to emphasize children's need for natural play environments to promote mental well-being and encourage explorative opportunities. A sterile environment of fixed play equipment and safety surface does not allow children real opportunities to experiment and investigate the natural environment. Consequently providers with any number of children and in any location must continue to find inventive solutions to the limitations of their environment and be creative in developing new ways to work with parents and carers that promote outdoor experiences.

Case study

A voluntary playgroup uses a community centre without any outside space; staff members set up daily activities in the sports hall. Activities include wheeled toys, tunnels, hoops, large wooden construction, balls and beanbags as well as smaller construction and other 'physical' toys. The group spends an hour in the space during each session. Small groups of children with staff from the playgroup also walk to the park on the same site and spend time feeding the ducks and playing on the grassy slopes each day.

It is widely agreed that physical activity is a naturally enjoyable and rewarding occupation for the EYFS age range and essential to enable babies and children to develop socially and intellectually (Edgington 2002, 2004; Doherty and Bailey 2003; Bilton 2004; Palmer 2006). However, changes in parenting culture and our society in general have led to a decrease in activity even for babies and toddlers. Babies need physical opportunities and stimulation from the start; these should include grasping, eye and head movements and right and left coordination such as crawling (Goldschmied and Jackson 1994; Doherty and Bailey 2003; Macintyre and McVitty 2004; Lindon 2005). Parents and providers who follow the sleep advice for babies to be placed on the back may be reluctant to place babies on their front, even when awake, and hence reduce their opportunities for strengthening muscles in preparation to crawl. The increase in baby seating, such as electronic rockers, and health and safety fears may mean that infants are strapped in one place for unnecessary amounts of time (Palmer 2006). These limitations on children's natural desire to explore illustrate the need for those working with young children to have a very good understanding of growth and development. Adults delivering the EYFS need to create opportunities for the next steps in a child's development of coordination and movement, allowing children sufficient risk to challenge their own boundaries across the full range of physical development – **stability, locomotion and manipulation, fine and gross motor skills** (Doherty and Bailey 2003). This offers greater challenge for providers when a child has specific physical needs but it is equally important that providers find ways to allow children with physical disabilities the chance to explore and take risks in physical activity with their peers, while continuing to provide for their individual needs.

Case study

Ben has **cerebral palsy (hemiplegic)**. His right-hand side is very weak and he has little sight in his right eye. Ben has fine motor skill exercises which he practises daily in the EYFS class at school. The teaching assistant and teacher include other children in these activities too and make them into games e.g. popping bubble wrap between finger and thumb, pegging toys, numbers, letters etc. out on the line, manipulating dough and picking up small objects. During outdoor play an adult watches Ben from a distance so he is able to build social and physical skills independently. The steps to the whole school playground have been painted yellow and a handrail added. For physical development opportunities the teacher adapts all the activities so they can be accessed in different ways at different levels rather than isolating Ben by giving him work with a teaching assistant or a different activity to the other children.

After all this physical activity children in the EYFS will need opportunities for rest and relaxation. While naps are perhaps not practical in Reception classes, some provision for rest and peace should be made throughout the EYFS. Quiet areas with beanbags or large cushions are ideal. Even in settings where the younger EYFS children are cared for, aspects of practice need to be examined. Comfortable, individual, safe spaces for babies and toddlers to sleep in are essential. Providers must find a way to ensure that children are well monitored but separated from those who are playing. They should also consider how to offer flexible sleep times to suit individual needs (Palmer 2006). In **Reggio Emilia** settings in Northern Italy children are able to choose their own sleep times by crawling into their own sleep basket or nest (Dowling 2005).

Emotional health

Emotional well-being is so important for learning, social development and even physical health that it could easily take a whole book to examine the links between it and the Early Years Foundation Stage. This aspect will be considered in more depth in other chapters particularly Chapters 5, 8 and 17. However, in the context of overall health and well-being some key areas must be addressed. Early years providers need to understand the importance of children's self-esteem for their ability to learn and form relationships with others and they should provide a whole environment and ethos that supports the development of this. Generally theorists and researchers agree that **emotional literacy, emotional health** or **emotional intelligence**, whichever term they favour to describe children's mental well-being, requires a combination of factors: **self-awareness** and **self-esteem, empathy** and **positive discipline** (Goleman 1996; Mountford and Hunt 2001; Roberts 2002; Mortimer 2003; Panju 2008). Some of these can be enhanced through planned teaching and learning opportunities but many rely on the behaviour, relationships and emotional role models of the adults in the EYFS.

Children need a secure relationship, usually with a key person. To build this feeling of security children must feel accepted under any circumstance and treated as individuals (Roberts 2002; Bruce 2004b; DCSF 2008a). This means that all their feelings should be acknowledged even when the provider is not happy with the resulting behaviour. Children must be helped to cope with uncomfortable feelings. Adults should avoid trying to distract children from their feelings or suggesting that children are 'being silly' or 'making a fuss'. Instead, feelings, including those of non-verbal children and babies, should be acknowledged through adult responses using expression, tone and gesture (Dowling 2005; Lindon 2005). For example, even the younger members of the EYFS can be given physical reassurance after a tantrum, thus sowing the seeds of managing their own anger and frustration (Roberts 2002). Children should be allowed to make mistakes without fear of personal rejection and disapproval and have meaningful discussions with adults about how to avoid such a thing happening again. They also need real praise, which may need to be gradual, subtle or non-verbal, to be accepted and to be valued for personal qualities rather than being 'good' or doing as they are told. Alongside this, children need to have clear and consistent boundaries for behaviour which are appropriate for their own stage of development and understanding (Mountford and Hunt 2001; Roberts 2002). Some important dispositions can be encouraged by the way that adults behave and what they praise children for. Finding ways to encourage children to take care of one another and being positive when they do this spontaneously can improve children's relationships and self-esteem (Macintyre 2001). Similarly, children throughout the EYFS must be encouraged to explore, experiment and suggest, so that they can become confident, independent learners. That does not mean that children have complete freedom of choice but one within limits where explanations will be given if an activity is not safe or feasible (Barrow *et al.* 2001).

Much has been written over recent years about listening to children. This is not just listening to verbal communication but using our observations, play interaction and intuition to understand how children are thinking and feeling (Lancaster 2003; Mortimer 2003; Clark *et al.* 2005). If providers take time to do this they will be able to help children manage their emotional needs through physical reassurance, role modelling behaviour or talking about problems. They should not intervene in every altercation but also allow children time to work out some solutions for themselves. Providers should not underestimate the strength of children's feelings in a world where they may have little control. Emotional well-being underpins children's ability to learn, form relationships and even remain physically healthy.

Reflections

- Which area of health and well-being does our setting give the highest priority?
- How are we balancing individual needs for sleep or food with our need for routine and organization?
- How flexible are we in responding to different parental expectations?

Part 2

Positive Relationships

5   Respecting each other

This chapter covers ways to make all families feel welcome; choosing and using resources that promote diversity and equality; helping children to value their own and others' individuality and build positive relationships.

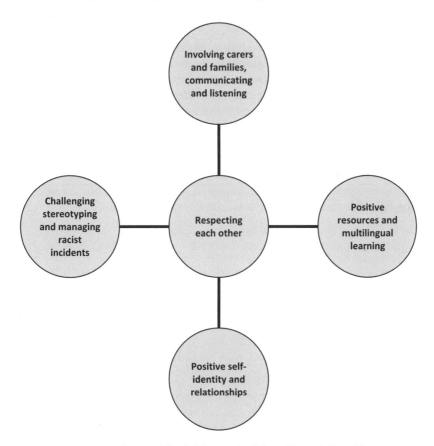

Strategies that enable children to build positive relationships

The Early Years Foundation Stage (EYFS) document (DfES 2007a) highlights the need for practitioners to consider the relationships that they make and the role models that they offer as a crucial factor in the quality of their provision for birth to 5-year-olds. The key areas where this may be addressed are:

- understanding the needs of parents and carers and working with them effectively;
- helping children to form relationships and have a positive understanding of their own identity and that of others;
- ensuring that staff, parents and children from diverse groups are valued and feel supported by each other;
- ensuring that staff members are able to maintain professional relationships with parents and colleagues.

Addressing assumptions, building identity

The first and most difficult step in creating an ethos that truly models respect for children, staff and families is addressing those assumptions, stereotypes and prejudices that influence our daily views and behaviour. In any EYFS environment children, staff or parents are likely to differ in their social economic status, their experience of family life, their language, culture, ethnic origin, religion and sexuality. Any one, some or all of these potential differences may be known to others or not. Consequently it is essential that all early years educators consider their own personal viewpoints and question how these might influence the experiences that they offer to the children in their care.

Reflections
- What is your view of girls' and boys' natural play?
- What do you do to challenge children's view of stereotyping based on gender or ethnicity?
- Where are single parents, same-sex parents, foster parents or other relatives in a parental role represented in your environment and resources or annual events and celebrations?
- How might your expectations of childhood and home experience be affecting the way that you view children's behaviour and play?
- What can you do to understand more about the children's home lives and cultures and encourage children to get to know one another?

Not only will early years educators need to question the role models that they provide but they will also need to find ways to counteract existing stereotypes that children hold. This may include questioning and explanations such as asking why one child says that another has to be the nurse in the children's role play; selecting children for jobs contrary to a 'gendered' role, for example asking a boy to help with the cooking; and sharing stories, pictures and anecdotes in which these roles are changed. In the

EYFS, children are likely to have strong views, already shaped by their family life and the media, about gender roles and ethnic identity. Research shows that these take some time and persistence to counteract (Schaffer 1996; Siraj-Blatchford and Clarke 2000; Knowles and Riley 2005) and practitioners need to explain to parents and carers how the setting approaches these issues (see next section).

Working with children to address stereotyping and promote the positive aspects of diversity in our society can allow children to develop a positive self-image and an open and accepting outlook that will help them to form successful relationships. When babies are 'listened' to by staff responding and tuning into their non-verbal messages, when they are carried and comforted or laid down to sleep in the way that is familiar from their home this increases their confidence in the support of those around them and encourages them to express preferences. When toddlers have the opportunity to make faces in the mirror, or hear home language words and music or to see a photograph of themselves and their family displayed in the setting this affirms the importance of their own differences and home background (Siraj-Blatchford and Clarke 2000; Klein and Chen 2001; Roberts 2002; Knowles and Riley 2005). Children need support to show respect to one another. Adults can model positive relationships by using praise and reassurance, sensitively intervening to promote sharing and turn-taking, talking about the feelings of themselves and others and how individual actions affect others. These relationships cannot be imposed upon children but will be learned through consistently caring and respectful adult/child, adult/adult relationships. Staff should take care to show how they look after one another, how they manage their own feelings and how important their varied home life and culture is to them as well as how interested they are in the lives of the children in their care (Barrow *et al.* 2001; Mountford and Hunt 2001).

As many experienced EYFS educators will agree, social and emotional skills are not automatically established in children. Some children as young as 2 or 3 can show empathy and consideration for others (Dunn 1993, 1998; Kantor *et al.* 1998), while others find it difficult to allow for peers' wants and some children may find themselves rejected by their peers (Dowling 2005). In most cases children throughout the EYFS find managing anger particularly problematic, which is not surprising when one considers the difficulty this poses for many adults. Clear and consistent expectations and boundaries are one important part of helping children to understand what constitutes acceptable behaviour in the EYFS environment. However, this is insufficient to enable children to develop the emotional skills required to form friendships. Children need to be taught, through games, pictures and stories, to recognize their own emotions and should learn acceptable ways of managing them. In the youngest children this may be by comforting them when they are upset, giving them time and space to calm down or offering examples of coping strategies. There are also planned teaching methods such as using persona dolls, circle time and SEAL materials which can be useful for the 3–5 age range (see Chapter 17).

It is important that children get the right amount of adult support with their early relationships. Research shows that children's friendships can be more stable and long-lasting than assumed by many adults, sometimes lasting for several months from the age of 2 and over (Dunn 1993; Children's Society 2007). Children need the emotional

Figure 5.1 Children can be supported to sustain interaction with one another independently, if given suggested roles to play.

support of peers and secure friendships contribute to children's mental well-being and therefore their ability to learn (Dunn 1993; Children's Society 2007). Choosing friends for children is unlikely to be successful but observing children's play and supporting appropriately may make a difference for those children who are having difficulties making links. One intervention of this kind does not solve all problems but regular support can help children to find ways to interact with one another (see Figure 5.1).

Case study

Junaid was playing close to Tristan using the model farm animals. The staff member observed as they played alongside one another that Junaid was watching Tristan's play but seemed unsure how to get involved. The staff member joined in playing alongside then started to narrate the game. 'Wow, Tristan's cow is on the roof. My cow is too.' Initally Junaid copied the play on his own, then he moved closer and put his cow next to Tristan's. Tristan said, 'My cow's jumping now' then looked over at Junaid, 'Come on.'

Some children will experience life changes during their time in the EYFS. These can be those that appear to adults to be positive, such as the birth of a sibling, or moving house, or negative such as family breakdown or bereavement. It is important that EYFS educators help children to cope with these issues and the EYFS setting is often a safe place, away from those concerned, in which to explore feelings. The youngest children will usually show how these issues are affecting them through changes in behaviour. EYFS staff should continue to maintain expectations for behaviour while talking to the child about his or her feelings (Barrow *et al.* 2001; Mountford and Hunt 2001; Dowling 2005; Lawrence 2006). A good way of finding out about children's concerns in a child-friendly way is by using 'what' instead of 'why' questions (Roberts 2002), such as 'What is making you so angry today?' and offering verbal support, physical reassurance or suggestions for action. Some children will need extra support beyond the usual measure available in the setting. This may require sensitive collaboration between the setting, family and outside agencies.

Case study

Michelle had a sibling who had recently died, her parents had separated and she now spent time in two homes each week. Michelle was outwardly cheerful and popular in her EYFS class; she liked to help the teacher and play with others. However, she would regularly fall out with her friends and her arguments with them were violent. In the classroom she would scream and swear and cry when frustrated in her play. On the playground she would attack her friends when the play went wrong. Staff tried the usual rewards and sanctions to manage her behaviour; she responded to this in the classroom but not at playtimes. After a series of incidents they involved support from the local authority who put the family in touch with a charity that supported family bereavement. Michelle brought a photo of her sister into school for the first time and talked about her with staff and children. EYFS staff members took turns to spend time on the playground at lunch time and offered her extra activities away from the large playground.

An informed perspective?

A possible product of stereotyping and assumptions amongst the staff in an EYFS setting can be low expectations, as a result of specific beliefs about groups of children and families (Siraj-Blatchford and Clarke 2000; Klein and Chen 2001; Brooker 2002;

DCSF 2006b). It may be that some adults give children less intellectually challenging experiences if they are not yet able to communicate fluently in English or assume, for example, that a lively boy would not wish to settle down and look at a picture book with them. EYFS settings need to invest time in training and open discussion about equality and raising attainment for all children. Practitioners need to be aware that their expectations may disadvantage groups of children from diverse ethnic backgrounds and prevent them from showing their true potential (Siraj-Blatchford and Clarke 2000; Klein and Chen 2001; Brooker 2002; DCSF 2006b). This can be because practitioners have not taken into account the varied family life and experiences that some children have before joining the EYFS. For example, some children may be mostly used to helping adults and older siblings around the home but in the EYFS quiet behaviour or following adults around the class may be interpreted as to be lacking in initiative and independence (Brooker 2002). Such assumptions can be addressed by making opportunities to carefully observe children's strengths in the setting and find out more about their life at home, as well as questioning our own culturally influenced expectations of early learning. Ouseley and Lane (2006) argue that early years practitioners have the opportunity to influence **community cohesion**. They suggest that it is vital that providers address their own fears about communicating with parents from ethnic backgrounds different to their own and actively encourage children to play with peers who may have a different gender, language and ethnicity to themselves in order to help them overcome stereotyping and counteract racist views.

Case study

A maintained nursery school arranged home visits from a teacher and bilingual support assistant in the term before each child joined the setting. This allowed the staff to find out more about the children's likes and dislikes and home experiences as well as to talk to parents/carers in a setting where they were comfortable. Once the children had joined the nursery they took turns to take a digital camera home and record their life outside the nursery. This was then made into a photo album for each child to discuss and add to during their time in the group.

The younger members of the EYFS may also be affected by culturally held assumptions. These might include when it is appropriate to walk or talk, when children should be ready to use the toilet independently, or eat solid food. Milestones that have historically been viewed as developmental markers are often a reflection of the expectations of the particular society and culture in which we live (Siraj-Blatchford and Clarke 2000; Klein and Chen 2001). This can mean that those caring for children in the EYFS have very different expectations from the parents and carers they are working with and the treatment of children can be quite contrasting between home and the setting. It is in the child's best interests for the EYFS provider to work closely with the parents and carers to explain their routines and find out those of the home. Some level of compromise on either side is often needed and this will once again draw upon the need for sensitive and respectful relationships with parents and carers.

Every Early Years Foundation Stage provider will need to have a 'Diversity and Equality' policy and a procedure for recording, monitoring and managing racist incidents. While this is not a new expectation, good practice in this area is shown by proactively sharing and reviewing policy and procedure so that it influences every aspect of the setting and all staff, parents and carers understand what the expectations are from the start. It is crucial that staff do not ignore racist or other discriminatory language and behaviour and allow children's remarks to go unchallenged (Siraj-Blatchford and Clarke 2000; PLA 2001). While EYFS children may use racist language without full understanding, staff must explain why certain remarks are offensive without punishing the child concerned. They must also comfort and explain the situation to the victims of such comments, making sure that they continue to feel positive about themselves. Parents or carers on both sides will need to be informed sensitively about their children's interactions (Siraj-Blatchford and Clarke 2000; PLA 2001).

It is particularly important to explain the duty of schools and early years settings to promote equality outlined in the Race Relations Amendment Act 2000 (OPSI 2000). Recording and monitoring incidents allows the setting to tackle any commonly occurring issues with individuals and also through teaching opportunities. It is also vital that settings show equal care for their staff and manage discrimination towards and between staff by explanation and discussion if a remark or behaviour is implicitly discriminatory and by taking disciplinary action for overt discrimination. Settings should also work proactively to recruit a diverse staff including men and women from a range of different ethnic, cultural, religious and linguistic backgrounds. These staff will provide positive role models for the children and potentially create a more approachable setting for different parents and carers. Using other local services and information to access different communities may make it easier to recruit from a more diverse group (Siraj-Blatchford and Clarke 2000; PLA 2001).

Positive messages

The relationships that are forged with parents and carers are crucial to the happiness and security of the children within the EYFS setting. One aspect of this that is highlighted by the EYFS document is maintaining a professional relationship between staff, parents and carers. Staff must work within safeguarding guidelines but maintain a professional and approachable relationship with families who may not conform to their expectations of parenting behaviour. Equally, they should find ways to build strong relationships without becoming over-familiar with parents and carers. By pointing out this tension, the document emphasizes how difficult it can be for EYFS staff to cope with the emotional demands of working with parents and carers while maintaining a professional role. The key is to focus on the need of the child, especially where a problem arises, and also rely on support from the staff team. Sometimes a member of staff may be struggling to cope with maintaining a healthy relationship with perhaps demanding or stressed parent and carers, or may feel overwhelmed by the needs of a particular child (Goldschmied and Jackson 1994; DCSF and NHS 2008a). Systems will need to be in place to support anyone in this situation as well as new colleagues and those members of staff who may be struggling to work well together. These may involve one-to-one debriefing or 'supervision' in which staff can discuss and work through any issues. Mentoring can be useful but needs to be monitored so that experienced colleagues do not dominate others. Senior management have an important role to play but other staff must also feel secure in sharing information about difficult relationships in the setting and know the mechanisms for doing so. By emphasizing this area as part of the EYFS principles the document acknowledges how important adult relationships and feelings are in allowing children to feel safe and nurtured (DCSF and NHS 2008a).

It is also important to consider the way in which providers convey a message of respect and equality. In particular, ways of welcoming and including those who may not feel comfortable in the EYFS setting need to be planned. While multilingual notices are useful it is far from sufficient just to display a welcome poster! Positive promotion of bilingualism and ethnic diversity should be part of all staff roles, policies and planning in the setting (Siraj-Blatchford and Clarke 2000; DCSF 2007a). Settings that assume all parents and carers will understand the routines and conventions of the dominant culture disadvantage those who don't (PLA 2001). These issues can be addressed by carefully thought-out communication between providers and parents or carers (see Chapter 6).The first messages about each setting's ethos are available before a child joins the EYFS, through publicity materials such as websites and prospectuses. The values and beliefs of the provider should at this point include a commitment to inclusion and equal opportunities and this will need to be supported by positive visual images of all kinds of families. Providers will need to make arrangements for translations and interpretation where possible, sometimes in published materials but more usefully in person during visits and admission. Sometimes using other parents is necessary but staff must do their best to ensure that these ad hoc interpreters are conveying the messages they intended (DCSF 2007b).

Providers must consider the needs of all families when admitting children, in particular those who may have recently arrived from another country or those who move from one school to another regularly as part of a travelling community. Arrangements can be made easier for these families by having photos of the uniform, making clear where to purchase items or even lending spare clothes to children who will only stay in the school for a few weeks (Kiddle 1999). It may help the child's transition to the setting if staff first meet with the family and then admit the child or children to the setting the next day. This gives the staff time to prepare a space for a new child's belongings, make any name labels, perhaps introduce more home language words and let the other children know to expect a new friend (DCSF 2007b). All of these simple strategies can help a child to feel reassured and valued.

Too often providers will assume that they know a child's first language, home experience or religion from the predominant local community or from their experience with other similar families. Of course no two families have the same set of circumstances and assumptions such as these are extremely detrimental to appropriate care and learning for these children, so specific information about family languages and religion should be recorded. Providers should take care to explain to parents and carers why this is important, in order to get the most accurate information. Without reassurance and explanations parents/carers may omit specific details, such as choosing not to mention that their first language is a community language that is not widely used (DCSF 2007b).

Resources and language

In order for all children and families to feel valued and respected the EYFS setting must feel familiar and reflect their lives (Datta 2000; Conteh 2003; DCSF 2006b). This can be achieved by evaluating and selecting resources that reflect a range of cultures and family circumstances (Knowles and Riley 2005). Common difficulties with attempts to reflect different ethnic backgrounds include using narrow images of people in other countries without showing their counterparts involved in daily life in Britain, using national costumes as part of the role-play area or depicting Traveller families in old style horse-drawn caravans (Siraj-Blatchford and Clarke 2000; Knowles and Riley 2005). It is important to ensure that the characters in stories and images on view are really a positive and up-to-date representation and link to children's real-life experiences. It is not always necessary to purchase special resources for this purpose for example providing pieces of fabric such as sari material or something with strong patterns and bright colours can be useful for children to create their own dressing up and photos from home can also be used as positive illustrations. Dual-language texts and tapes can be created with the help of bilingual parents or assistants.

Case study

Agatha found a cassette in the music box at her childminder's house. When she put it in the cassette player she discovered that it was a tape of Polish nursery rhymes. At first she looked shocked, then she sat down next to the tape player, listening intently, laughing and smiling.

Misbah was alone in the home corner concentrating on wrapping herself in a piece of sari fabric. She came up to teacher and asked for help. 'What are you doing?' the teacher asked. 'I am grandma, going shopping', she said.

Multilingual signs and word books show children and adults that their home language is valued but only when they are used as part of everyday reference and not as a token gesture. Staff members should also use positive and correct terminology and pronounce names correctly (PLA 2001; DCSF 2007b); if unsure they should ask parents how they describe their own ethnic origin or pronounce their child's name. Practitioners should also understand the importance of continuing home language development for children who are learning **English as an additional language**. They should use play opportunities to encourage language development in both the home language and English as well as responding sensitively to any **silent period** (DCSF 2007a; Drury 2007). This may require additional staff training and well-planned use of bilingual assistants where available. Managing multiple language needs is challenging for EYFS providers but is an area where a small amount of effort can at least help children to feel comfortable enough to take risks and learn. While many strategies can benefit all the children in the EYFS it is important to plan to address language needs on an individual basis and not assume that all EAL learners will need the same treatment. They are most likely to succeed in an environment that starts from their existing knowledge and interests than one that assumes they are entering education as empty vessels (Siraj-Blatchford and Clarke 2000; Andrews and Yee 2006; Drury 2007).

Many of these strategies are already being used in good EYFS environments. The expectation of the new document is that this good practice will be consistent throughout the curriculum so in all activities and experiences there will be frequent opportunities to explore and understand other cultures and affirm children's own positive identity. This moves away from the sometimes tokenistic approach in early years settings of marking festivals and food tasting. Providers need to develop their ideas further so that they do not only address the cultures and languages present in their setting at the time but present a balanced view of the diverse society in which we live and model respect through their relationships with children, parents/carers and each other.

6 Parents as partners

This chapter will describe successful strategies to enable a partnership with parents to exist. These will include assessment strategies, booklets, family learning and groups, home/school projects, open days, fayres, celebration events and maintaining shared dialogue. It will also describe how to use the environment of the setting to promote cooperation and collaboration to enhance the progress and development of the children. Attention will be given to developing relationships with harder to reach groups such as fathers, working parents or those who do not speak or understand English.

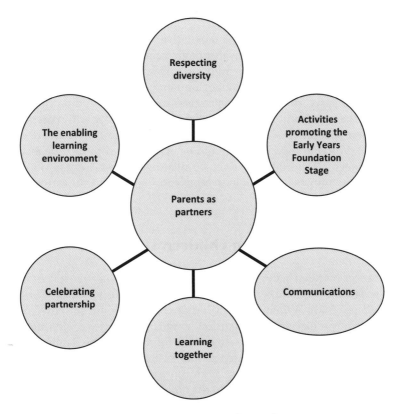

Strategies to foster a partnership with parents

This chapter forms part of the Positive Relationships area. It is underpinned by the EYFS principle that 'Children learn to be strong and independent from a base of loving and secure relationships with parents and/or a key person.'

Good practice

According to the EYFS framework, 'Parents are children's first and most enduring educators. When parents and practitioners work together in early years settings, the results have a positive impact on children's development and learning.' Research by Osborn and Milbank (1987) identified the positive effects of partnerships with parents to provide a shared concern for children's learning and progress. The EPPE project (Sylva *et al.* 2004) noted the importance of a home background in which children's intellectual and social development was enhanced by the active engagement of parents in activities with them. In 2006 the Parents as Partners in Early Learning (PPEL) project reviewed current provision. The key messages from the report included the emphasis on the importance of establishing effective partnerships with parents. Parenting networks established in some authorities were also highlighted as encouraging good practice in disseminating effective strategies.

Good practice is established through the building of an appropriate environment and atmosphere to foster successful, collaborative partnerships. This can be planned and implemented in a variety of ways through a foundation of trust and honest relationships. These relationships have implications for the children in the setting and how secure they feel in a new environment, and for practitioners to be able to ascertain a child's point of entry, so that experiences can successfully build on those gained at home and in the community. There is a shared responsibility with parents/carers to provide the best possible conditions to allow for optimum and all-round development for each child. Working together, it should be endeavoured to provide as wide a variety of experiences as possible in a rich, stimulating yet secure environment to help children develop, enjoy their explorations and learning and become caring, thoughtful members of society.

Communication – sharing children's progress

Communication between parents/carers and the EYFS setting is vital in supporting children's progress. Successful communication can be established before a child attends the proffered provision. When a parent has accessed the form for entry or declared interest in securing a place in the provision, a welcoming letter could offer a time for a visit to the facility or suggest an arrangement for a visit to the family home. When visiting a home appropriate safeguards should be followed based on a knowledge of the area. A small gift could be brought from the setting to enable the child to have a positive recollection of the visit and help the child prepare for entrance to the setting. Families can often feel more at ease in their environment, which could support sharing of key events or achievements in the child's life. This could help to identify strategies to aid the transition to the setting from home and plan and prepare for the child's needs. Visits arranged to the setting can help parents and carers gain an understanding of the setting and its aims and ethos. They can encourage networking between parents/carers and the facility, and encourage them to feel a valued part of the setting. A booklet can provide an outline of the facilities and identify adults working in the setting in order to promote a rapport from the outset. Parents and staff can discuss routines to encourage a knowledge of the activities in which their child will be participating, while practitioners gain an understanding of the child, such as possible health issues, concerns voiced by the family and the achievements of the child.

On admission the parents/carers and the child should be able to:

- get to know the staff, routines, environment and activities in the setting;
- have access to a named person and time for discussion as needed;
- relate to and participate in the enabling environment of the setting.

The importance of the relationships, ensuring continuity and shared understanding between home and school, should be demonstrated as an ongoing part of the experiences of the child. Practitioners should do their utmost to welcome parents/carers and children and encourage children to want to come. A key person can support new visitors to the setting by showing them the facilities, helping them to get to know some of the children and the resources available. If the child does not attend frequently procedures should be in place to ascertain why. Colleagues can promote liaison by planning, cooperating and working well together.

Respecting diversity

Effective partnerships with parents/carers are vital to ensure that children develop in a happy and secure environment. There are many ways practitioners can take a proactive stance in promoting this crucial aspect of work. A warm, welcoming atmosphere can be fostered through a stimulating and inviting entrance. Sharing information with parents/carers regarding routines, times, objectives and planning will promote shared dialogue. It is part of a practitioner's role to respect parents/carers as a significant component of a child's life and be aware that the home life provides a basis for children's understanding of the world. In such a way children's backgrounds should be valued and celebrated as part of the richness of the diversity in the setting. This can be utilised in planning the partnership of care between practitioners and parents/carers. Posters in a variety of languages could be purchased or designed to help make parents/carers feel welcome when they begin to use the provision. Resources, for example books, can be bilingual to provide access for children as well as aid communication with parents. Parents/carers can be encouraged to share their views through ongoing discussions at the beginning and end of sessions, reflection sheets following activities achieved at home, diaries of certain events, shared themes such as holiday photographs, or more formal meetings with the staff at the setting. A key person, responsible for individual children, can also help to forge relationships with the adults surrounding the child and act as a contact with whom they can share or celebrate any events which might concern them. Parents can be asked for their views about the provision and encouraged to support changes and improvements. Newsletters are a useful way of contacting parents to keep them informed if they are unable to visit the setting themselves.

Fathers can be welcomed by ensuring they are aware they are valued in the provision. Discussions can lead to an understanding of their fears or interests for their children. Family support groups, such as meetings, literacy, numeracy or language workshops can be used as a means of including fathers in their child's learning and development. Expertise could be harnessed through materials made or events supported, always ensuring that the necessary safety procedures are covered.

The ethos of the setting should be built on the Every Child Matters agenda, which highlights five areas of *being healthy, staying safe, enjoying and achieving, making a positive contribution* and *achieving economic and social well-being.* Strong partnerships with parents help to facilitate these issues through liaison regarding health concerns, joint working to ensure children remain safe and secure, promoting achievements and sharing the enjoyment of learning and developing. It is important to build on strengths described by parents prior to a child starting a setting, provide a firm foundation for future progress through strong relationships between staff and parents, and promote a sound background for the development of every child. Provision for individual children can be fostered through partnerships with parents to ensure that all children feel included, welcome and part of a community with a strong ethos and vision for the future of the setting.

Learning together – the shared learning environment

An initial opening for shared discussion could be a booklet covering key aspects of the setting's practice.

The following checklist suggests some strategies for developing strong partnerships with parents.

Achieved	Strategy
	On-entry shared discussions between practitioners, children and parents/carers
	'All About Me' booklets compiled with children as individuals
	Record of achievements in place and shared
	Noticeboard demonstrating diversity, to share information
	Partnerships with parents considered as part of ongoing dialogues
	Open days, events planned etc.
	Visits and visitors used to broaden children's awareness
	Activities to share with setting/parents
	Routine links forged with parents

Practical suggestions

Every effort should be made to develop good relationships with parents and carers. These can be encouraged through the following strategies:

- Provide time, possibly at the beginning and end of sessions, to talk about the children with parents/carers and receive regular information about their child's progress.
- Discuss any concerns.
- Encourage parents/carers to look around the setting at appropriate times to see children's efforts and achievements and gain further insight into the rationale and ethos of the environment.
- Work together to provide a happy start for children with parents and carers who are reassured that the children are given an excellent provision facilitated by caring staff.
- Share strategies for promoting the welfare of their child to provide a well-rounded environment both at home and in the setting.
- Parents and carers could provide further help and support if they wished to do so. This could be with outings or making apparatus for games or activities, such as storysacks.
- Effective communication can be shared through a parents/carers noticeboard, showing photographs or examples of the planned curriculum from the Early Years Foundation Stage, details of the planned overview of the week, activities for the day and any relevant newsworthy events, such as an open afternoon.

Effective practice

This section describes successful strategies such as open days, fayres, parent/carer groups, displays, booklets with a theme such as Literacy in the Environment and shared activities based on the Early Years Foundation Stage.

Open days

These can be organized as part of a celebration of children's activities and achievements, possibly following a theme. Individuals could be hosts to distribute refreshments. Care needs to be taken for the children's safety during this time, with reference made to procedures while the visitors are in the setting and to ensure children leave in a supervised manner.

Fayres

These are a pleasant way to enjoy the relationships forged and celebrate the work of the setting. Games and activities to enjoy during the fayre can be carefully planned, for example Hook a Duck or face painting. The local council might have resources that could be made available, such as Catch the Ball equipment.

Any monies obtained would need to be audited.

Parent/carer groups

These could meet to carry out activities such as making equipment for the children. This should be checked to ensure it is safe for the children to use. There are a range of relevant activities in which parents could be involved. They could include parent/carer and toddler groups or family literacy, numeracy or language groups. Again, relevant procedures would need to be followed to ensure awareness of children's safety and the setting's responsibilities and liabilities.

Displays

Reference to partnerships with parents can be made through the display of models or artefacts made at home, incorporated with those made in the setting. Articles to enhance the display can be brought from home, such as photographs and collage work of children's grandparents or older friends, a favourite toy or teddy bear.

Home/setting activities

A wide range of ideas are available in books or articles regarding activities that can be shared between the setting and the home. Examples could include such themes as Homes, in which model homes could be made at home and brought to the setting. Activities based on 'Ourselves' could include comparisons with other family members, for example comparing sizes of feet.

Pressure should not be placed on parents to complete the activities with their child as this is not always possible but those completed can be celebrated while others are given the opportunity to attempt the activities within the setting.

Children's own books could be made at home to illustrate their experiences and imaginations and shared with other children in the provision. Books can be shared to describe aspects of practice, for example supporting an awareness of literacy in the environment.

Challenges and dilemmas – extending liaison

Effective liaison with parents can develop links with other agencies through existing practice. Organizations such as **Portage** can be accessed and information shared on children's progress for those who are involved with the support. Links with health and social services can also be fostered through relevant provision for children. This framework builds on parents' experiences and shares their concerns and delights in a child's progress, providing secure and caring support for parents and children.

Fathers need to be made welcome and included as some settings might need to encourage them to participate if activities are female-dominated.

Celebrating achievement

Achievements can be celebrated through display, for example an 'I can' wall where children's successes both at home and in the setting can be acknowledged. Records of achievement can be organized in such a way as to promote the sharing of a child's experiences; keeping a diary of events and evidence of activities achieved can be used to encourage the child's progress.

7 Supporting Learning

This chapter considers the ways in which the practitioner enables the child to learn.

By the end of the chapter, practitioners should see themselves as facilitators of learning and should begin to reflect upon what that means in terms of engaging with the learning process.

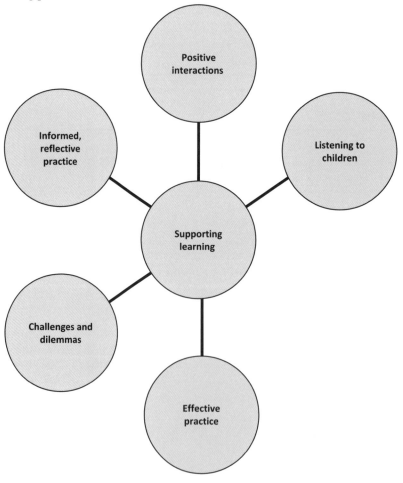

Empowering young children to learn

The role of early years practitioners is to support the learning process of every individual child in their care. It is essential to build warm, trusting relationships with the children, their parents and carers, on a foundation of mutual respect, and to have high expectations of every child based on assessment of each individual's personal strengths and areas for development. This involves talking and listening to the child and observing the child within the setting, encouraging and extending curiosity and learning. Activities and resources based on the child's interests or on **assessment of prior learning** are the **starting point stimuli** from which the child's robust knowledge and understanding is extracted and used to set subsequent **learning challenges**. The child will appreciate and benefit from frequent opportunities to revisit activities or to extend earlier learning opportunities further and to consolidate learning by testing **hypotheses**.

Positive Interactions

Babies and toddlers show their enthusiasm for a task with smiles, gurgles and limb activity.

Case study

Harpreet, aged five months, is lying on her back. She sees her childminder kneeling next to her holding a shiny red rattle. She calls out in delight. Momentarily, she focuses on the rattle then makes bicycling movements with her legs. She smiles and shouts. Her childminder shakes the rattle from side to side, making a new sound. Harpreet makes a connection between the rattle and the sound. On subsequent occasions, the rattle is left near Harpreet's feet. Initially she moves her legs to show pleasure and when she incidentally makes a physical connection with the rattle, she hears the shaking sound. Momentarily she is still, listening. Then she kicks again, expecting to hear the sound. After several repetitions, she is able to choose to make the rattling sound.

Crucially, parents, carers and practitioners are regularly engaged in reflection, dialogue and decision making with the child. The child's physical, mental and spiritual needs are met because learning only takes place when the child's **reptilian brain** is satisfied in a warm, friendly and comfortable or 'enabling' environment.

Listening to Children

Unconstrained 'dialogic' learning (Alexander 2008a), or learning involving a dialogue with children, is crucial in order to understand what children like and dislike and how this affects them and their learning. For this to be effective, the child needs to have a positive relationship with the adult carer without fear of ridicule or failure. There is a difference between conversations that involve people speaking at each other and dialogue that involves focused conversations related to the task in hand. This has implications for children with, for example, speech or developmental delay or hearing impairments, children with verbal dyspraxia or those who are elective mutes. In these circumstances, referring to a **picture exchange system** or **Makaton** helps children to communicate with staff. It also has implications for the percentage of time that adults spend watching, talking and listening to the children. Through verbal communication with children, professionals can discover information about aspects of their lives at home or with their extended family and can use this information to extend the learning process, with reference to familiar elements of the child's life-world experience. The amount of knowledge known about the child impacts on the practitioner's ability to support the child's learning needs and to personalize the learning experience. All shared information is confidential to the setting. The task of the professional is to design a series of activities to stimulate the child to talk about the world that he or she knows and to question the boundaries of that knowledge. A philosophy that incorporates the child in the centre and at the heart of the learning process is essential, in contrast to considering the child as a passive recipient of knowledge, an 'empty vessel' to be filled. Managers should ensure that all professionals are engaged with the children rather than each other. Children do listen to conversations between adults. Within this dialogic process, the professional models and extends the child's vocabulary and grasp of language and language conventions so that dialogues become increasingly meaningful.

Children respond to the questions that they are asked, usually trying to give the answers that adults expect. These can be closed questions, such as 'Are you warm enough?' to which the reply is simply 'Yes.' This kind of questioning is useful for testing. Open questions, such as 'How can we make the water flow across to the sand pit?', in which the child has either to use resources to show their meaning or describe the process of moving water from one place to the other, explore information with no set answer: reasoning, hypothesizing and evaluating experiences. The child might give insights into his or her understanding by mentioning, for example, 'The pipes have to flow downwards because water doesn't go up.'

It is important to model listening to a range of information from the children to gauge when they need more time to repeat an activity, when they feel confident, when learning is taking place and when they feel scared, bored or frustrated. Conventions should be observed such as taking turns in the conversation, not butting in and respecting what the child has to say. Professionals tune in to, rather than talk at, children.

The children's conversations give the starting points for the next steps in learning. These keys to understanding will include the following:

- *Feedback*, which includes children's evaluative comments on their own achievement and what might be the next step in their learning. For example, the professional asks: 'William, can you tell us about your good idea?' William enthusiastically sets out his thinking in language understood by his peers. His enthusiasm is the motivating factor for discovery learning. The professional acknowledges the good idea and enables William to develop this further by interacting with others.

- Professionals should be aware of the impact that negative or humiliating comments can have on learners' confidence and enthusiasm. All feedback should be as constructive as possible. Constructive comments should focus on the work rather than the person to enable both learning and motivation.
- *Specific judgements* about their own attainment or how they estimate attainment. Children frequently underestimate their own ability to solve problems because adults are too ready to give solutions rather than setting challenges that enable the children to learn. Professionals should take account of the level of children's communication skills, their level of confidence and competence in English, their level of understanding and their ability to express what achievement means for them.
- *Self-evaluation.* Children appraise their own performance and are encouraged to talk about the things that went well. Notice that children are quick to compare their achievement with that of others in the setting.
- *Psycho-social questioning.* For example, to encourage non-participating children to engage, professionals may ask, Susan, you have a new puppy?' Careful listening will ensure that the practitioner understands when children feel that they have made real progress, or the significance of the picture drawn. Young children are able to express pleasure at producing their best work.

Reflections

- How do I shift the power balance to 'cede' the power to decide what happens next, to the children?
- How does dialogic learning and teaching improve the range of activities provided for the children?

Effective teaching

The process of learning and teaching children is cyclical. Consider the model below as a wheel turning in a clockwise rotation from the top.

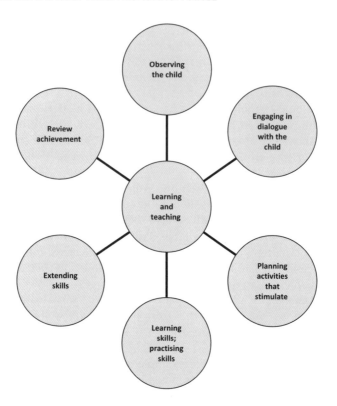

Case study

A skilled practitioner announces that the new focus will be on Nick Butterworth's *Percy the Park Keeper*. She is using the theme of Autumn and the natural resources freely available to plan interesting activities. The children listen to the story and plan a role-play corner. From the story, they identify the items that Percy must have in his shed and a few more from their own experience of sheds. For instance, they suggest that he needs:

a park keeper cap and scarf;
a folding chair;
a carpet or rug;
a table on which to pot plants;
a trowel;
seeds;
a wheel barrow – which Courtney has at home and volunteers to bring;
a newspaper and shelf of gardening books to read when he has a cup of tea and a teapot and mug for his tea.

Notice that the children draw out the ideas of what goes into the role-play corner and are encouraged to bring in items from home or to make representational artefacts. Children must be involved in the choice of tasks that they are offered so that they develop their ability to think and plan independently. The practitioner adds to the items to extend the learning potential of the activities and to motivate the children to concentrate and takes some items away over days or even weeks so that the role-play area evolves in response to the children's suggestions that bring their home life and setting life together. This area is their special place, which they are encouraged to keep tidy. Seasonal elements are added, as the children are introduced to a world without violence or fear, for example using natural resources (such as the leaves that Percy has collected). These can be used for clay templates, pressing the ridges of the veins into clay, leaf pictures, colour matching, sorting by size, scrunching, language extension, matching to the trees in the outside area. Seeds can be sorted, colour matched or manipulated with tweezers to develop fine motor skills and hand–eye coordination, or planted to experience a variety of plants and conditions for growth. Percy has a recycling bin and eats five pieces of fruit or vegetables per day. His milk is semi-skimmed. He uses a laptop to communicate with the local council and a **digi blue** to record the growth of his plants.

The professional needs to plan ahead for learning to take place so that the learning opportunities are presented sequentially and necessary skills are pre-identified and developed. A professional's planning should provide opportunities for both learner and teacher to obtain and use information about progress towards learning goals, as outlined in the six areas of learning of the Early Years Foundation Stage *Setting the Standards for Learning, Development and Care for Children from Birth to Five* document. Curriculum planning needs to take account of available space and resources, including human resources. It also has to be flexible to respond to initial and emerging ideas and skills. Planning should include strategies to ensure that learners understand the goals they are pursuing and the criteria that will be applied in assessing their work. It is also important to consider how learners will receive feedback, how they will take part in assessing their learning and how they will be helped to make further progress.

To achieve this, it is useful to consider the potential variations of each resource. For example, paint can be used for teaching colour mixing skills; add glue or soap suds and change the consistency and experience. Liquid paint, powder paint and tempera blocks can be used. Children can experience free painting with brushes or finger painting, paint with big brushes, small brushes and sponges. They can 'rag-roll', roll marbles in paint and add cornflour. They can paint with icing sugar on black paper.

These different creative suggestions can be used sequentially to offer variety and skill extension. However, if an activity is popular and children are benefiting from engaging with it, it does not make learning sense to take the activity away from them in order to follow a prepared planning sequence. Thus planning has to be flexible, responding to the specific needs of the children at any time.

In time, children need to know about the adult world but this can develop in response to the questions that children explicitly ask. This has implications for the content of informal conversations between members of staff and their choice, modelling and reinforcement of appropriate language.

Children often prompt their own learning by talking about what they know. Parents, carers and practitioners scaffold the learning process by providing suitable resources that extend learning but are still within the child's reach to use independently such as books, video clips, plant pots, magnifying glasses, growing medium and tools. The adult role is that of an enabler, or facilitator of learning, helping the children to choose activities that challenge their thinking or existing skills. This places an understanding of progress and achievement at the heart of developing the learning process.

By modelling and decoding language in context and with a specific purpose, children learn to behave appropriately, aware of the professional's expectations and able to understand how to develop particular practical skills. Language and jargon can also be a barrier to understanding. Frequently, children are asked 'Why' or 'How' questions, assuming that children understand these abstract words.

Effective Practice

Professionals need to consider the variety of influences that affect children's perceptions and ability to thrive. *Every Child Matters* (DfES 2003) and the Children Act (DfES 2004a) have formalized multi-agency working, bringing together childminders and early years settings with social services, formalizing the transition into school. **Extended schools** and **Wrap-around care** are designed to give further support to children and families outside the normal school hours. The result is a social policy designed to reduce child poverty and increase educational attainment through its five outcomes, with a high priority given to social inclusion. Everyone working with children must demonstrate through the inspection process that they are working towards meeting the five outcomes. More recently, Children's Trusts led by a Director of Children's Services have been introduced.

All practitioners need to develop an awareness of the variety of cultural mores and traditions of the children within the setting and of children from the six major world religions. They should also familiarize themselves with the reasonable adjustments needed to support children with a range of learning differences, building respectful and caring relationships with all children and families while focusing on learning and achievement. They should 'put into practice the written policy of listening to children who are non-verbal, or use alternative communication systems'.

Challenges and Dilemmas

It is difficult to allocate sufficient time to gauge the children's response to tasks set. Professionals are challenged to make that balance using their assessment of the value of the current activities compared with a series of new activities.

Resourcing activities on a limited budget can also be challenging. It helps to put in place a two-year cycle of themes that can be revisited so that resources are prioritized according to the themes.

Inclusive practice means offering activities to all of the children in a setting. There is a dilemma in deciding whether an activity that is unsuitable for a child with particular needs should be offered to other children in the setting.

Children's Needs

- Children need sensitive, knowledgeable adults who know when and how to engage their interests and how to offer support at different times.
- Children benefit from a range of experiences, including those that are predictable, comforting and challenging.
- When children's physical and emotional needs are met they are more ready to take advantage of the play and learning opportunities on offer.

Reflecting on Practice

Reflection, or 'assessment', can take a variety of forms. Initially, professionals tend to describe the behaviours that they see. This practice can be developed by highlighting key issues that are drawn out of the description and then effecting change by concentrating on managing change of practice. The professional compares achievement to benchmarks of expectations of children at a specific age or stage of development. This assumes that development is uniform and unproblematic, which it is not. Each child develops uniquely, at his or her own pace. Children with access to the same resources and with similar support from adults may progress at different rates.

To record this, many settings use digital photographs and MP4 digital video clips as evidence of achievement. As technology advances, children in the later foundation stage can be taught to respect and use digital cameras and 'tuffcams' to record their own achievements or to share their learning on the interactive whiteboard in schools, as a follow-up to a learning session. Central to the role of the practitioner is knowing when to watch and listen and when to prompt learning. Children are able to identify what they feel they can and cannot achieve independently. They sometimes stand back and observe others until they feel able to take part in the activity but the observational element can be a necessary phase in the learning process.

As the knowledge and skill of the practitioner develops, the child begins to take the lead in directing his or her own learning.

8 Key person

This chapter discusses the different roles the key person might have. A consideration is given to key qualifications and the standards they cover. Key features of the role are considered, for example leading the team, preparing for activities in a play-based environment and ensuring aspects of the Early Years Foundation Stage are covered.

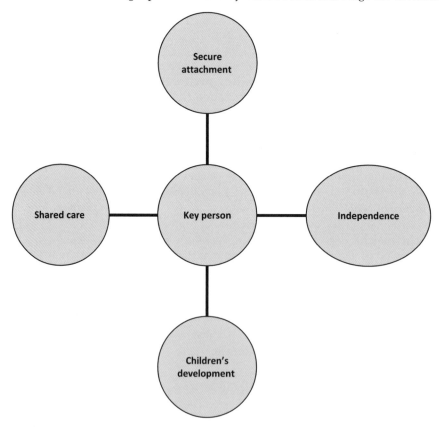

Aspects of the key person's role

The *key person* chapter is part of the Positive Relationships section, which is based on the EYFS principle that 'Children learn to be strong and independent from a base of loving and secure relationships with parents and/or key person.'

Secure attachment

Children develop in different ways, have special interests and dislikes, have their own identity and are unique. To nurture this unique perspective children should have a key person to care for their welfare and progress while they are in the early years. A strong bond can be formed, which would ease transitions, share progress and development and provide a base from which the child can grow, linking closely to the Every Child Matters agenda. The key person can liaise with parents, track a child's progress and form a base from which to identify a child's achievements and needs. The adult identified can be a familiar person for the child to have as a secure point of contact with the wider world, while sharing the child's development with the parents/carers. These relationships promote the development of children as individuals as a basis from which they can realize their potential. This is important throughout a child's early years, in a birth to 5 setting and as they progress through primary school.

Fostering links with a key person throughout these years can help to support seamless provision to enable transitions to be part of the continuous process with harmonious relationships. Bowlby's research based on attachment theory in 1953 emphasized the effects of a relationship between a child and the mother. While the findings could be controversial, the importance of relationships with key adults in a child's life are considered in the EYFS framework.

Case study

The observation of a 4-year-old girl identified how she needed the security of her key person yet was able to gain confidence during the day to lessen contact with the adult. She began the session by using coloured pencils to draw a picture of an animal she had seen on a previous visit to a farm. She showed the key person. She started to use wax crayons to draw a picture of the animal and again showed the key person her achievement. She then painted over the wax crayons with water colours to complete her picture. She put the picture to dry and this time found a friend to work with when drawing pictures of animals they had seen on the visit. She wrote about the visit and the animals using some recognizable letters including her first name.

Shared care

It is crucial that good relationships are forged at the onset. A child's experiences on first leaving home could be a challenging experience or one where the child feels well supported to cope with the next stage of development. Children who feel supported are able to develop the confidence to explore and attempt their own discovery and creativity. These close links with the child and those surrounding him or her will deepen the key person's knowledge and enable the professional to respond appropriately and sensitively to perceived needs, interests and requirements.

Case study

A child entering early years provision was anxious and upset about the prospect of leaving his mother. She was also anxious about his ability to cope with the social situation in the setting after spending most of his time at home with her. They attended an open afternoon and played together with a variety of resources available. A visit was made to the child's home where he was introduced to his key person, who left a booklet describing the routines, discussed what the child might achieve, and left a memento from the early years setting. When the child visited the setting he and his mother were warmly greeted by the key person, whom they were pleased to meet again. The parent stayed for a short while until the child had found he enjoyed playing in the sand, then left, returning later in the morning at the end of the session – the arrangement that had been agreed when the child was at home. He played in the sand, watching others in the setting. Later he made and decorated a hat, discussing the materials with a few peers and encouraged by the key person. At the end of the session he proudly displayed his hat, was keen to take it home when his parent returned, and eager to come the following day. Later, the parent joined a meeting group for parents associated with the early years provision and became a helper in the setting.

Transitions to a setting might not be as straightforward as the one described above. Further liaison might be necessary in the initial stages to reassure parents that a child has settled and that their role continues to be vital and valued, as they could feel a sense of loss as the child gains independence.

Challenging circumstances at home can also need much sensitivity, support and awareness of confidentiality while the events are being addressed and resolved. Children could need further reassurance during such times and the continuation of familiar routines and the support of the key person could make a significant difference to the well-being and progress of the child.

A key person can liaise with other adults involved with the child to provide a source of contact and shared dialogue to consider ongoing learning, development and care. Observations, assessments and records of learning and development can be compiled as a team, shared and available to those responsible for the child's care. The differing, complementary roles should be viewed as aspects of the whole provision. The role of the key person should complement that of the parents, who can be reassured that their child is cared for and supported in his or her explorations and be content that an adult is there for their child. The awareness of differing roles should be acknowledged by the practitioner to negate any feelings of jealousy or desire to have the child dependent upon the key person.

Independence

The key person's role facilitates the child's ability to grow in independence in a secure and caring environment where reassurance can be sought when necessary.

Case study

In an early years setting each child is allocated a key person. Parents/carers and children are aware who their key person is and will meet the practitioner during the initial visits. Once the relationship is established, ongoing dialogue takes place. At the start of the sessions the key person is ready to welcome the children and their parents/carers. This provides opportunities to discuss any concerns or events that might have occurred. The session begins with the child and key person discussing the start of the activities, the key person ensuring the child feels happy and content in the surroundings. Throughout the activities in the session the child has a contact nearby if needed. At the end of the session the key person is able to greet the parent/carer and provide an overview of the child's responses while at the setting.

Growing independence can be supported throughout the early years. Babies will need love and attention from the adults in the setting and require much time spent with them to give them the emotional and physical care they need. By working with, observing and forming relationships with the babies, knowledge can be gained of each unique child in the setting. This constant care and attention gives a sound basis for valued opinions about the child which can be shared, based on the deep understanding the practitioner will have gained through the constant and daily communication and interactions in the setting.

With this strong foundation of knowledge about an individual child a practitioner is able to plan appropriate steps, including the development of confidence building and independence. This continuity of care can help children to feel secure and able to take risks, and to design their own activities. The development of independence needs to be observed carefully to assess areas where a child might need continuing support to gain assurance. Children can be encouraged to use the whole space in the setting or certain areas if required. They can plan their learning activities and share their learning with their peers and with adults. However, some children might need to be encouraged to have the confidence to do this as early years settings can occasionally appear large and confusing places to a small child. Examples of independent activities could include taking responsibility for their physical independence such as feeding themselves, using the toilet, dressing, putting on a coat or shoes; emotional independence, such as having the confidence to attempt new activities; social independence when approaching others in the setting, interacting with peers and adults, or taking the initiative to care for other children in the group or provision. Observations can check which areas individuals are using and the amount of social interaction taking place.

Children need to be assessed in terms of independence on an individual basis as some might be nervous in the company of many children or need specific help, such as children for whom English is an additional language. Care also needs to be taken to ensure children can access resources offered and that some are not excluded from activities through unintentional difficulties with storage or access. However, individual children might appear confident yet require reassurance and attention to maintain their self-esteem and feelings of worth.

> It can be argued that achieving the best for young children is a matter of adopting a respectful and inclusive attitude to all aspects of provision and practice.
>
> (Nutbrown 2006: 116)

Key person

According to the EYFS framework, 'A key person has special responsibilities for working with a small number of children, giving them the reassurance to feel safe and cared for and building relationships with their parents.' The key person could have a range of qualifications based on the early years. Some of the many key qualifications are Qualified Teacher Status (QTS), Early Years Professional Status (EYPS), BTEC levels 2, 3, or 4, educational psychologists, portage workers, speech therapists, health visitors and social workers. Those working with young children should have the appropriate sensitivity and understanding to do so. In 2001 minimum National Standards were set to ensure a baseline for quality (DfES). The Office for Standards in Education (Ofsted) is responsible in the UK for the inspection of early years providers in line with the requirements of the National Standards. In 2006 the Children's Workforce Development Council (CWDC) aimed to ensure that people working with young children had the appropriate skills to provide care in a multidisciplinary framework. The EYPS provided a pathway to achieving graduate-level qualification for working with early years children. With the introduction of the EYFS, training has been given in a multi-agency approach for those with QTS in maintained settings and those working in private, voluntary and independent provision.

Practitioners work as teams to provide appropriate provision with differing features, for example who is leading the team, preparing timetables, chairing meetings, ordering resources, providing activities and ensuring that aspects of the Early Years Foundation Stage are covered.

All adults working in an early years setting should be suitable to do so. They must have the appropriate skills, knowledge, qualifications and training to be able to fulfil their role as an early years practitioner. Staffing should be organized to provide a suitable standard of provision for all the children in the setting.

Reflections

- Are all members of the team aware who is responsible for each child?
- How is the information shared?
- Who is responsible for ensuring each child is developing to his or her full potential?

Part 3

Enabling Environments

9 Observation, assessment and planning

A wide range of strategies for observing and assessing children are described, for example the use of photographic evidence, tape recordings, children's recordings and achievements, tracking individual, small or whole-group activities, observing an area of learning or an aspect of the environment. Strengths and weaknesses of each strategy are discussed. This leads into a consideration of the assessment and planning cycle of development and progress. Examples are given of ways to use the evidence to complete the Early Years Foundation Stage Profiles. Implications of the profile scores will be considered to enhance future planning.

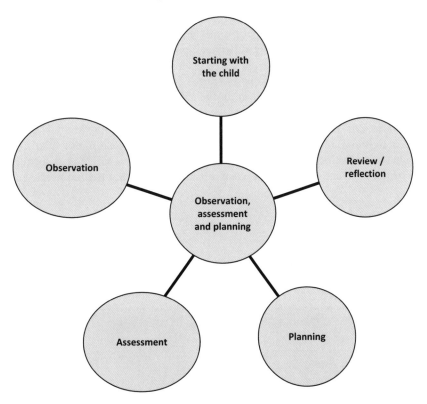

The observation, assessment and planning cycle

Observation, assessment and planning is part of the EYFS principle based on Enabling Environments, which states: 'The environment plays a key role in supporting
and extending children's development and learning.'

Starting with the child

According to the EYFS framework, 'Babies and young children are individuals first,
each with a unique profile of abilities. Schedules and routines should flow with the
child's needs. All planning starts with observing children in order to understand and
consider their current interests, development and learning.' Each child brings its own
unique strengths and achievements to the early years provision. Partnerships with those
involved in their prior care can form a basis for the supportive development of the
individual and ensure appropriate provision is fostered to meet the developing needs
of the child.

Initial collaboration to share a child's development can forge strong bonds between those who care for a child at home and those in a setting. Children's progress is
enhanced by the knowledge that those responsible for their care are working in partnership to promote it. While in the setting collaborative sharing of a child's achievements
between home, the setting, those working within the setting and the wider agency
network can help to strengthen the appropriate provision and address any issues that
might arise. Liaison can be encouraged between providers to maintain a coherent transition if needed, when a child has to move between settings. Work in observations,
assessments and planning can also be reference points when a child moves into Key
Stage 1 to facilitate a smooth transition for the child, drawing on abilities and supporting needs.

The enabling environment incorporating adult-led, adult-initiated and child-
initiated activities can be used as part of the observation, assessment, planning, reviewing cycle. Practitioners can become participant observers where they form part of
the structure of the activities or observe as a bystander viewing the happenings.

Observation

Observations can form part of the everyday life of the setting, helping practitioners to
assess children's development and to determine what the next steps could be.

Case study

Example of an observational tracking
    Kay takes a triangular-shaped polydron and sings while she fixes the pieces
together. She chooses a book about a tractor then continues fixing together the

polydron shapes, making a pyramid shape. She continues to join the shapes and shows an adult her achievements.

Later in the session Kay is observed at the graphics table making a map of a farm she had visited. She talks with her friends about what she saw. Five children make a large map of the farm and use the shapes she made earlier as part of the farm buildings and equipment, including a tractor.

Observations can be organized to identify what is to be assessed, who will undertake the assessments and the time they will take place. Informal assessments could include observations while something else was the focus or those of a colleague who happened to notice an aspect of provision or children's development in the process of carrying out other activities. They could occur while routine procedures are in progress, such as an aspect of personal, social and emotional development while children are sharing fruit or caring for others. Observations to note could include those identified while an adult is pursuing an adult-led activity where the focus was designated as another area of the framework. Planned observations can be conducted in a variety of styles or for a range of reasons. It might be thought beneficial to observe a child's progress during the day to ascertain factors such as relationships with peers or involvement with activities. This could be for set periods throughout the session of a certain time limit, for example five minutes for each observation. It would provide an overview of the child's experiences during the session and enable early years practitioners to discuss the child's development. In this way practitioners are able to gain a broad understanding of the abilities and achievements of the child, building on previous knowledge, in order to design an appropriate range of facilities to meet his or her needs and interests.

Case study

A group of children were excited about their water play and keen to continue with the activities in the following session. Others in the setting were also eager to participate in the water play. An observation of the activity revealed a complex social fantasy play with 'potions' in the capacity equipment available and a story line to which the children enjoyed returning. Their activity incorporated consolidation of concepts regarding capacity, showed a high level of interaction and developed into story writing and making models to support the story created.

Observations can provide a wealth of knowledge and information about children's development, in a relaxed atmosphere where children do not feel pressured. Specific areas in the framework could be identified for further investigation; for example, more input might be felt to be needed in the *communication, language and literacy* strand. Observations could then be focused on activities that promote this area of learning and development. Through observations, discussions can be focused on matters that have arisen, to promote shared dialogue between practitioners. Observations can also broaden the understanding of adults as observers, giving a valuable insight into the perceptions children bring to the settings that might be unfamiliar to the adult observer, therefore forming opportunities for greater understanding and shared dialogue.

An area of provision could be examined to ascertain whether it is fulfilling its original purpose or needs to be changed. Is it used? How often? For what purpose? How are the available resources utilized? This area could be observed for a certain amount of time at short intervals to create a valid record and inform future planning.

Assessment

Assessments can take a variety of forms. They can include information from the observations described earlier or other evidence such as:

- photographs;
- creative activities such as mark making, recording, or modelling achieved by the children;
- video;
- tape;
- observation of the area of the setting a child is visiting;
- observation of independent activities;
- during practitioner-directed activities;
- during routine activities;
- parental/carer observations and knowledge of the child shared formally and informally;
- information shared at planning meetings;
- multi-agency collaboration.

It is useful to annotate evidence as a point of reference when reviewed at a later date. Assessments might be formative, summative or diagnostic. Formative assessments can be made through ongoing practice, such as during daily routines, through discussions with parents or carers or through evidence outlined above. Discussions with children could lead to the identification of skills achieved and progress made, or questioning can result in gaining further knowledge of what a child can do.

Where there is a particular area of concern it might be necessary to gather more information through a diagnostic assessment. This might initially take the form of an individual observation but the involvement of colleagues could help to create a better understanding of the nature of the concern and a clear picture of what it entails. Support could be sought to provide further guidance on the next steps for the child and involvement with the **Common Assessment Framework (CAF).**

The learning, development and care framework enables early years practitioners to track the children's progress through the areas of learning towards the Early Learning Goals. Records should be kept and maintained in an appropriate condition. **The Early Years Foundation Stage Profile** provides an assessment at 5 years of age, usually when the child is at the end of the Reception year. The Early Learning Goals in the EYFS were not designed as assessment criteria, rather as goals to be attained as part of a continuous, seamless process of development. The Early Years Foundation Stage Profile (EYFP), however, provides a summative assessment combined with progress to the Early Learning Goals as a set of 13 assessment scales, each of which has nine points. They do reflect progress and development in the EYFS.

The first three points in each nine-point strand describe a child who is progressing towards the Early Learning Goals in the development stages. The following five points are drawn from the ELGs while the final point is taken as a child working beyong the ELGs who has attained the previous points.

The EYFP can provide a useful means of assessing the progress a child is making and address any needs that might be highlighted. Care should be taken to complete the assessment. A child's progress can be tracked throughout the stay in the early years. This forms relevant information when beginning to complete the profile over the final years of the Early Years Foundation stage. When this is completed as an ongoing strategy it does not become an onerous task but one that fits into existing practice.

These assessments provide a useful means of summative assessment to inform colleagues working in Key Stage 1 and highlight any talents or concerns a child might have, enabling preparations to take place for further support. For example, very low scores in certain strands of the profile could identify a need for special provision for the child, while children having scores of nine points in certain aspects could have access to an appropriate curriculum in those areas in Key Stage 1.

Planning

Planning occurs to provide organization and management in the provision while reflecting on and enhancing the quality obtained for each child. Teams can share ideas in the regular meetings organized. Consideration can be given to the timing of the meetings. Team meetings ensure that provision is appropriate for the children who frequent the facility. Observations can be discussed within the team about a child's abilities and interests, with further information supplied by the formative assessments made by practitioners. This can be used when reviewing how to support a child's next developmental steps. An appropriate environment and suitable resources and activities can be devised to enable the child to experience, discover and enjoy the play-based learning. Plans can be shared with parents and provide a reminder of objectives as part of a display on a noticeboard or in newsletters to keep those involved with the children informed of the pedagogy of the setting. Planning can be organized to provide a holistic experience for the children. Long-term plans can incorporate aspects of an action plan to improve provision. Medium-term plans can provide overviews of what can be achieved in a few weeks, while short-term daily and weekly planning can identify specific strategies to support children's individual needs. Daily plans can be incorporated into the routines to provide ongoing experiences for the child.

Planning can be organized into themes, responding to the needs and interests of the children at the setting. They can foster relevant links with parents/carers.

Review

Review of the observation, assessment and planning cycle is crucial to provide a dynamic system where response is made to the changing needs of the individual children and the requirements of the setting. Formative observations, linked with other forms of assessments, could provide a broad, deep knowledge of the children as individuals. From this knowledge, teams can assess children's learning and reflect upon the next steps for the child. These assessments can inform strategies to build on a child's learning, care and development. These strategies can again be observed to assess their effectiveness and progress. From the observations further assessments can be made to assess progress, and again used to devise further steps in planning. In this way a child's development and progress can be tracked to indicate how a child is faring. It can indicate a child is thriving and that appropriate strategies are in place, or an area of concern could be highlighted that could warrant further investigation through observations to identify appropriate provision. Records can be kept to identify how a child is developing and what areas might require further support. They can also identify the speed of development, which could again highlight any concerns. A child could vary in stages of development, taking time to consolidate a concept or skill before building on his or her learning further. However, unexpected discrepancies could indicate a requirement to readdress achievements, where perhaps the assessments had not sufficiently allowed for the extent of a child's abilities or to take action to respond to concerns.

Evidence can be kept in a variety of ways, through dating achievements or compiling lists of progress in different areas of development. Records of Achievement provide a useful means of sharing a child's development with the child, other practitioners and parents or carers. Contributions to the records can be made through the early years team, parents/carers and wider agencies where appropriate. It is useful to date and possibly annotate evidence to give meaning to the sources kept. Children can share their achievements with others and be proud of their successes. They can become aware of their own abilities and the next steps. For example, in an early years setting jigsaws were given labels indicating levels of difficulty, as a resource for children. When questioned, the children were aware of the significance of the labels, knowing which jigsaws they could complete and those which they would be likely to find harder. Levels of questioning beginning with easily answered questions to those requiring critical thinking can aid children's reflections of work they have achieved and can develop in future sessions. This can be organized as part of the early years routine where older children consider the resources they will access and discuss their activities and achievements at the end of the session. Displays of the children's work can also support children's understanding of their progress by enabling them to change mark making, models and outcomes of other activities by themselves, thus discerning that they have made progress in an aspect of learning. The evidence collected in the Records of Achievement can support decisions regarding aspects of the Early Years Foundation Stage Profile achieved in the summative assessment.

The process could also identify changes needed to the layout, the resources and the manner in which they are organized, routines, provision for individual children and a whole range of issues which could be raised following such ongoing observations and assessments. These can be changed informally, following discussions with the team working in the setting or written as part of an Action Plan. An Action Plan could formalize the changes, identifying a time scale, those responsible for the proposed changes and the outcomes that would deem the project successfully completed.

Reflections

- Is a record system for formative assessments in place?
- Does this support the tracking of children's development and progress?

10 Supporting every child

This chapter covers children's experience of transition and ways to support this, as well as using observation of play to plan for future learning. It offers practical examples of interaction between practitioners, parents and carers and other agencies when supporting children with additional needs.

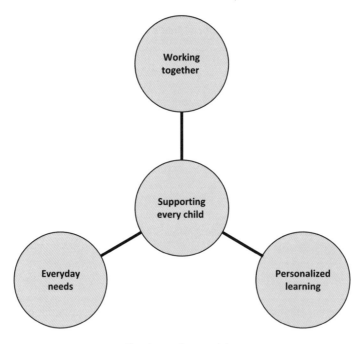

Key issues to consider

The Early Years Foundation Stage (EYFS) (DfES 2007a) reinforces several of the aspects considered in other principles within the broader framework of supporting every child. Sensitive adult support and the consideration of individual physical and emotional needs are highlighted. The importance of planning experiences that match individuals' needs and interests is also emphasized as part of creating a learning context that is flexible and responsive. Settings will need to work well with other professionals and families in order to tailor support for children. They will need to pay particular attention to children's individual needs when managing transitions within and beyond the setting.

Working together and transition

Children in the EYFS will experience a range of transitions. These may be daily between child care and education settings, such as from home to childminder to school and back again or based on part-time care arrangements such as attending a children's centre in the morning and school in the afternoon, or moving between a special playgroup and home. Children will also experience permanent transitions from one education venue to another, for example from nursery to primary school, or a pre-school to a Reception class (Neuman 2002; Johansson 2007). There will also be transitions for individual children and family circumstances such as those experienced when families break down, or move house.

Ensuring that every child is well supported during these transitions may have a significant impact on their later learning as difficult transitions and adjustment, particularly when starting school, may be a predictor for later difficulties in education (Neuman 2002; Margetts 2007). Boys in particular may have more difficulties with the move from one setting to another, while having a strong friendship or an older sibling may help to avoid some potential difficulties for children of either gender (Margetts 2002, 2007). It is important to recognize that problems that children encounter are not only a result of the anxiety of coping with the unfamiliar, although of course this is a potentially anxious time for parents or carers and children. Difficulties for children are most likely to be evident when the expectations of school or the early years setting are at odds with those the child experiences elsewhere. For this reason, although the focus of concern has historically been on the transition from early years setting to school, transitions within the EYFS can also be problematic. Bronfenbrenner's theory of environmental influence (1979) describes the various factors that impact on children's learning, which include both the interaction experienced within the setting and the external forces of society and cultural expectations. This complex combination of factors means that the expectations of early years providers may differ greatly from those of parents and carers and from one location to another (Johansson 2007).

The EYFS document itself goes some way to enable practitioners to support every child by maintaining some consistency of pedagogy and expectation. Aligning this with home experience and parental understanding is crucial, as parents are most likely to base their expectations of early education on their own experiences of school in another era or in another country. Settings will need to ensure that systems are in place to help parents to understand and contribute to their organization of care and learning (Dunlop 2002; Margetts 2007). This should start around the point of entry to the setting where children and parents are able to visit, and can take many forms depending on the age of the child and the setting. They could include: individual visits to settings where parents stay and play with their child, group activities with new parents and new entrants, visits between settings with groups of children for shared stories or performances, home visits from key workers, information meetings, individual consultation and entry plans (Dalli 2002; Peters 2002; Clarke 2007; Margetts 2007). Some thought also needs to be given to the allocation of key workers, as this process needs to be clear to all concerned; the role of the key worker should also be well defined at this time (Peters 2002).

Reflections

- Should the key worker be the only point of contact for the parents or carers of a child?
- Should the key worker plan activities for the child during the transition period or leave this to the child to initiate?
- How should the key worker incorporate information from home into the child's experiences at the EYFS setting?
- How is our setting helping children to make smooth transitions between home and different childcare and education providers?

Case study

In a large multilingual infant school the staff members hold an entry meeting for parents and carers of children in the EYFS. The EYFS staff members show a video of a typical school day and explain the principle of learning through play. They give information on routines for P.E., assembly, lunch and break time. They explain the home reading scheme and opportunities to help the children in their home language. The talk is supported by visual reminders and examples of books and book bags, P.E. kit and so on. Many elements are translated and multilingual staff members are available to answer questions. A programme of activities with the nearby nursery school is in place throughout the year, of shared musical performances, assemblies and visits of groups of children, accompanied by staff members, from one setting to another. The adults from both settings meet to share information and plan in the summer term. When the children start Reception they attend for half days for the first few weeks and can access wraparound care at their previous nursery if their parents or carers are working.

Case study

In a small village school with a mixed age EYFS and Y1 class the children who are due to start school are invited to weekly 'stay and play' sessions for two terms after school with their parents or carers. These take place in the room that will be their classroom with the teacher and teaching assistant. Younger siblings come along and each child takes an activity pack home to bring back the following week. There is an opportunity to get to know family members and to ask and answer questions informally. After this, one or two new entrants at a time are invited to join the class for some summer term sessions, negotiated with their parents, so that they can experience the class without a flurry of new members.

The main consideration for any of these arrangements is that they need to be flexible and prolonged, building up to significant amounts of time spent in the setting and also over a long enough settling-in period. Such arrangements should be negotiated with parents to meet their needs and not approached in a regimented and enforced way (Margetts 2007). Understandably, there are difficulties with some of these approaches because of staff availability, ratios of children and adults and disruption to the existing children in the setting. While these cannot be taken lightly, it is simply insufficient and potentially damaging to admit a child to any early years setting without enough thought and time allocated to this process. This initial entry transition to a new setting should not be seen as the only transition that requires thoughtful collaboration with parents and adults from other settings. Parents should be consistently involved in contributing information about their children's learning, interests and progress at home that can be included in documentation, assessment and forward planning. Similarly, groups of EYFS providers should establish links that enable them to share information during the course of time when children are attending more than one setting. They should also find ways to share their own values and expectations so that the children in their care receive the same messages about what is important. This may be through sharing documentation, visits or network meetings. Forming supportive and collaborative relationships is particularly important in England as suspicion and difficulties with collaborating between providers may be exacerbated by the differences in pay, status, training routes and qualifications as well as environment and resources available in different EYFS settings (Neuman 2002).

Ensuring that practitioners and parents and carers work well together will support children but there are also strategies within settings that may help children to prepare for moving on. Staff in the earlier part of the EYFS can help the children in their care to prepare for changes by focusing specific learning opportunities on the topic of transition, such as sharing stories as a basis for using thinking skills and discussion to help a character who is not sure about what to do in a new situation. Exploring questions such as 'What might Susi be worried about? What does she need to know? How can she find out what to do?' can enable children to work through anxieties and solutions before they are in the new environment (Fabian 2002). Margetts (2002) also suggests including school uniform and book bags in the role-play area of the early years setting as another way to familiarize and prepare children. These ways of working can also be employed to support children with life transitions such as the arrival of a new sibling or moving house. EYFS providers can help children to develop skills such as a willingness to ask for help and the ability to share and take turns. This may help children to adjust more easily to arrangements as they progress through the EYFS, where the adult to child ratio becomes gradually less favourable. However, it is not fair simply to expect children to be ready for school, as their ability to cope with the additional expectations of independence will vary according to their individual personality and experiences (Dockett and Perry 2008). Adapting to a new setting may be particularly challenging for those who are working in a new language or who have specific areas of difficulty. For this reason staff should adapt their provision to meet the needs of their new children and not simply expect children to adapt to fit in with the setting. Children with specific needs are likely to benefit from an individual transition plan where arrangements for sharing information with all staff, liaising with parents and other professionals involved with the child and planning for appropriate routines is organized collaboratively.

Personalized learning

The principle of supporting every child within the EYFS requires a personalized approach to learning. It is important that EYFS providers do not interpret the curriculum and the continuum towards the early learning goals as a restrictive straightjacket, as doing so will reduce opportunities to be flexible and truly inclusive (Jones 2005). Opportunities to meet the learning objectives within the EYFS should be planned for in response to observations and understanding of children's needs and interests. Some time before the advent of the EYFS, early years educators such as Hurst and Joseph (1998) stressed the importance of exploration, child-initiated play and holistic learning experiences. These ideas are very much part of the underpinning principles of the EYFS. Children's learning should not be restricted to one area at a time and the focus of provision should not be on formal large group instruction but on the skills that adults can use to maximize learning, whether this is in groups or one to one (Sylva *et al.* 2003). Real inclusion is not only about supporting the needs of children from potentially vulnerable groups but ensuring that the play and intervention that is available matches the needs of all the children, whether in a special pre-school or catering for mixed ages in a childminder's home (Nutbrown and Clough 2006). For this way of working to be successful, practitioners need procedures that link observation and planning. They will need the skills to observe objectively and understand early learning enough to be able to identify, support and extend the next steps for the child concerned. Parents and other adults should be part of this process and any staff members who are new to using these strategies are likely to need continuing training to ensure that they are effective.

A valuable model for all EYFS educators could be that each new learning opportunity follows a cycle of explain, model, rehearse, reinforce, practise, reflect (Jones 2005). Within this cycle there are opportunities for child-initiated exploration and adult-led experiences, there is talk to link new and familiar ideas and practical and visual reinforcement. Perhaps most importantly, children need to be allowed time to try out new skills and knowledge in a range of different contexts. EYFS providers will need to offer open-ended activities with appropriate challenge for the most able and create a culture where children are encouraged to ask questions and take risks (Porter 2005; Sutherland 2005).

The following case studies demonstrate how observations of child-initiated learning enable practitioners to plan for future learning and adult support. Some of these examples are taken from an Early Years Foundation Stage setting where the learning stories and accompanying photographs are regularly displayed and updated for parents. Parents also have daily access to children's portfolios that are used to document their learning. They are encouraged to record their own observations of children's progress at home. One entry read, 'H rode her bike without stabilizers for the first time this weekend. Mummy, Daddy and Grandma were so proud.' Record keeping and written planning and observations may help practitioners to track, support and share children's learning but should not be completed for their own sake. They should be used at key moments to inform and guide the practitioner.

Learning story 1

During child-initiated play John chose a drum from the creative trolley. He began to play the drum using a steady beat, singing 'We're marching to the drum' (Creative development (CD), sing simple songs from memory). He then called to some of the other children, 'Let's make a band. . . We're a marching band' (Personal, social and emotional development (PSED) dispositions and attitudes: initiates ideas).

He then continued to sing the song he had learned during music. He marched to the beat of the drum '. . . march, march, marching until the music stops!' Stopping the music and standing still, he turned his head to check whether the other children had stopped (CD, matches movement to music).

After he had led the band around the garden twice he then called, 'Who wants to be the leader now?' (PSED, making relationships: takes turns and shares).

Figure 10.1   The practitioner observed John spontaneously initiating a follow my leader game.

Figure 10.2 The practitioner noted John's musical awareness (CD) and his ability to organise others and take turns (PSED).

From this and her other experience of working with this child the practitioner identifies a need to plan for further work on repeated sounds and sound patterns, including sharing a computer programme where John can make sound patterns. There are clearly other opportunities that may also be capitalized on at other times. This is where practitioners must tune into the child and use their professional judgement about which avenue to follow.

Learning story 2

Melissa decided to make a tiara on the making table. She selected her own resources independently and arranged them on the table and started to create (PSED: displays high levels of involvement in self-chosen activities, selects resources independently).

Melissa said 'Sleeping Beauty does have golden hair but you didn't have gold so I had to use yellow.' She then used a variety of ribbons which she cut well with the scissors and sellotape and glue to join her tiara together (Physical development: handles tools safely and constructs with basic control).

Figure 10.3   Melissa shows her skill in joining materials.

Figure 10.4   Melissa is able to select and manipulate appropriate tools and material for the task

Melissa then used her own head to measure her tiara to see if it was the right size. She gauged with her finger where she should put the final piece of tape (PSRN: measuring, KUW constructs in a purposeful way).

Figure 10.5 Melissa uses practical problem solving to measure her creation.

This example shows how children with strengths in a particular area can benefit from open-ended experiences. In this instance the practitioner chose to focus on measuring as a next step to extend this child's understanding and interests.

Observation may also be the means to plan provision for children who are experiencing difficulties, with the help of other professionals and parents. Under Every Child Matters this collaboration is an essential part of the role of EYFS practitioners (ECM 2006). The **Early Support Family File** (Early Support 2008) offers a record that can be updated and shared with all professionals when working with a child with complex needs. Practitioners will link with social workers to carry out **Personal Education Plans** for **Looked After** children (DfES 2006a) or plan targets for children with special educational needs. EYFS providers will normally be expected to liaise with other agencies and share information using the **Common Assessment Framework**, **ContactPoint** and the **Integrated Children's System** (ECM 2007). This can be challenging as there are different expectations and language at work within different services (Whitmarsh 2008). However, finding successful ways of working together is essential to offer individual children the support that they need (Siraj-Blatchford 2008).

Learning story 3

Perry was supported with home visits from the local **Portage** service after being diagnosed with a genetic condition that affected his growth and development. This support would end when Perry's mum went back to work and he joined a child care setting. When planning for his entry to the local children's centre, staff arranged an information-sharing meeting with the Portage worker and Perry's mum.

Initial planning meeting with: Portage worker, Perry's mother, setting manager, Area SENCO

Perry is 2 next month. He has developmental delay and in most areas of his development is around nine months of age. He can crawl and pull himself to standing. He eats small pieces of food and has milk from a bottle. He makes few noises but will communicate by facial expression and tapping an adult. He may become frustrated if his communication is not acknowledged or misinterpreted. He has been cared for by a childminder and has been receiving support from the Portage worker fortnightly. She has requested an **Educational Psychology** assessment in order to commence **Statutory Assessment Procedure**. Perry's mum has just begun to receive weekly respite care for one day for Perry. He is due to have a splint on one leg to help him put his foot down flat. He has physiotherapy exercises.

Transition planning

- Perry to phase in attendance, starting with short visits, accompanied by mum, and getting to know key worker and environment.
- Key worker to observe Portage worker with Perry in a handover session then continue to work on **Individual Education Plan (IEP)** targets set by the Portage worker until staff can tune in to Perry's needs.
- Staff members to use basic **Makaton** signs and offer clear visual choices, so that communication is consistent.
- Key staff to access Makaton training as soon as possible.
- Incorporate physiotherapy exercises in daily routine with Perry.

A few months later when Perry has joined the setting the staff are able to draw on their own observations and information from his family and other professionals to plan experiences that will support his learning.

Review and observations from staff

The physiotherapist has visited Perry and wants staff to work on encouraging him to bend from the knee. The **occupational therapist** is due to visit in the next few weeks. Perry is now walking freely although stiffly. He is able to pass objects hand to hand and is now working on making a pincer grasp. He smiles and chuckles but does not babble sounds. He does not startle at loud noises. Perry's third IEP target is to join in action rhymes; he waves his hands and likes music but rarely copies actions. Staff members have started to use signs with him and are now introducing picture cards as a means of communication.

Actions

- Coordinate the IEP with the other specialists and include some physiotherapy or occupational therapy targets.
- Arrange for professionals involved to meet at the centre and discuss this with mum and key worker.
- Work towards the new target for fine motor skills gradually, use textured materials like sand and pasta from which Perry likes to fish out other textured objects and gradually decrease the size, e.g. ball of paper, small sorting shape or large bead. (Physical development: manage body to create intended movement).
- Encourage Perry's mum to pursue a hearing assessment and use the same photo cards and signs at home.
- For action rhymes hold Perry's hands and actually help him to make the movements if he is happy to do this. If not, start off by giving him a shaker to use as this will also strengthen his grip. Then perhaps try to get him just to clap or pat his knees rather than introducing more complex actions.
  (Physical development: manage body to create intended movement and Creative development: express themselves through physical action and sound, begin to move to music, listen to or join in rhymes and songs).
- Ensure all staff members have photo cards to use for communication
  (Personal social and emotional development: begin to indicate own needs, for example by pointing).

This example shows how careful joint working and consideration of individual needs can enable practitioners to help children with complex needs to access the EYFS areas of learning in a way that is appropriate to them.

The concepts of inclusion, working with parents and professionals and documenting and responding to children's learning needs and interests are clearly inseparable. Practitioners must use the EYFS and their own professional knowledge to personalize learning so that it is meaningful for individual children and their families, and maximizes their engagement and potential. In order to make this happen effectively, there must be supportive systems and procedures that link collaboration, planning and observation in a holistic cycle. There is no doubt that this is a challenge that requires dedicated and knowledgeable early years practitioners who can tune into children and support them along the way. It also requires the practitioner to use the EYFS curriculum as a tool and guide, a sort of magnifying glass that enables practitioners to notice what the children are showing them and then points them to the next step.

If practitioners view the EYFS in this way they can use it to support every child's learning in a purposeful and informed way.

Reflections

- What else can we do to use our observations of individuals to support our provision?
- How do we use information from other agencies to plan for individual needs using the EYFS?
- Are we being guided by the children or the document? What is the right balance between the two?

11 The learning environment

This chapter covers appropriate ways to organize the learning environment both inside and outside and suggests flexible use of resources to support learning across all age groups in the Early Years Foundation Stage.

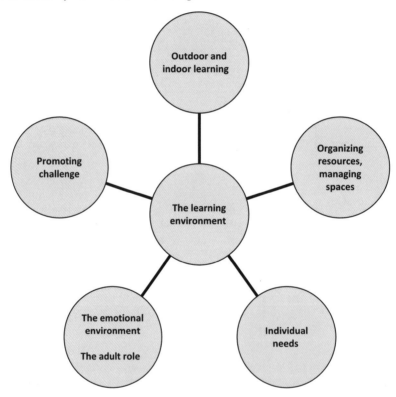

Learning is promoted through thoughtful use of all these aspects

The Early Years Foundation Stage (EYFS) document (DfES 2007a) emphasizes the importance of the learning environment for the provision of high-quality learning experiences for all children. It is not expected that the diverse range of early years settings, including home-based care and education, will be able to provide purpose-built environments with new resources. Instead, the aim is that practitioners will ensure that their provision is well maintained and flexible, taking into account the individual needs of children and finding innovative ways to overcome limitations presented by the building or location. Importantly, this section points out that the effectiveness of the learning environment includes the people and relationships within it.

Outdoor learning

The obvious connection with outdoor learning for children in the EYFS is the opportunity that it can provide for physical development. Being outside can offer children room to move in ways which are not safe or practical indoors and to develop strength and new skills from these gross motor movements such as pedalling, climbing and swinging. As mentioned in Chapter 4, the increasing concern for children's health and lack of exercise means that parents, carers and staff are generally now familiar with the need to encourage vigorous physical activity to ensure that they become healthy adults (Edgington 2002; Bilton *et al.* 2005; Garrick 2004; Palmer 2006). Research suggests that children need physical activity each day but not in the same way as adults, who require a period of sustained physical activity to contribute to health. Instead, children will benefit from frequent bursts of activity, such as that which naturally occurs in their play. This can most easily be offered through free access to outdoor provision (Sleap *et al.* 2000). However, outdoor learning offers potential for learning in all areas of development and the benefits are far greater than simply offering a chance to burn calories.

The outdoor environment can stimulate the many types of learning that occur inside, such as language and communication, fine motor skills, spatial awareness, early mathematical concepts and social skills. Not only can activities be carried out inside and out but the outside area can offer special learning potential for some children. Bilton (2004, 2005) and Edgington (2002) suggest that some children show increased concentration, perseverance, communication and even imagination in an outdoor environment. This makes particular sense for those groups of children who may spend large amounts of their home time out of doors, for example Traveller children and those from some refugee families or rural communities in the UK and abroad. Research (Schaffer 1996; Garrick 2004) also supports the observational belief of many practitioners that some boys, in particular, may need opportunities to be boisterous and engage in physically demanding play but these are not the only children who benefit from learning outside. There are other possibilities for play that are not so readily available inside such as spontaneous exploration of natural objects, insects and plant life; creating dens; growing things; constructing with large materials; experiencing the weather and seasons at first hand. Children may also gain both cognitively and emotionally from close contact with the natural environment (Edgington 2002; Bilton 2004, 2005; Garrick 2004; Palmer 2006). In other countries this understanding of how children gain from being outside is also evident and given a high priority. In the Italian early years settings of Reggio Emilia the environment is so important that it is described as the third teacher (Rinaldi *et al.* 2005), while the **forest schools** of Norway include time spent in all weather engaged in activities in the wilderness beyond the school grounds (Garrick 2006). The value that is attached to these experiences for early childhood education in other countries is an example that some EYFS providers are already attempting to follow.

There is general agreement that to be of maximum benefit for children the outside area should be well planned, flexible and accessible for children. Providers will need to evaluate their outside space, perhaps by observing which areas are used and the types of play that occur within them, and make changes in order to provide the best range of activities. Fixed equipment can limit play opportunities, as children run out of ways to use it creatively. However, adults can help children to use such equipment differently and prolong its usefulness.

Case study

In a large infant school planned activities to extend the use of the fixed climbing apparatus were included every week, such as covering the frame with a tarpaulin and adding role-play equipment to make a den; weaving in and out of the bars and creating collage mobiles and streamers; hanging different objects from the frame and using them for percussion e.g. pans and spoons; painting the frame with water and draping it with large material as a canvas for a mural; adding obstacle courses around the frame leading up to and off it such as low balance beams and stepping stones.

Organizing the outside area should include designated areas for different resources and types of play with accessible storage such as wheeled crates that can be brought inside at the end of the day (Edgington 2002; Bilton 2004, 2005). Bilton (2004) and Edgington (2002) suggest areas for the garden should include art; construction; quiet area; small apparatus; horticultural area; environment and science; and gym. Other possibilities could be areas for wheeled toys; small world play; sand and water. In general, outside activities should be as varied and imaginative as possible. In one nursery school this included an outside stage, a low platform that children used for their own role-play activities. Practitioners can also exploit the natural features of a site in various ways such as encouraging children to roll down or transport objects over a grassy mound; creating an intentionally muddy area for children to dig in; offering children opportunities to examine puddles; or using a cluster of logs and stones to attract insects. These are all simple ways to offer real exploration. Practitioners can encourage children to make creative sculptures and patterns with bark or small pieces of wood, shells, pebbles and feathers. These activities encourage children to explore natural materials in a different way. Similarly, den-building underneath trees or using a fence or even a clothes horse and blanket can allow children the experience of their own private space outdoors. Children need to make links between learning in and outside; this can be encouraged by bringing familiar resources into the outdoor area, such as writing equipment and books, or running an activity in both spaces, for example a role-play market area with stalls inside and out (see Figures 11.1 and 11.2).

While the provision and resources make a difference to the children's experience, they do not need to be on a large scale. In a limited space, without a grassy area, children can still experience digging and planting using builders' trays, large plant pots or an

Figure 11.1 Giving the children maps to use in outdoor play has been a stimulus for imaginative play around journeys.

old tyre. Children can pour and splash and create puddles on tarmac with a water tray and buckets. They can chalk and paint and weave against a fence or the wall of the building. If the space can only contain a few activities at any one time these can then be regularly rotated. Some outdoors activities can even occur indoors if the space is larger; some settings have an indoor climbing and sliding frame or use moveable resources such as crates, boxes and wooden frames for large construction (Edgington 2002; Doherty and Bailey 2003; Bilton 2004, 2005).

Adults outside

The adult role in this play is crucial for its quality. The findings of Researching Effective Pedagogy in the Early Years (REPEY) (Siraj-Blatchford *et al.* 2002) and the Effective Provision of Pre-School Education project (EPPE) (Sylva *et al.* 2003) suggest that the balance

Figure 11.2 Following the introduction of maps to the outdoor play resources, many of the children have been inspired to use other play equipment and reclaimed materials as forms of transport.

between adult-led and child-initiated activities influences the progress of children in early years settings and that children can gain maximum benefit from one-to-one inter-action. In order to achieve an appropriate balance when learning outside, adults should take time to observe children's play in order to plan experiences that may extend it; they should intervene spontaneously but sensitively and when asked for help. They should not always be passive onlookers nor feel that they should oversee or direct all the play.

Case study

Jack and Mariam found frozen rainwater inside a tyre. They investigated it with sticks, tried to prise it out of the tyre then tried to break it, eventually smashing through the frozen layer. The practitioner stood back but then went to talk to them about what had happened and offered magnifiers to look at the ice shards more closely. The practitioner then planned an activity for the children to fill different containers with water and leave them overnight to see if the water had frozen. She also introduced ice cubes and ice balloons containing leaves to the inside water tray.

Adults should also plan systems that enable children to use the space independently and develop cooperative skills; this is likely to be important when using bicycles and tricycles! In many settings children compete for wheeled toys and avoid other activities, often riding them with little regard for others. Some ways of improving this situation are to use them less frequently; to create a bike track; to have a ticket and parking system for bike changeover that is managed by the children; and to add trailers/extra seats to the bikes so they must be used cooperatively (Bilton 2004). Adults should also ensure that, when outside, children are given opportunities for physical challenge and are trying out a range of skills with varied equipment. This can be when using fixed equipment or by changing small apparatus and being involved with the play, such as encouraging different types of throwing; inventing games that involve throwing or rolling on target; adding monkey bars or small **'A' frames** to clamber over and floor-level planks to balance on.

Thought should be given to the accessibility of the outdoor area for children who have mobility difficulties or sensory impairment. Planting safe, tactile and perfumed plants in raised beds or window boxes can be enjoyable for all children. Similarly, hanging wind chimes and percussion and ensuring that areas are clearly demarcated with clear spaces for travelling in between will help everyone (Garrick 2004).

Challenges

Other issues that affect the outdoor provision in the EYFS are provision for children under 3 years of age, timing and weather. Babies and toddlers also need freedom to explore outside. For safety, this may be more easily achieved when separate from the older children; however, as with indoor learning there are social advantages to playing as a mixed age group (Robson 2004). If possible in a setting where the whole of the EYFS is represented, some opportunities for play outside with and without older children would be ideal. Practitioners are understandably concerned about the health and safety of the youngest children when they are outside but it is important that this does not prevent babies from making contact with the natural environment such as feeling the grass on their bare feet, grasping and releasing leaves and flowers or mouthing a large, smooth (and well-washed) shell (Renowden 1997). Early physical and sensory experiences provided by outdoor learning will enable babies to make new connections and understanding as well as strengthening the development of muscles and joints (Goldschmied and Jackson 1994; Renowden 1997; Doherty and Bailey 2003; Lindon 2005). The method of using designated areas for resources can be equally appropriate for this age range, with the physical expectations and resources adapted appropriately.

Soft balls and bean bags, flat stepping stones for balancing and low-level benches and tunnels for crawling and climbing can be part of the physical equipment, for example, while digging in sand and mud and water play are good for all ages if well supervised.

EYFS practitioners should try to find ways to make the most of the changeable weather conditions. Awnings, parasols and even temporary plastic gazebos can provide shade while children should be asked to bring in woollies, wellies and waterproofs for other times of year. Some settings have invested in all-in-one waterproof overalls which can be used by any of the children; others will have spare wellies, hats, gloves and coats of different sizes so that no child is disadvantaged and unable to go outside. Children can learn a routine for removing and cleaning boots and using an extra large door-matted area to keep the mud at bay. In poor weather, planned activities may have to be replaced by those that make use of the conditions and short bursts of outdoor activity with smaller groups may be more manageable but these should offer new possibilities such as channelling puddles; making simple flags, kites and mobiles; making patterns in frost or a light layer of snow (Bilton 2004).

Inside

The principles of good outdoor provision in the EYFS really mirror that of indoor op-portunities. The concept of separate areas for different activities is one that most EYFS providers are familiar with; within a home-based setting it is likely that childminders will provide different boxes of play materials e.g. **small-world play**, construction or dressing up and a space for messy activities such as cooking or painting, which may well be the kitchen table. Most authors are in agreement about the areas that should be rep-resented: sand, water, paint, print, collage, clay and dough, graphics (writing, drawing, mark-making), workshop for technology using reclaimed materials, construction large and small, small world and fine motor tasks, role play, reading area, music and displays which offer interactive learning opportunities including children's own use of display (Drake 2003; Edgington 2004; May *et al.* 2006; Holt 2007). As with outside play, these activities may need to be available at different times depending on the space available. Practitioners should also consider how ICT as well as mathematical opportunities and scientific exploration are used throughout the different areas.

Quality is frequently mentioned when reading about EYFS resources. This means different things to different people. It may reflect the resilience of equipment when being used daily. For some it may be the use of natural materials or the way in which they reflect real life. A balance of views seems sensible, for example some children will prefer the open-ended nature of construction with plain materials, while others will enjoy the colours in plastic resources. Similarly, some children may like to sort or thread real beads and buttons because they are familiar and from the adult world, while others will choose to work with large plastic dinosaurs as threading shapes and make roaring noises while doing so! Variety is the key to meeting the needs of all children. However, if working in a smaller setting where budget is limited, resources need to be chosen with a range of uses in mind and utilized inventively. Simple pots of large beads and laces, for example, can be used for counting, sorting, matching, threading, 'cooking' for dinner and wearing during role play, excavating from sand, sieving from water and rolling in paint or pressing into dough for pattern making. It may be useful to use reclaimed materials from the home: even an unwanted phone or kettle may work well in a home-corner area with the cord and plug safely removed (Isaacs 2007). With all resources, health and safety must be considered by ensuring that there are no potential dangers, that equipment is easily cleaned and from a hygienic source. Of course, some resources will not be safe for all ages, particularly very small objects which may be swallowed or inhaled, but practitioners should try to allow the use of many materials in a developmentally appropriate way with all children in the birth to 5 age range (Fogarty 1997; Renowden 1997; Holland 1997). It is entirely appropriate, for example, that children under 3 access paint, glue and dough. These materials can be offered in different contexts and with different tools from the older members of the EYFS, perhaps for children to explore with fingers. Even the natural response of mouthing a paintbrush is exploratory and harmless if the paint is non-toxic. Just as in the outdoor environment the birth to 3 age group benefit from a chance to watch and mix with older children inside (Renowden 1997).

The EYFS guidance mentions the accessibility of resources as a key factor in the successfulness of an EYFS setting. Ideally, settings will have open low shelves where resources can be viewed and accessed independently by children. If not, containers may need to be laid out for children to choose from and put away at the end of each session. Again, if space is limited, these will need to be rotated. Containers may be transparent or labelled with photographs of the contents. In order to promote the most child-initiated and flexible use of these resources, areas should be grouped together. Small-world play and construction in close proximity are a good example, as children will develop their play by combining these resources (Edgington 2004; May *et al.* 2006). In general rules and routines should be established for tidying, numbers of children working in a given area and places where resources should be stored. Using music for tidy-up time, having work stations for mark-making tools, or coloured cut-outs of large apparatus on shelves which children can match and using a coloured band or apron to limit admission to a certain area are all simple ways of encouraging children to manage these expectations. Prescriptive use of certain materials in certain areas can restrict some interesting learning opportunities and instead children should be allowed to transport objects (small-world people to the sand, for example) or, if in doubt, be encouraged to check with an adult beforehand (Drake 2003; Robson 2004; Wood and Attfield 2005). **Visual timetables** are useful for all children especially those with language needs or who require clear structure. Children can contribute to these by planning some sections of their own timetable, following the **plan, do, review** process of High scope settings (Holt 2007).

For the youngest children in the EYFS the principle of balancing natural and man-made play equipment and allowing for independent exploration still applies. Of course, with babies the organization of the room and access to resources will rely heavily on the adults involved. Staff will need to plan to offer a range of learning experiences to babies and toddlers each day, some allowing the children to investigate objects without intervention and some involving sensitive and responsive adult interaction. Consideration should be given to the use of **heuristic** play for mobile under-3s (Godschmied and Jackson 1994). This involves letting toddlers investigate a collection of everyday objects uninterrupted but accompanied by an adult. Non-mobile babies can also be offered a **treasure basket** of safe objects to explore. This allows both age groups to follow current interests using all of their senses (Holland 1997).

Case study

In a children's centre, space was available for babies, toddlers and 3–5s to be cared for separately. In practice the setting adopted a more family-structured approach. Babies slept separately with adult supervision and moved freely around a small baby room exploring objects and playing one-to-one. They were also regularly moved to be involved with the older children in the morning session (birth to 3), for example sitting with a staff member and sharing a story with a group of children, investigating blocks in the carpeted area while others played nearby. In this large room toddlers accessed many of the activities at their own level alongside their key workers and ate lunch with the older children. In the afternoon session more 3- to 5-year-olds attended and the babies and toddlers moved to another area of the centre.

Promoting learning

The final and perhaps most significant emphasis of the EYFS regarding the learning environment is that of the adults within it. May *et al.* (2006) and Wood and Attfield (2005) point out that though most EYFS practitioners would claim to support the idea of learning through play, their practice does not always allow this. Adults may provide a play environment but still focus on working with children to produce expected outcomes and to structure the play towards a particular piece of learning. Understandably adults may be anxious about meeting the expectations of the EYFS curriculum and feel that channelling children in a particular direction is the best way to ensure this occurs. In fact children will direct their own learning and despite adult intentions they are likely to interpret an activity in a way that serves their own current schema or interests (Nutbrown 2006). In order for practitioners to create an environment that truly offers learning through play they must learn to observe, empathize with and play alongside children rather than attempting to take control of the learning. Adults can stimulate learning through their interaction, responses and questions as well as providing unusual displays and objects to spark a new interest or idea (Edgington 2004). Children need sufficient time inside and out without the interruptions of a school-based timetable to really pursue an area of interest. They need to engage in **sustained shared thinking** with an adult who is able to listen fully and pay attention to their concerns (Edgington 2004; May *et al.* 2006; Nutbrown 2006).

Reflections

- How open-ended are the activities on offer?
- How can children move resources freely from one area to another (inside and out)?
- What systems do we have that encourage children to plan their own learning?
- How do we support children of all ages to explore an area of interest?
- What choices and control do babies have over their environment?
- What benefits might there be for babies and older children to be together at times?

12 The wider context

This section focuses on the increasingly multidisciplinary approach where practitioners with a range of expertise and experiences with young children work in collaboration to support children's learning and development. The chapter includes ways to engage with other agencies and the wider community in order to support transition between different care and education settings. This includes planning experiences that involve going out into the community or linking with work in the community. Suggestions are made about best practice for working with a range of other professionals, sharing information-seeking guidance and enriching the children's learning experience through work with others. Examples are given of ways to support children through transition between settings and to work in partnerships with other providers.

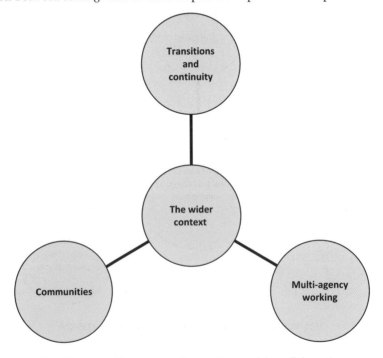

Practitioners with a range of expertise work in collaboration

The *wider context/multi-agency collaboration* is part of the Enabling Environments section of the EYFS and is based on the principle 'The environment plays a key role in supporting and extending children's development and learning.' The framework states:

> Working in partnership with other settings, other professionals and with individuals and groups in the community supports children's development and progress towards the outcomes of Every Child Matters: being healthy; staying safe; enjoying and achieving; making a positive contribution and economic well-being.
>
> (DfES 2007b)

Transitions and continuity

The environment for children now plays an important part in their understanding of themselves and their place in it. It is important for young children to have some understanding of their surroundings and feel welcome and secure there. From this base of security children can develop and be confident when moving to a new situation. The EYFS framework supports transitions by providing a common basis for provision and records to form a dialogue with colleagues to ease the change of providers. To enhance transitions parents/carers and children should be informed of the process of the transition where possible, to share the experience, which will hopefully be a positive one. Communication with colleagues can help support the transition by enabling them to gain a sound knowledge and understanding of the child before he/she arrives at the setting. The Early Years Transition and Special Educational Needs (EYTSEN) project in 2005 built on the work of the EPPE project and identified the 'positive impact on cognitive attainment' which remained at the end of Year 1. Intervention in pre-school with good transition strategies to continue the framework enhance children's ability to access activities in school in Key Stage 1.

Children will respond differently to change. Some may view it as an exciting adventure while others will be apprehensive and unsure. Adults, particularly the key person, can ease the transition and maintain continuity through sensitive and kind planning and preparation to help the child feel confident in his or her next steps. If collaboration and liaison has been effective it can be viewed as a process in the child's journey of development and growth.

A range of strategies can be used to support transition issues. Practitioners can support a child's initial visit through carefully planned activities to enable both the child and the parent to feel confident that he or she will be cared for and supported. This can include visits to the home, preliminary visits to the setting to gain an understanding of the routines and a knowledge of those who work there, invitations to events to help children and adults become familiar with the provision. Good practice can be forged at an early stage through such activities as sharing items made at home or school or key events. These could be displayed in the setting to provide something familiar when the children start to help them feel a valued part of the setting from the onset. It is sometimes hard for parents or carers to leave their child even if the child is quite happy to attend the provision. This can be handled sensitively while reassuring the adult that the role is just as vital and can be viewed as a success that the child has gained in sufficient confidence to feel able to deal with a changing environment. Children who are quiet might need time to get to know the routines and happily watch others while they learn about the setting.

Practitioners who liaise regarding a child's achievements can use a variety of ways to share information about the child. Discussion of the tracked development of the child in the Early Years Foundation Stage could be a start. It is helpful if practitioners contact each other and liaise about their settings to support the child through the transition.

Case study

An early years teacher has a rota of visits to different providers to develop relationships with other providers and children who will be coming to her setting. When the children arrive they greet the teacher: as one child claims, 'We know her already.'

Settings might have a range of strategies to facilitate transition issues and support continuity, responding to the needs of the provision and other providers.

In a Reception class children can be invited to short weekly visits to build up their knowledge of the class gradually before the term starts formally. Again activities can be shared and routines discussed. In this way time can be given to interacting with the children and forming relationships with them, listening to their interests, hopes and concerns. Parents/carers can be invited to attend a session to learn about the class and address any concerns they might have. It is useful to have a booklet describing key features of the provision to provide a source of reference if needed at home and as a point of interaction for parent, child and practitioner. Consideration can be given to any specific requirements or special needs the child might have. If this is planned in sufficient time agencies can be contacted and provision made in good time, before the child starts. This will also give sufficient time for those involved with the child to gain information and knowledge about any requirements that might be needed. Collaborative practice with other agencies can be successfully maintained in this atmosphere based on respectful, ongoing liaison. Colleagues, parents and the child can share the learning and development achieved to enable the next practitioner to continue to build on prior knowledge and understanding.

There might be networks of practitioners to share practice in the local area, such as training sessions held locally, or in a small group of providers.

Further examples of effective practice are given in DfES (2006b).

Communities

Engaging with other agencies and the wider community supports children's progress and their transition between different settings. Experiences can be planned to promote cooperation and collaboration, linking work with the community. For example, a garden project might support a community's desire to enhance the surroundings. It could be based in the early years setting or be located in an area in the community.

Children learn through their interactions with the environment. They gain an understanding of the diversity of the community, places and events as well as the material and physical surroundings. They learn to play together cooperatively and constructively, relate positively to their peers and take part in activities with confidence and respect for others.

Practitioners could have a variety of early years experience, including differing settings such as childminding with a range of expertise, for example in health, education, or social care. The Children Act 2004 (DfES 2004a) highlighted the importance of integrated services. Therefore it is part of the remit of the setting to incorporate collaborative working as a significant factor in the ethos of the provision and demonstrate this view through open and shared work with the community.

Best practice is promoted when working with others is based on honesty and trust, sharing information when appropriate, seeking guidance and enriching the children's learning experiences and development. Liaison can be strengthened with other providers who can work in cooperation between facilities for the care of the children, such as liaison between childminders, maintained and private nursery providers and schools.

Multi-agency working

The Children Act (DfES 2004a) formalized a commitment to multi-agency working. The practice of working collaboratively with other agencies had been in operation but the new legislation gave it a recognized structure. It endeavoured to work in partnership to achieve the Every Child Matters agenda successfully, that is: be healthy; stay safe; enjoy and achieve; make a positive contribution; achieve economic well-being. It provided a legal obligation to have multidisciplinary services working collaboratively and to implement a programme of integration of services over the following ten years.

The legislation fostered a range of strategies to implement the framework. The integration of services was given a high priority, encouraging practitioners to develop successful ways in which to ensure effective liaison and communication. The child's key person played a significant part in this development and could track an individual's development. This way of working supported early assessment and possible interventions for further provision for the child where necessary. Training for early years work has increasingly highlighted the need for multi-agency working where it is an accepted component of the different roles, for example responses in Initial Teacher Training to working with others and courses such as Early Childhood Studies which are based on a holistic approach to the child.

The early years 'hubs' of the community encouraged cohesion of services, ease of collaborative practice and benefits to the community they served. Family activities could be planned with parental/carer views sought. To achieve this aim professionals from a range of backgrounds work together to ensure the welfare of the child, for example educational psychologists or speech therapists. The shared commitment to the child can deepen the understanding of the development of the young child. Challenges to the collaborative systems suggest that practice will facilitate a common vocabulary regarding issues involved in the implementation of the EYFS and integrated services. There could be questions of differences in pay scales, meaning of language used and unsure perceptions of various roles within the multidisciplinary services. Abbreviations and common language used by one service provider could confuse others and cause a negative response. However, work centred on a child demonstrates concern for his or her welfare. This leads to discussion of strategies to plan the next steps to help, with action plans and successful outcomes formulated and agreed. This shared dialogue strengthens relationships and further collaborative work. Communities concerned with young children can be fostered and developed to share expertise outside the integrated services group, bringing new perspectives if necessary.

Settings differ in the amount of multidisciplinary working that might be apparent. A children's centre might be entirely integrated with various services using the same building and facilities, while a Reception class in a school could have links with appropriate services.

Reflections

- What strategies are used to liaise with other agencies?
- How is communication between practitioners with differing expertise and experiences maintained? Are there difficulties in this communication?
- How can they be overcome?

Part 4

Learning and Development

13 Play and Exploration

This chapter highlights the need for children to be involved in designing and extending language-rich play experiences. By the end of the chapter, practitioners should reflect on their understanding of 'play' and 'learning'.

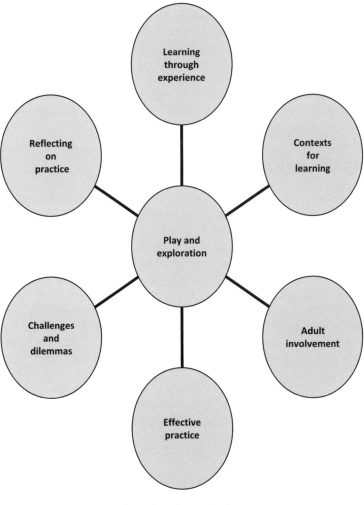

Learning through play

Equal opportunities with regard to culture, ethnicity, faith, gender, family background, disability and special educational need are implicit within the EYFS framework. The Child Care Act (2006) builds on the findings of the Effective Provision of Pre-School Education Project (EPPE) (Sylva *et al.* 2004) and concludes that planned, purposeful play with a balance of adult-led and child-initiated activities underpins all development and learning and is the vehicle through which children explore the six areas covered by the early learning goals. These are not separate subjects and no one area is more important than any other. Neither do the children see artificial barriers between the areas. As unique individuals, the children approach play in their own ways, based on prior experience. But what is 'play?'

Sutton-Smith (1998) suggests that practitioners plan activities based on an intuitive belief of what is needed for young children to make progress in cognitive development. Often it is socially situated, involving open-ended experiences that involve an element of imagination and creativity in trial and error learning. The more 'play' is defined, the more elusive a definition seems. What is accepted is that it is a form of behaviour preferred by young children that is 'flexible, ever-changing, instinctive, active and culture bound, characterized by the free choice and ownership of each child' (Moyles *et al.* 2001).

There are specific legal requirements, encapsulated in the EYFS framework, regarding the physical space required to provide opportunities for free movement and well-spread activities. These are discussed in Chapter 16.

Learning through experience

Experiential learning was explored in depth by Bruner in O'Hara (2003), whose research suggested that children make sense of the world by interacting with it and developing patterns of repeatable behaviour. This engagement reflects the children's current preoccupations chosen from wide-ranging interests, which may change. For example, a child who was observed running in circles in outdoor play was then observed regularly painting circles. The same child was fascinated by toys and artefacts that were broadly round. Not every child reacts in this way. Athey's (1990) research suggests that some children explore more than one schema or repeatable pattern at any one time. Some children diagnosed as being on the autistic spectrum may follow particular play behaviours such as lining up toys in rows. Interference from other children or adults in this patterning process can trigger extreme reactions from the child.

Bruner suggested that children pass through three stages of development which are not static as previously outlined by Piaget, so that experience and engagement, including guiding a child's understanding by breaking down the learning into small, progressive steps, has a positive impact on the child's rate of cognitive development and maturational progress.

The enactive stage

This stage is based on experiential understanding where children are presented with a variety of active learning challenges to gain first-hand experience. For example, children experience objects and materials in a variety of contexts to explore their senses, feelings and reactions. Young children turn towards sources of light or bright shiny objects that catch their attention and reach out towards these. Sound effects and a variety of music gain early attention and a range of textures of natural and man-made objects can be the starting point for learning. For example, compare scrunching leaves in a feely box with the inside of a conker shell. Young children need to be introduced to an infinite number of life-world examples with enthusiasm.

The iconic stage

This is dependent upon gaining a variety of life-world experiences and having the vocabulary to make associations between objects of a similar shape or outline. The child links visual representations and illustrations from books and films to real objects and can develop imaginative play from 2D representations of real objects. For example, the child links his or her impression of the large cow in the field to the small illustration of the cow in a book.

The symbolic stage

Children progress to expressing words and numbers as these are encultured and develop the art of conversation, having moved from single words, to **echolalia**, to short phrases and then to sentences. Oral language is at the heart of competent literary skills and is therefore of fundamental importance. The child uses small-world representations of large objects, such as small plastic farm animals which are sorted into sets of the same sort. The children attribute farmyard sounds and create conversations between the animals. Sometimes the animals are counted or arranged in numerical patterns.

Klugman and Smilansky (1990) strongly advocate the importance of the links between the physical and emotional experiences of play and the need for children to explore trusting and respectful relationships in familiar settings. Young children need opportunities to express fears and relive anxious experiences.

Case study

Fiona was the key worker for Sean whose family home had been destroyed by fire. Although no one in the family was injured in the fire, Sean was anxious about the whole experience. Fiona put out the doll's house as a play opportunity, with no pressure on Sean to engage with it. She also added a fireman's helmet to the role-play area and displayed a story about Fireman Sam as opportunities for Sean to begin to talk about his experience. After several clingy days of ignoring the house, the helmet and the story, Sean recreated the fire experience in a number of ways, evacuating the family and taking them by toy ambulance to hospital, then trapping them in the fire, then escaping out of the door.

Notice that it was important for Sean to try out a variety of scenarios to answer 'what would happen if..?' for himself. Through the small-world toys he was able to try things out, solve problems and take risks in order to make sense of an overwhelming experience.

Small-world representations help children to explore their emotions safely. For example, a doll's house allows the child to explore the relationships within the small family that lives in the house. Klugman and Smilansky (1990) suggest that children grow in confidence with familiar equipment which helps them to extend fine and gross motor skills.

Rummelhart and Norman (1978, 1981) and Harlen (2000) describe learning as thinking that something is true until new information comes along. The old understanding is confused into what Harlen describes as a state of disequilibrium and Rummelhart and Norman describe as accretion. New ideas have to be restructured and tested out against what is robust knowledge. Fine tuning then allows the child to transfer understanding into new situations, at which point the new understanding becomes robust knowledge. This is why it is important to allow children time to play with the same equipment so that they can reinforce their new learning to accommodate new ideas. The adult observer will know when there is a need to add new stimuli to move learning forwards.

Case study

The practitioner sets out the small-world farmyard on day one. The youngest children explore the shapes of the animals with fingers and mouths. Later in the week, different coloured paper (green, brown, blue and yellow) is set out to represent muddy fields, grass, water and sand. The children sort the animals into different types and areas. One child tells the practitioner that the Daddy one is very cross and must go on his own. The others in the group put all of the beasts with horns on their own. The practitioner explains that cows can have horns too. Mummy cows have udders. This is new knowledge for the urban children. The beasts are explored more carefully to look for udders. The activity is extended by putting out mirrors to represent water. The children notice the udders reflected in the mirrors. With support from the practitioner, they also notice that the cows are upside down in the mirror.

They also express a need to build walls between the various sorts of animals and, through trial and error, use the wooden construction bricks as fences. On a subsequent occasion, the cows are added to the sand pit. The children build sand walls between sets of animals.

Different levels of physical and mental challenge need to be experienced to promote problem solving, a sense of personal responsibility and independence.

The youngest children usually play on their own. This is known as solitary play. By the end of the foundation stage, children should have opportunities to play next to other children, which is known as parallel play. With an adult, children will begin to share and engage with other children in a small group. These are necessary social skills to equip the children for life.

Contexts for Learning

Babies and children learn by doing, taking part in authentic activities from which they learn. For example, babies act and react to moving faces and expressions, showing their pleasure with smiles and gurgles. Toddlers and young children need plenty of space indoors and outdoors to interact with each other, resources and materials in a stimulating and exciting way. Research from the Effective Provision of Pre-School Education Project (EPPE) (Sylva *et al.* (2004) discusses how children learn about their world, adjusting their understanding in the light of new experiences which they then test out in new contexts. This fits in with Rummelhart and Norman's (1998) theory of learning previously mentioned.

Case study

Following the story of *We're Going on a Bear Hunt* by Michael Rosen, Jonathan, the Early Years Foundation Stage practitioner, put a box outside, in the outdoor play area, containing various lengths of material such as an old pashmina shawl, a curtain, a bed sheet, various hats and dressing up clothes and a picnic set and travel rug. The children explored the content of the box, sorting piles of clothing from the picnic set, choosing items to make a bear cave and choosing articles of clothing to wear. Rules for the activity were set by the children, deciding who was who, how they were going to follow on in a line, who would be the leader and where they were going for a picnic. On this occasion they were going to a bear cave. They enlisted Jonathan's help to cover the climbing frame with the bed sheet. One child suggested that shoes which had been through imaginary sticky mud should be left outside the cave. The travel rug was spread inside the cave, having first checked for bear occupancy. Children took individual roles, playing next to each other but not necessarily with each other. One fetched a torch to check for bears, another fetched the digi blue camera to film any bears who might be found. Jonathan added to the activity by using the blue pashmina to make a stream. The children had to find a safe place to cross the 'stream'. A plank was requested, to make a bridge. Jonathan asked where one could be found? The children remembered the long pieces of wood next to the sand pit. Jonathan reminded them that two people would need to carry the plank. The children put the plank across the water. Jonathan took several digital images to keep on file as evidence of the children solving problems and cooperating with each other.

To make outdoor facilities more accessible in inclement weather, many settings add an outdoor play canopy or large conservatory to an existing building.

Children need to interact with new resources before using them for problem-solving activities in order to explore their possibilities. Too often, practitioners put out a variety of new resources and are frustrated when the children are more interested in exploring what they can do with these rather than working towards a preferred learning outcome. If they are allowed exploratory time, children are more likely to engage in a learning activity and solve a learning challenge successfully.

Often problems can be solved through role-play activities that mimic the child's life and world experience. Making dens and dressing up are part of this experience, helping children to explore new and unfamiliar roles.

Adults are also influenced by media stories of accidents that happen to children and consequently prevent children from learning by taking risks, whereas an element of considered risk is essential for development. Allowing the children to use a plank as described in the case study above is an example of this.

A young child in an Early Years Foundation Stage setting can be adequately supervised using real tools, such as hammers and saws, provided that a risk assessment identifies potential dangers, supervision is vigilant and minimizes harm to the child. Skilled professionals think through the risks and the progression of skills needed and introduce these before giving free access to tools.

Case study

Jane wants the children in her care to learn to use a small hammer responsibly without hitting their fingers or each other. As a preliminary step, she reflects on the group of children involved and the children who are likely to need the closest supervision. She teaches the necessary skills first by modelling, speaking about what she is doing, using golf tees and blocks of polystyrene with a light, wooden hammer. Jane talks through health and safety issues such as 'Hold the tee at the bottom, not where you will hit your fingers.' The children are individually supervised as they knock tees into the blocks. Then they are offered free choice opportunities to practise the skill with an adult positioned close to the activity to check the level of risk. The activity is extended by making patterns with the tees, for example alternate colours of tees or shape patterns. Subsequently, she introduces the children to a set of pre-cut card shapes, pins and cork mats to make shape pictures. Finally, she introduces real nails, hammers and wood to build the three little pigs' house of sticks, under close supervision, outside.

Notice how Jane has pre-identified the progression in skills with the intention of protecting the children from unacceptable risk, building the skills necessary to work with real nails and real hammers in a real context eventually. The adult is aware of the potential danger of the real tools and positions herself with the group in order to minimize the risk. This also affects the other learning opportunities offered on that day so that these contain less risk and can be accessed independently. Being overprotective can prevent children from learning about their environment. Practitioners need to have regard for policies and procedures within their own setting that guide acceptable practice.

Reflections

- Have I read the relevant policies, including Health and Safety and behaviour management within our setting?
- How do volunteers and visitors know about our policies and assessing risk?
- Do I consider safety, supervision and the progression of skills as well as ideas for activities?
- Have I considered the need for close supervision and staffing implications of potentially hazardous activities?
- Have I listened to the children's ideas and incorporated these into the activity?

The first consideration for every practitioner should be how much space the children will need to safely complete the activities outlined in the planning. Most practitioners mentally divide the available space into a variety of areas, for example role play, messy activities, sand and water, malleable activities, physical activities, creative activities and different learning opportunities at different times. The division could be loosely labelled, 'role play', 'outdoor', 'messy' and 'everywhere'. Riding on wheeled vehicles such as bikes and tractors develops gross motor skills but creates a number of hazards. With limited outdoor space, it may not be practical to have free access to bicycles and ride-on toys at all times. Limited outdoor space may also be needed for other things, for example a dance activity. The two activities may not be carried out safely at the same time. Therefore it is sensible to plan to use the space differently at different times. When ride-on toys are in use, practitioners need to introduce a circuit or roadway so that the vehicles move round the space in the same direction. Even so, crossing to find a favourite bike can be hazardous. Early road safety rules can be taught, for example by introducing a safe place to cross with a zebra crossing. (It may not be appropriate to talk about crossing roads independently with the youngest children who will not be encouraged to do so on their own.)

Equally, there needs to be careful planning of the indoor area. For example, an activity involving messy materials needs to be situated near to a sink so that the danger of a wet or slippery floor is minimized. Warm soapy water needs to be added to the bowl in advance of children becoming covered in paint or glue. Sleeves need to be rolled up and clothing covered by an apron.

If the setting is a shared space, for example a community hall, the outdoor environment should be checked before each session for potential hazards such as broken glass, excrement or needles. Sand pits should be covered. Dog and cat faeces, for example, contain a serious health hazard for children.

Different hazards at different ages

As babies develop into toddlers, their mobility and dexterity increase. While crawling is common from six months of age, many babies develop an ability to move around by kicking and rolling from about four months. This means that they should never be left unsecured and unattended on a raised surface and at floor level practitioners should expect that they will explore everything in their local environment. In the home, radiator pipes, fires, electrical equipment, stairs, animal dishes and sharp objects are potential hazards. For example, the crawling baby will hold on to a hot radiator pipe, crying with pain. He or she may not have developed an association with letting go of the pipe because it is hot. It is therefore important for a risk assessment to be taken of potential hazards so that everyone working in the setting is aware of the associated dangers when supervising young children.

Adult involvement

In a child-centred setting, all practitioners need to consider the provision and resources required to match the children's learning needs. This includes human resources. The relevant age- and stage-related skills that they need to teach, from the EYFS framework, should be reflected upon in order that the children have the opportunity to learn from planned starting point experiences. While the terms work and play are interchangeable in the early years, play cannot be considered simply in terms of skill enrichment. This means giving consideration to what the child has as robust and transferable knowledge, so that new understanding can be developed, based firmly on prior knowledge. All adults within the setting should be encouraged to engage in continuing professional development in order to have a thorough knowledge of children's growth and development, enabling them to track learning along a developmental continuum.

Curtis (1998) adds that the attitudes of staff towards each other, and towards visitors to the setting, the children and parent partnerships, also affect the quality of the possible learning outcomes from planned experiences. The children need play opportunities that help them to gain knowledge and understanding of people in a variety of contexts. They need to learn to gain control over their bodies and senses, understanding their feelings about others and situations, growing in confidence and self-esteem. Watching the children's engagement with resources and equipment is the starting point for the planning of all play experiences. An appropriately challenging and stimulating environment extends appropriate play activities. Bruner's (2003) social constructivist research suggests that adults should become involved in play activities to extend and challenge thinking because, in his opinion, learning is socially situated and developed by interactions with others. He emphasizes the importance that language interaction plays in intellectual growth. He also recommends a spiral curriculum in which children revisit topics and themes, advancing levels of understanding.

Therefore it is important to work towards an enabling environment that considers or assesses what children bring to the learning experience and the aspects of development that predominate by keeping and reviewing records of prior achievement and planning sequences of learning opportunities that identify the next small steps in learning. The problem with this is that learning is not always a linear progression and children develop at different rates. Some aspects of development can be anticipated. For example, when joining materials, children need to learn a variety of skills before they can choose the most appropriate join for the material in hand.

Talking to parents and previous carers and transferring records with each child helps the practitioner to plan appropriately for each child.

Play should be natural and spontaneous. Sometimes, when adults intervene, they can add a new dimension and encourage the child to continue to be engaged in the activity. While children gain significantly from joining in with respectful adults who engage sensitively, Moyle and Adams *et al.* (2001) and Fisher (2005a) sound a note of caution. Practitioners can easily take over the learning experience and answer challenges in a way that limits the child's or children's opportunity to solve problems. An important reason to intervene is to teach a new skill or to extend language and vocabulary. This necessitates sensitive observation and then appropriate intervention. As practitioners become increasingly skilled, they step back for longer periods, often playing in parallel to the child, modelling preferred outcomes, respecting the children's rules and punctuating play with additional resources as these are required, encouraging non-verbal prompts and verbal prompts and cues as language extension. Children often invite the adult into the 'play', on their terms.

Practitioners must intervene in play if it is racist, sexist, offensive, unsafe or violent, or involves an act of bullying.

Effective Practice

In order to manage the variety of resources identified as appropriate for the developmental stage of the child or children, equipment needs to be stored effectively. Many settings choose similar large, colour coded plastic boxes that are clearly labelled with pictures and words to identify the contents.

Colour coding often identifies boxes of resources that are thematically connected or that can be accessed on particular days to give variety to the setting. For example, on a red day, the children select only large red boxes and on a blue day, the boxes are blue. Most toys are made of hard plastic that is brightly coloured, machine washable and durable and are divided between small-world representations, construction materials, mark makers and art and craft materials.

Challenges and Dilemmas

One of the main challenges for carers, practitioners and teachers is to value all play, including noisy and messy play. Bennett *et al.* (1997) caution that many practitioners lack awareness of how their own carefully considered interventions can empower or diminish the quality of the learning experience for the child.

Bruner's findings (2003: 9) suggest that practitioners need to be aware of what a child can do and understand independently but should also be prepared to intervene, 'questioning, guiding and instructing in an effort to extend and challenge thinking'.

Bruner also suggests a social dimension to cognitive development, stressing the importance of interactions between children and of communication and language development in learning.

Noisy play can be a source of irritation for others, particularly when a child chooses to practise screaming or wants to bang a percussion instrument repeatedly. Collectively the staff team must decide on appropriate rules for the setting that are applied consistently. For example, some settings allow noisy experimentation and messy play outside but not inside the building and painting on walls and floors is considered outside the boundaries of what is considered acceptable.

Some settings set boundaries related to violent television themes and choose not to allow the use of weapons such as guns and knives into role play. Where the boundaries are clear, children will remind each other that 'We do not play fighting games here.' This also impacts on the computer games chosen, television programmes accessed and dressing up materials available in the role-play area.

When an activity becomes aggressive or confrontational, staff need to decide whether to intervene or not. Over time, children should learn to diffuse their own situations. As a rule of thumb, practitioners are responsible for the health and safety of all the children in their care. Inappropriate language and threatening behaviour is never acceptable. However, the adults must ensure that they explain why they have intervened, without implying criticism of the child's home circumstances or blaming the child for repeating words that are used freely at home.

Staff must intervene, use reasonable force only and record incidents of:

- attacks by the children on members of staff;
- attacks by the children on other children;
- fights between children;
- children who are choosing to damage or vandalize property (or are about to);
- children at risk of harm through misuse of equipment, for example taking electrical equipment near to water;
- children running indoors in such a way as to risk injury to themselves or others;
- children who are choosing to leave the premises.

Staff should also be aware of gender stereotyping in play and avoid promoting male and female roles. Staffing in the early years often includes more women than men in caring roles. Practitioners must be aware of this imbalance and consciously choose books and toys that will appeal to both sexes.

Reflecting on Practice

High standards of learning and play are achieved by professionals who regularly reflect upon the effectiveness of the learning opportunities given to the children. Through reflection and discussion with the staff team, planning can be adapted to meet the individual needs, interests and next steps in learning of the children. Staff need to identify their own strengths, which can be shared with others in the team, and areas that can be developed as next steps through setting personal targets for achievement. Practitioner research encourages all members of the team to identify the impact of the learning opportunities on the cognitive development of the children. It is therefore important for the team to discuss their planning for play and their findings and to engage with current research.

14 Active learning

This chapter explains the theory of active learning in simple terms. Links are made to planning and personalizing learning based on individual interests and experiences. Examples of activities which are overly adult-directed and may inhibit learning are given alongside a positive alternative for each of the possible areas in an early years setting. Suggestions are made for developing responsive and flexible planning strategies and readers are encouraged to question their current practice with a brief self-audit of the way learning opportunities are presented in the setting. Consideration is given to sharing children's achievements and encouraging them to be aware of the next steps in their learning.

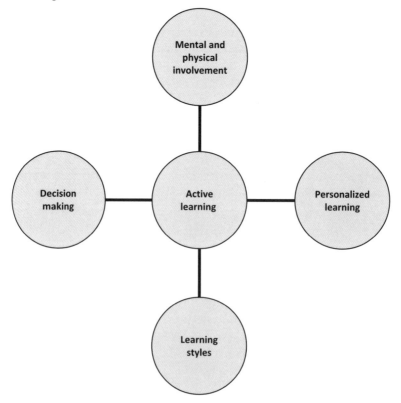

Active learning based on individual interests and experiences

The *active learning* chapter is part of the EYFS Learning and Development area and is based on the principle that 'Children develop and learn at different rates and all areas of learning and development are equally important and interconnected.'

Personalized learning

The EYFS framework states that 'Children learn best through physical and mental challenges. Active learning involves other people, objects, ideas and events that engage and involve children for sustained periods.' Children learn and develop differently and have individual natural talents and strengths, which can be fostered in numerous ways. Initial contacts with parents/carers and the child can provide valuable insights into the child's interests, strengths and achievements. These can be used to support planning for the child's progress; for example, an interest in ships and boats could be encouraged through stories linked to the theme, model making, fiction and non-fiction books, shapes, capacity, floating and sinking and this could lead into other forms of transport, different types of boats, the local environment and areas of the world. These ideas could be incorporated into a theme which could have a generic topic, such as travel. Ideas from the children could be developed in their own terms, supported by the adult. It is important to draw on these when children first enter the setting, helping them to develop their potential to the utmost. Observations and assessments would identify whether the child was making progress and the observation, assessment and planning cycle should be reviewed regularly. This personalized learning demonstrates awareness of the child as unique, with responses made to individual needs. Observations of individuals will indicate those who are thriving in the environment and those who might require further input to ensure they are making the most of their time spent in the setting. Careful support, encouragement and interaction could help those children develop their use of the resources available to reach their potential when playing.

Formative assessments can be tracked to gain an understanding of how the child is progressing, areas where the child is developing well and those where further support might be needed. This also provides a time scale of progression, indicating whether the child is having a spurt of development or consolidating what has been learnt. Concerns over progression can quickly be addressed through this system, used within the setting in an ongoing basis.

The plan (see table on p. 136) was based on children's interest in toys, their surroundings and their curiosity with colours. This occurred when children helped to colour the water in the water trough, as they were fascinated by the changing colours when they were mixed. It gives broad outlines for the plan but allows opportunities to develop events and interests to be incorporated as they might arise. Within the short term, plan provision was included for children who had special requirements and needs.

In order to facilitate play it is important to allow children to have access to a variety of resources that can support different learning styles. Care should be taken to reflect critically on the provision offered to the children, and to question practice to ensure that all learning styles are catered for.

Plans for a group of 3- to 4-year-old children following observations

	Week 1	Week 2	Week 3	Week 4	Week 5
Personal, social and emotional development	Welcome new children	Support learning routines	Help children to become independent in setting	Caring for others	Care for our environment
Communication, language and literacy	Discuss holidays/visits – make postcards	Favourite toys Make puppets	Shopping lists Toy shop	Red Riding Hood	Festivals
Problem solving, reasoning and numeracy	Counting	3D shapes	Patterns	Sorting – colours	Sorting/matching/counting fruit
Knowledge and understanding of the world	Our setting	Textures/materials	Changing seasons	Maps and plans/making dens	Shopping
Creative development	Pictures of visits and visitors	Textures of puppets	Paintings, drawings of toys	Colours – printing/colour mixing	Observational drawings of fruit
Physical development	Moving around the setting – our environment	Large apparatus	Fine manipulative skills	Pathways	Pathways with large apparatus

Learning styles

The social construction theory states that learning is the active construction of understanding and knowledge by the learner, through experiencing things and reflecting on those experiences. What is learning? According to the construction theory, learning is the construction of neural networks in the brain. The neuron consists of a cell body containing the nucleus and an electricity-conducting fibre, the axon, which also gives rise to many smaller axon branches before ending at synapses, which are the contact points where one neuron communicates with another. The neural networks have growth spurts, particularly *in utero* and for the first eighteen months and roughly between the ages of 10 and 14. The brain changes physically as it develops. The neural networks have critical periods. The hard wiring of different parts of the brain depend on genetic potential, maturation and the environment. The implications for early years provision are obvious with regard to development of the brain during the early years and the importance for children's development and progress of the environment created. The neural networks have 'plasticity', with the brain having a capacity for change. It adapts to the environment by developing and pruning connections and even generating new neurons. It can adapt to its surroundings. 'If the environment is enriched and interesting then our brains will become enriched, interested and efficient at working in that environment' (Burnett 2002: 92).

Ten key brain bytes are noted in Burnett (2002: 93):

- Every brain is an intelligent, individual, biological organism. No two brains are the same.
- Our brains have a quality called 'plasticity', which means they constantly change and grow according to the stimulation they receive.
- Relaxation and 'composure' is a critical state of mind for learning.
- Music can aid in creating an appropriate state of mind for learning.
- Oxygen is crucial to brain functioning.
- Drink lots of water – dehydration causes loss of concentration.
- Sleep cements learning and makes us alert.
- Emotion is a key to forming long-term memories.
- Connections and multiple 'representations' matter more than numbers of brain cells.
- Every brain is a beautifully sophisticated, unique and miraculous work of creation.

The construction of knowledge and understanding is supported by social interaction. We also learn best when we are in a state of 'relaxed alertness', that is when we are not anxious or frightened but, in the same manner, not bored or tired. Therefore a calm yet stimulating atmosphere where all feel valued and happy to be there does have positive effects on children's learning, and possibly the health and well-being of all who are there!

Gardner's theory of 'multiple' intelligences (MI) has implications for practice in the early years. He suggested nine aspects of intelligence including:

- linguistic;
- visual spatial;
- musical;
- bodily kinaesthetic;
- logical mathematical;
- interpersonal;
- intrapersonal;
- naturalist;
- existential.

Children might be more adept in some areas than in others, so opportunities could be provided which address a range of styles of learning. These are commonly referred to in the early years as provision for VAK (visual, auditory and kinaesthetic). Access to a range of learning styles will enable children to participate readily in those they find easier, as well as giving them opportunities to experience those with which they might be unfamiliar.

This has implications for planning and personalizing learning to enable children to reach their full potential. Chapter 1 gave information regarding prominent theories of learning. Children can be active participants in their learning and construct meaning from their world. This can be achieved through interactions with peers and adults to scaffold learning. Questioning, such as Bloom's Taxonomy, which described a hierarchy of questions from simple to thought-provoking questions, can aid thinking skills and speaking and listening. Language has an important role in developing cognitive concepts and internalizing thoughts and ideas. Activities which are overly instructive can have a negative effect on young children. Consideration can be given to developing responsive and flexible planning strategies. Observations can identify whether appropriate strategies are in use; for example, provision should be made to ensure children's learning styles are in evidence in their play, such as investigations, creativity and consolidation of what they have learned. Children should be motivated to learn. This can be observed in the manner in which they ask questions, demonstrate enthusiasm, listen and communicate their involvement in their learning.

Physical and mental activity

When children feel safe, secure and valued they are able to engage fully in their learning. The early years environment should appear bright and welcoming to all who enter and be a pleasant and exciting place in which to play and work. All aspects of health and safety should be given careful consideration, including regular checks of equipment and appliances as well as cleaning routines performed by children, practitioners or the cleaning services.

15 Creativity and critical thinking

This chapter covers definitions of creativity and critical thinking and how they link to learning. It suggests some practical ways to help children to develop these attributes.

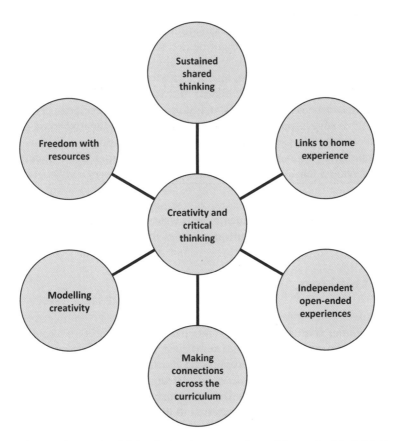

Contributing factors in children's development of creativity and critical thinking

The Early Years Foundation Stage (EYFS) document (DfES 2007a) makes clear the distinction between fostering children's creativity in everything they do and *creative development* as part of the curriculum. Practitioners are encouraged to respond to children's interests by offering open-ended activities and allowing children to use resources in unexpected and inventive ways. Opportunities for independent, child-directed learning need to be a consistent part of EYFS provision. However, this should not be interpreted as learning without adult support. Children develop critical thinking by working closely with adults who enable them to explore avenues of interest and make connections in their learning, across the curriculum and to experiences at home. In order to do this effectively adults will need to use observations and skilled interaction and model a creative approach to problem solving.

What is creativity and why do we need it?

Creativity can be interpreted in different ways but there is some agreement about its essence. It includes the discovery of new possibilities, through looking at familiar objects or ideas in a new way (Fisher 2005a), and may result in an original or innovative suggestion (McGregor 2007). This might be in a way that challenges current thinking and has global significance, such as the ideas of Einstein, but does not have to be at this level (Duffy 2006)! All children and adults have the potential to think creatively about smaller scale problems and interests and generate ideas that are new to them (Cole 2006). In order to think creatively children need to be confident enough to take risks and to move away from existing patterns and routines. Creativity can occur in any area of the curriculum but often needs a practical outlet or purpose (Fisher 2005a; Cole 2006). Encouraging children to think creatively may be particularly relevant in current society where varied family structure, mobility between careers and geographical locations, and frequently changing technology require the ability to adapt and cope with a variety of different situations (Craft 2002; Fisher 2005a,b; Duffy 2006). Therefore, early years practitioners should nurture creativity as a foundation for learning and a fundamental disposition for coping with modern life.

Critical thinking

Critical thinking usually involves analysing or evaluating a given object, information or situation rather than generating a new idea (McGregor 2007). Children who are thinking critically may use particular skills such as careful observation, comparison and memory. They are likely to make suggestions and give reasons for their ideas. Critical thinking could also lead to a child offering a creative solution in response to questioning what is already in place. For example, he or she might suggest an improved system for taking turns in the role-play area. Both creativity and critical thinking can be focused on practical applications and experiences but critical thinking may also be more abstract and philosophical, for example, 'Why does time go so slow sometimes?' (Institute for the Advancement of Philosophy for Children 2008). Children may be naturally philosophical but on reaching school they can learn to focus on providing curriculum-based responses to adult questions rather than truly reflecting on their concerns (Lipman 2003; Fisher 2005a; Sedgwick 2008). This could equally be the case in any EYFS setting that does not encourage children to pursue their own interests and questions.

Educational theory refers to critical thinking and creative learning through exploration in a number of guises. Piaget described **schemas** where children **assimilate** and **accommodate** new ideas through a process of application in different contexts (Piaget 1954) while Vygotsky and Bruner emphasized the need for social interaction and language to support learning and moving on to a higher level of understanding (Bruner 1966; Vygotsky 1978). More recently Lipman (2003), Costello (2000) and Fisher (2005a, 2005b) have promoted ways for children to philosophize and consider big ideas using story, group work and dialogues. While the detail differs in each model the belief that children benefit from having the freedom to express and explore their interests and concerns is consistent. In order to achieve this, practitioners need to encourage children's individuality and pay attention to their ways of communicating. Reggio Emilia and the work of Loris Malaguzzi emphasize the potential that all children have to express themselves in individual ways, calling this the 'one hundred languages of children' (Rinaldi *et al.* 2005). However, for this to work in practice, practitioners will need to interact carefully with children, ensuring that the learning opportunities available meet their individual needs and interests and offer scope for new avenues of discovery.

The role of the practitioner

Knowing about creativity and critical thinking is not enough to ensure that children in the Early Years Foundation Stage develop these skills. While children may possess a natural desire to explore and make sense of the world they are also likely to believe the teachings of adults in an unquestioning way (Costello 2000). The EYFS practitioner must strike a balance between imparting important information and necessary rules such as 'Do not eat berries from the hedge because they will make you ill' and encouraging children to challenge and question why things are so. In general the authors referred to in this chapter agree that critical thinking and creativity can be actively taught to the youngest children. Perhaps most important in fostering a creative approach in the EYFS is the practitioner's attitude towards creativity. In order to feel confident enough to develop innovative ideas children will need to be in a climate that supports their self-esteem. Practitioners may need to examine the way that they interact with children so that more in-depth conversation and discussion is encouraged (Alexander 2008). Adults will need to listen with genuine interest to children's unusual ideas. They should challenge these suggestions with open-ended questions and encourage experimentation. **Open questions** can be related to problem solving for a practical course of action, for example 'What would happen if ...?' 'How can we make it better?' (McGregor 2007); these sorts of questions stimulate children to predict and hypothesize. Open questions can also require children to reflect and explain. These add a further dimension to critical thinking, such as 'What do you mean?' 'How do you know?' (Costello 2000).

Case study

At his childminder's house Joshua (age 4) noticed the pips in the orange at lunch time. He collected them all on his plate. 'Will these make oranges?' he asked. 'How can we find out?' asked the childminder. Together they planted the pips following Joshua's interests and suggestions and were eventually rewarded with small seedlings. The interest and support that Joshua experienced encouraged him to experiment with planting a number of seeds found in different fruit and outside. He was able to tend the seeds and observe their different growth patterns, making his own suggestions about why the growing investigation was more or less successful in each case.

This example shows supported creativity in Joshua's thinking as he discovers something new to him rather than an original idea unknown to the adult. The practitioner is able to extend Joshua's thinking by joint planning and meaningful questions following the principles of sustained, shared thinking (Nutbrown 2007).

Encouraging children to use language to reason and explore ideas is an important part of critical thinking and creativity (Costello 2000; Fisher 2005a,b; Taggart *et al.* 2005) but children who cannot yet express themselves fully in language can also be creative and use the cognitive skills necessary to reason and problem solve. Research into peer collaboration suggests that, from some time between the ages of 2 and 3, children are able to work together in imaginary play or collaborate on a simple task such as moving objects from one place to another to make a road (Brownell and Carriger 1991; Dunn 1998; Ashley and Tomasello 1998). This indicates that young children can begin to problem solve and reason from an early stage, if given an appropriate stimulus. Critical thinking in older children may also take the form of internal dialogue where the learner independently works through the process that a skilled teacher would create with questions and evaluation (Lipman 2003). If this is the case, the role of adult talking through the process of critical thinking in the early years helps children to work through a similar process later when faced with challenges independently (Alexander 2008). Children also need to develop specific language about thinking so that they are able to categorize and explain their own learning processes. One way of introducing this vocabulary is by adult modelling; another is by using stories in which the character is described as using different types of thought such as deciding, wondering or comparing (Taggart *et al.* 2005).

Adults in the Early Years Foundation Stage might assume that all play is creative but this is not the case. Play comes in many forms and can involve repetition, consolidation, investigation and practice of new skills without being creative (Craft 2002). The adult role in play can offer new opportunities for creativity by extending children's thinking and encouraging risk taking. They should ensure that activities and interaction are not focused on an end product. Instead they can help children by demonstrating new ways of working with given materials, discussing the child's ideas and facilitating shared work with other children. An important part of this is giving enough time and attention to one child or a small group to enable them to get really involved in what they are trying to achieve. It is also important to be open-minded and not unwittingly convey adult judgements or scepticism about a new idea either verbally or through body language and facial expression (Duffy 2006). Sometimes the adult may support children by standing back and allowing them time for solitary play, particularly that which involves imagination and representation, as these elements are clearly linked to creative and critical thinking (Taggart *et al.* 2005; May *et al.* 2006).

It may seem essential for early years practitioners to promote creativity by being creative. This is only partly true. Of course early years practitioners who do not stimulate creativity and limit and prescribe resources, activities and outcomes will make creativity more difficult for the children in their care. However, practitioners who are individually very creative will not automatically transfer this disposition to the children. They will need to be prepared to be led by the children's ideas and act as co-constructors (Costello 2000; Craft 2002; Craft and Jeffery 2004; Taggart *et al.* 2005). Practitioners will also need to be aware of their own problem-solving and thinking styles and consider how this may influence the way that they interact with the children in their care (Taggart *et al.* 2005). This need for sensitivity and responsive, supportive adult interaction is the key to developing creativity with the youngest members of the EYFS. Babies need to experience control over their environment and the people within it by watching adults imitating and repeating their noises and actions. Later, attentive adults can make sure that opportunities are available that link to individual interests and schema. As children develop **representative play** and verbal communication, adults can extend their imagination by participating in the play and providing new and interesting links to the wider world through carefully chosen resources (Duffy 2006).

The creative environment

A further extension to the adult influence over creativity in EYFS is their role in planning for resources and the use of the environment. As mentioned in Chapter 11, practitioners should aim to provide opportunities for children to combine resources when pursuing avenues of exploration. This may involve grouping areas of the room together such as malleable materials, reclaimed materials and art resources; sand and water; role play; music and reading area; large construction and small-world play. There are many ways of arranging resources and some decisions will need to be made after observing and consulting the children about how they use the areas. To provide a creative environment the early years staff will need to encourage unexpected combinations of resources by ensuring that most are accessible and portable and children feel free to use them inside and outside (Duffy 2006; May *et al.* 2006). This can be achieved by considered use of storage and regular rotation of available resources for the children in smaller and home-based contexts. In all EYFS settings adults should ensure that the resources available are useful enough to be motivating, such as checking that the paints on offer have not all become a shade of brown from misplaced brushes. Children need time to use one type of resource proficiently and can sometimes be overwhelmed by too many materials to

Figure 15.1 These children are skilled at selecting and joining materials from frequent access to the technology area. This allows them greater potential to plan and execute creative constructions.

choose from, so practitioners will need to observe and plan when to introduce new possibilities (Cole 2006). (See Figure 15.1.)

Providing new and interesting resources can inspire children to creativity. Consider how the resources on offer appeal to all the senses and choose everyday objects that have an interesting texture, smell, sound or visual quality. Adding shells, flowers, stones or glass pebbles to construction, sand, water or role play can provoke a response. Even ordinary objects in an unusual location can stimulate new ideas, such as a rubber glove in the painting area, cotton reels and buttons in the flowerbed! Keeping containers of open-ended materials for spontaneous creations can also be useful especially if thought and support is given as to how the children will join materials together. Blankets, pegs, ribbons, string, bulldog clips, carpet squares, cushions, large cardboard boxes and tubes can form the starting point for den building, imaginative role play and even mathematical and scientific investigation of forces, shape, space and materials as children develop new 'inventions' and work through problems (see Figure 15.2).

Another way of stimulating creativity may be to enable children to access child-sized versions of adult tools and resources. This could be using gardening equipment, raking, digging and watering, experiencing clay rather than play dough or using hammers, saws and wire cutters for technology (May *et al.* 2006). Of course these activities

Figure 15.2 The practitioner has invited children to use the 'thinking cave', an open-ended creativity that stimulates creativity, as children can use it in any way they wish.

will require adult involvement and careful consideration of health and safety but giving children the skills to use such equipment can open up a new range of possibilities as they incorporate these methods into their creative decisions.

Sometimes children's creativity may be hampered by lack of space to try out movements and construction ideas. This is another reason why significant periods of time available in a larger outside space can help children to work creatively. Practitioners can improve the chances of children working in a more creative way by removing excess furniture indoors and allowing children to use fixed outdoor apparatus inventively (see Chapter 11). In a smaller setting or home environment this may mean clearing the centre of a room, allowing children to build dens with chairs and tables, using outdoor space at home or taking resources to a community open space (Duffy 2006). Similarly, time itself is a valuable factor in providing the opportunity for creativity and critical thinking. Adults in any EYFS setting need to plan for sustained periods of uninterrupted time where children can pursue their own interests, with responsive adult support. In many later EYFS environments this may be compromised by the timetable and expectations of 'lesson' times (Duffy 2006; May *et al.* 2006). In other locations the routines of feeding, changing and using outdoor space may cause the same problem. For the younger members of the EYFS the principles of sufficient time, space, freedom with resources and encouragement to explore still apply. As mentioned in the chapter about the learning environment, using treasure baskets and making resources accessible for babies and toddlers at their own level is very important (Goldschmied and Jackson 1994). It is also necessary to consider how the blank spaces of floor and wall coverings can be used to stimulate the youngest members of the EYFS who may be less mobile (Rinaldi *et al.* 2005). Parents and carers will also need support to understand the benefits of creative approaches to learning. They may be concerned about the intellectual value of open-ended learning opportunities or messy activities. Practitioners will need to ensure that parents and carers are able to raise questions and discuss this aspect of children's learning with them and that children are provided with protective clothing and safe opportunities to allow them freedom to explore (Duffy and Stillaway 2004). Limitations in the EYFS as a whole may need to be addressed by reviewing and restructuring the day as well as the environment (Craft and Jeffrey 2004). This may require more flexible arrangements for snacks, drinks and toileting and a separate timetable for the EYFS when they are in school settings, so that children are not constantly interrupted when they are immersed in a new discovery.

Case study

In one Reception class, where the children attended school for half days during the first term, the teacher was concerned about the amount of time taken up by assembly, which occurred half way through the morning session each day. She negotiated with the head teacher that her class would only attend whole-school assembly once each week and would find other times for acts of worship with KS1 and the other Reception class during the week. This enabled her to plan for small-group activity with adults and sustained child-initiated activity for an hour and a half without interruption at the start of each morning.

Approaches to creativity

Some particular methods of teaching and planning have been connected with developing creativity in young children. One model, 'thinking actively in a social context', combines Sternberg's ideas about the development of thinking and problem-solving skills with Vygotsky's principles of scaffolding and enabling children to learn through questioning and partnered play (Wallace 2002). This model identifies six key aspects to problem solving that adults can use flexibly with different projects, building up the range of skills over a year. These include:

- **Gather** – children and adults share ideas, questions and prior knowledge and experience.
- **Identify** – the focus and purpose of the task is established.
- **Generate** – suggestions are made about a possible course of action and finding further information.

- **Decide** – the group selects 'the best idea' and suggests possible outcomes.
- **Implement** – the group carries out a process of trial and error with the selected idea.
- **Evaluate** – children suggest good and bad features of their chosen solution and whether this was the best course of action.
- **Communicate** – children explain what they have found out to others.
- **Learn from experience** – the group considers how it will use this new knowledge in the future.

(Wallace 2002)

This process can be applied to any curriculum area and use more or less of these different aspects depending on the chosen task. A similar way of working is also identified by Fisher (2005a,b), who describes a cycle of application, analysis, synthesis, evaluation. This process is very much in evidence in sustained **socio-dramatic play** or in classes that use the **mantle of the expert** (Heathcote 2002) as an approach to cross-curricular learning, drama and problem solving. In the EYFS practitioners can use a real-life starting point such as a visit to the shops or a farm then develop a role-play area and linked learning opportunities around it. New avenues of exploration can be developed by the adults posing problems and obstacles and following the children's ideas for change and new elements to the role play. Over a period of several weeks the children can use reading, mark-making, speaking and listening skills as well as critical thinking, reasoning and other curriculum opportunities such as knowledge and understanding of the world in this context. For example, creating a role-play garage with slightly older children enabled them to find out about the resources and activities that are found in a garage as well as letter writing, job applications, accident books and much more (Hall and Robinson 2003). Creative teaching using drama and role play can enhance learning for all pupils but also offers new potential for pupils to make their own creative suggestions about a task. At each stage of this socio-dramatic approach there are many elements of the problem-solving model outlined by Wallace (2002) in evidence, as the same skills are utilized to plan and develop a new role-play theme.

Another approach to creativity and critical thinking that is used within primary education and could be used in the EYFS is the **philosophy for children** model (P4C). This way of encouraging children to think creatively focuses on ideas and abstract concepts rather than practical problem solving. Children may be asked to respond to music, artwork or stories by generating their own questions to discuss and giving possible explanations. This approach involves children in working collaboratively to explore ideas, using talk to give reasons and clarify thinking, to evaluate and interpret their own and others' views and to make connections with previous experience (IAPC 2008). The same key elements emerge in each of the methods mentioned thus far: making links to prior knowledge, potentially including home experience; collaborative talk for raising suggestions and questions and evaluation and reasoning about the merit of suggestions raised. There is an emphasis within these methods on using genuine dialogue to extend children's thinking (Taggart *et al.* 2005). It is positive that such activities will encourage children in the EYFS to use language to explain and reason but the disadvantage of these primary-based approaches for the EYFS is the need for developed language to discuss and question. It is important that adults use appropriate scaffolding, visual prompts and practical activities in order to ensure that all children in the EYFS are able to contribute and gain from these experiences at their own level but even with adaptations these approaches may be most useful for the 3 to 5 age range or those children who have an early strength with spoken language. In order to find a method that has more potential with the younger members of the EYFS other approaches may be necessary.

The EYFS emphasizes the need to offer experiences that relate to individual children's interests and make links between the worlds of home and the EYFS setting. These ideals are supported by the philosophy of Reggio Emilia, where members of staff tune into the ideas and interests of children in their care by regular involvement and dialogue with the parents and carers as well as careful observation of the children (Knight 2001; Rinaldi *et al.* 2005). While the framework of education in England may be different and prevent the Reggio approach from being replicated entirely (Moss 2001), it is possible that a similar approach can be developed in EYFS settings. First the setting may offer a real-life task or experience as a starting point. Practitioners should then assist children in planning, gathering resources and constructing while following, supporting and questioning the children's ideas. Projects should be developed in line with individual and small-group interests and so EYFS practitioners would need to use a flexible and child-led approach to planning to achieve this. Other essential elements of the Reggio philosophy include the impact of the environment on children's learning and the involvement of skilled artists and craftspeople as a vehicle for learning (Abbott 2001; Knight 2001; Rinaldi *et al.* 2005). While EYFS settings are unlikely to have a resident artist at all times they are able to engage with skilled parents and carers, other community members and organizations such as **Creative Partnerships**. Short-term involvement with authors, musicians and artists may be the catalyst for a larger scale project or an individual area of interest and can be relevant for the toddler age group and beyond (Duffy 2006).

Case study

In an EYFS setting a community group visited weekly and worked with the 4- and 5-year-old children. The children learned to play different rhythms on large drums and to respond to physical and visual signals. They investigated South American culture, food, rhymes and songs. Many of the children could be observed taking these elements further in their own play by including songs and dancing. One child spontaneously organized a range of drums using upturned boxes and containers. He used critical thinking as he compared the range of noises that he could achieve and selected the different containers for his 'performance'.

Like this example, the Listening to Young Children project (Lancaster 2003) is an inspirational example of the range of ways in which children can express their feelings and ideas and develop creative responses. The work carried out at the Thomas Coram centre and associated settings in London shows practitioners, parents and dancers, musicians and artists enabling children, including babies and under-3s, to communicate ideas using dance, story telling, percussion, photography and video, art and design and movement. While stimulating creativity, this project emphasizes the need for adults to become really receptive to the views and needs of the children in their care. It seems obvious that it is only when such a relationship is achieved and children know that they are truly understood and listened to that they can be secure enough to think critically and creatively.

Reflections

- Do we agree that creativity is valuable for children's learning and development?
- What resources or areas do we have that could stimulate creativity?

16 The welfare requirements

This chapter covers the legal expectations and the Ofsted conditions of registration for Early Years Foundation Stage providers. It offers some examples of how these may be interpreted in a range of different settings and how they impact upon learning.

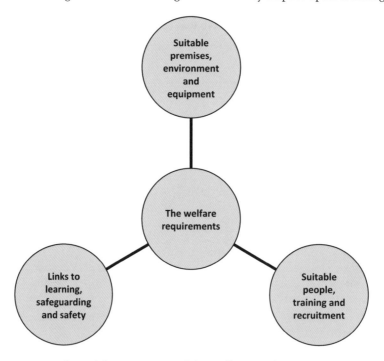

Essential components of the welfare requirements

It is important to remember that children's emotional and physical needs must be met before they are able to learn. Young children are used to the care and attention of their parents or carers and in a busy Early Years Foundation Stage setting or school, special thought and organization will be needed to ensure that children are nurtured and cared for. All providers, including childminders, settings in receipt of funding and private provision, must have due regard for the welfare requirements laid out in the *Early Years Foundation Stage Framework* (DfES 2007b:19). All settings are subject to regular Ofsted inspections in which the particular welfare arrangements will be checked for compliance with the legal obligations of working with babies and young children. They will also need to adhere to relevant legislation about health and safety at work, medicines, communicable diseases, fire regulations, food preparation, disability and equality. Detailed guidance on the legal expectations and how these should be interpreted is available from the Pre-School Learning Alliance (PLA 2008b) as well as from local authority child care and education teams. In schools and settings individual policies and procedures will outline how these expectations are met in practice.

How the welfare requirements link to learning

A child's brain is not a small-world version of an adult brain. In the process of maturation, many stages of development are passed through. Understanding what is currently known about the basic needs of the human brain offers an insight into the reasons for these particular welfare requirements for the babies and young children in our care.

The human brain is described succinctly by Dr Paul Maclean of the National Institute of Mental Health, Washington DC in Shaw and Hawes (1998) as triune, divided into three parts:

- The neo-cortex at the top of the brain, which is the 'thinking area', is divided into two hemispheres, joined by the corpus callosum. This is the problem-solving and pattern-seeking area.
- The mid-brain or limbic system deals with emotions, long-term memory and values.
- The third part of the brain is the reptilian brain, which responds to survival needs first and then learning opportunities. This area of the brain controls all routine bodily functions and instincts. Because of the physical need for survival, the reptilian brain operates beyond conscious awareness, controlling heart beat, balance, temperature and breathing and also responds to emergencies with a 'fight or flight' response, as discussed in Shaw and Hawes (1998). When the reptilian brain is under threat, higher order processes cease to operate and develop.

Practitioners need to be aware of this because children in their care will be unable to learn and develop fully if their basic needs are compromised. Threats can be physical, for example feeling too hot or too cold or too hungry or thirsty or being physically uncomfortable. Therefore, something as simple as wearing shoes that are rubbing, or feeling claustrophobic or uncomfortable in a crowded or noisy environment will constrain learning. Barriers to learning can also be emotional. These can be related to a sense of fear or anxiety, isolation, insecurity or injustice, so providing emotional security for children is vital. In order for learning to be effective, the reptilian brain's needs must be satisfied. Meeting the welfare requirements contributes to providing conditions in which children are safe and comfortable enough to learn.

Safeguarding and suitable people

Chapter 3 outlines further details related to safeguarding procedure. The requirements for suitable people are met by ensuring adults are appropriately qualified for their particular EYFS role. Childminders must attend a local authority-approved training course prior to, or within six months of registration and must hold a paediatric first aid certificate at the point of registration. They are also accountable for the work of any assistant and should think carefully about the ramifications of who they involve in their childminding role. First aid training towards a current paediatric certificate must be approved by the local authority and consistent with the guidance set out in *Practice Guidance for the Early Years Foundation Stage* (DfES 2007a).

All supervisors and managers of EYFS settings must hold a full and relevant level 3 qualification as set out by the Children's Workforce Development Council and half of all other staff must hold a relevant level 2 similarly defined (DfES 2007a:16). In Reception classes there should be a qualified teacher with no more than 30 children. In mixed EYFS classes in school settings, where the majority of the children will not reach school age during the year, this should be no more than 26 pupils with a teacher and a level 3 qualified assistant (DfES 2007a:16).

It is important to employ the right people to work with babies and young children without being discriminatory. The setting up of Early Excellence Centres, Sure Start programmes and neighbourhood nurseries has impacted on the expectations of providers to maintain settings that are multi-functional. For example, children's centres will need to 'combine nursery education, family support, employment advice, childcare and health services on site' (DfES 2003:7). Providers need to think carefully about the core values and beliefs that underpin their work in order to identify people with a similar vision and commitment to good practice. All employees need to understand collaborative practice or team work and effective communication. This includes the ability to work with people from other disciplines and services, as required by the Children Act 2004 which followed the Laming report (DoH 2003), clearly identifying the dangers of addressing an increasingly service-led rather than needs-led approach. Therefore the recruitment process needs to be considered carefully, deciding on the qualities that will complement the existing staff team to meet the needs of the children at different ages and stages. Evidence of suitability should be drawn from references, full employment history, qualifications, identity checks and other checks taken such as medical suitability. Where the applicant has a history of mental health problems, it may be necessary to ask them to attend a meeting with the occupational health officer for advice on their fitness to work with young children.

Recruitment and training

All potential employees must be asked to declare all convictions and/or cautions, as well as court orders which may affect their suitability to work with young children. Employers should not reject employees on the grounds of disabilities but can reject applicants who fail to provide adequate references or who are not able to receive enhanced clearance by the Criminal Records Bureau. All staff and visitors who work with the children in an unsupervised capacity must hold an up-to-date enhanced Criminal Records Bureau (CRB) disclosure that includes a Protection of Children Act list/list 99 check. Settings are advised to keep photocopies of these forms and copies of all staff qualifications and training on file with a log of the number and dates of CRB disclosures. It is important that all providers keep up with regularly changing requirements. From Autumn 2008 there is a new system of vetting and barring people from working with children and vulnerable people under the Safeguarding Vulnerable Groups Act (2006). Ongoing and induction training can support the welfare requirements by including clear expectations of all staff working within the setting with regard to health and safety issues, positive handling and physical intervention. All staff should receive first aid training that relates to working with babies and young children.

Suitable premises, environment and equipment

This standard is associated with health and safety and, of course, maintaining the security of a setting and children's well-being when using it is crucial. However, a suitable environment is also one that provides adequate space, age-appropriate resources and opportunities to learn through play. This includes sufficient access to outside space and appropriate food preparation, changing, toileting and sleeping areas. These premises should also be accessible and adapted to meet the needs of any children with disabilities. The choice of resources used should reflect a diverse range of family circumstances and cultural backgrounds (Ofsted 2008). The detail of how some of these aspects may be best provided is addressed throughout this publication. It is important to recognize that a suitable environment is not necessarily a perfect, sanitized or purpose-built one. It is just as likely to be the home of a childminder or a community hall if the practitioners have taken the time to consider the needs of the children and ways to address potential hazards (PLA 2008).

Early years providers face a significant challenge in working with the children and ensuring that premises consistently meet the exacting standards outlined in the framework. To achieve this, most providers keep paper evidence in the form of a log of all of the following:

- monthly inspections of buildings, outdoor equipment and perimeter fencing;
- six-weekly fire alarm testing and fire evacuation drills;
- annual tree management and PAT testing of electrical equipment;
- legionella bacteria management checks, regularly flushing through little-used water outlets;
- monitoring of water temperatures;
- rotational equipment checks;
- risk assessments and contingency plans.

Daily grounds inspections are also necessary to ensure that the outdoor area is secure before children enter the setting. Managers add the next inspection dates to the setting diary to plan ahead to ensure that the inspections happen. These are backed up electronically with a copy kept within the setting and a copy of important information, such as children's contact numbers, kept off-site, for example at the manager's home, in case of critical incident management.

Where a management committee or board of governors are involved in the management of the setting, individuals can be allocated responsibilities in the event of an emergency, for example in contacting parents and carers or in dealing with the media. Any changes in the provision that affect the use of space and level of care for the children must be notified to Ofsted. Not to do so is an offence. Most providers have a planning noticeboard, informing all staff of routine checks and planned inter-agency visits for the week in hand. This is particularly important in settings where staff work in shifts or on a rotational basis. There also needs to be a system in place, for example a hard backed notebook, for communicating unplanned maintenance needs such as replacing light bulbs or defective equipment, that is signed and dated when action has been taken. All log entries of the findings of these checks and interventions are made in ink so that any legal challenges show evidence of the last inspection date that cannot be subsequently altered. This protects both the staff and the children.

As discussed in Chapter 3, it is essential to check that outer perimeter and external doors are secure during contact sessions. Fences are needed to keep intruders out and children safely contained within the setting. Many settings choose to have two door handles on perimeter doors, one at child height and one at adult height to prevent children having unplanned access to the road or the outside world. It is essential for staff to know that all of the children in their care are safely contained and supervised at all times.

Buildings and equipment are subject to deterioration. For example, wire netting deteriorates over time and can become a health and safety hazard, so well-planned maintenance and monitoring is needed. Outside play equipment such as climbing frames and play houses need to be maintained and checked regularly for signs of wear and tear. Smaller equipment also needs to be checked periodically to ensure that it is safe and well maintained. This includes washing small-world toys on a rotational basis. Sets of bricks etc. can be put into a drawstring bag and washed on an economy washing machine cycle and air dried. Dressing-up clothes can also be washed and checked for loose buttons and trailing hems. Also check that low, single-glazed windows that have been in place for some time are fitted with safety glass which meets the minimum requirements.

Due care should be taken with potentially dangerous equipment and materials. All water trays should be supervised at all times and outdoor ponds should be fenced off from unsupervised access. Sand pits should be covered when not in use to avoid animal fouling. It is important to make parents aware of the dangers from animal faeces in order to implement a policy of no dogs in the grounds of the setting.

Fire safety

All emergency exit routes from the house or setting should be clearly labelled with large, green on white fire exit labels. Staff should be aware of their roles in the event of an emergency and should practise using more than one escape route. Emergency exits must be clutter-free and accessible at all times. It is helpful to talk to the local fire department about a particular building as they will be able to advise managers about possible exit routes, positioning of fire extinguishers of various types and locking mechanisms that can be opened quickly in the event of an emergency. They will also help to identify a safe evacuation point where the children can be counted and contained until they can be moved to a place of safety. It is sensible to have a contingency plan in place that hopefully will never be used. Each week the fire alarm should be tested and at least every six weeks a fire drill should check that all staff are aware of their responsibilities to the children so that when the fire alarm sounds the staff and children know their evacuation drill roles and responsibilities and undertake these without panic. Registers should be kept of all children in attendance. In an emergency drill, these should be taken outside to the predetermined, safe evacuation point where each name can be checked against the register. A log of the drill and the time taken to evacuate the building should be kept. In the event of fire, staff should be clear about who is leading the children to safety and who is checking the toilets are empty. Too often in a fire drill, a small child is left in the toilets, washing hands!

Smoke detectors should be fitted to childminding premises as well as to settings and the batteries should be tested regularly and replaced when necessary. Spare batteries should be kept so that there is never a situation where the detectors do not work. If the building contains open-flame water heaters, these should be checked regularly too and a carbon monoxide detector fitted. Think carefully about storage arrangements. For example, childminders should think about under-stair storage and whether cupboards contain materials that might compromise escape routes in the event of a fire. Fire is not the only hazard. In the event of a gas leak, it is essential to train staff to avoid using any electrical switches or trying to switch off electrical apparatus.

Access and collection

Some parents bring their child to the setting in advance of the time stated as an opening time. It is very important for providers to publish acceptable arrival and departure times and the need for parents to supervise their children until the published start time. Prompt collection of the children is to be encouraged. However, staff must stay on the premises with young children until they are collected. If children are not collected, staff should not transport the children to their home in staff cars.

In many purpose-built settings, there is an exterior door that gives open access to a receptionist and then there is a locked door with a key code or swipe card access to the area of the building in which the children work. All visitors who need access to the children or staff are expected to sign in to a visitor's book with their name, place of work, time of entry and exit, reason for the visit and signature. Most settings run by the local authority rigorously require visitors to wear a visitors' badge that is borrowed from reception and returned on leaving the building.

EYFS settings should, of course, ensure that all possible steps have been taken to prevent intruders accessing the premises. Many settings install a security intercom so that visitors identify themselves before being given access to the premises. The setting is within its rights to deny access to anyone who does not have a visitor appointment, does not have CRB clearance or cannot produce identification. Providers should also make it clear that they can only release children into the care of individuals named by the parent. Most settings have a policy that parents complete a form naming their replacement to collect the child. Staff must be confident that children are contained within the premises and supervised at all times. This means that staff should know which children they have responsibility for. When former members of staff are no longer employed within the setting, the return of all keys and swipes must be recorded to maintain security.

Outings

Children should not be taken beyond the perimeter of the premises without written permission being obtained from the parent or carer in advance. A full risk assessment should be made, identifying the necessary adult-to-child ratios, the nature of the outing and any additional clothing such as outdoor coats and wet weather protection required. Staff should keep contact numbers to hand, a first aid kit that includes disposable gloves and wipes, a mobile telephone and a change of clothing in case of toileting accidents. Records should be kept about the vehicles in which children are transported. These records should include insurance details and named drivers. Providers should not use their own cars without checking that their insurance covers them for this purpose.

Accidents and medicines

EYFS providers must have a system for managing medicines and dealing with accidents, injury or illness of children in their care (see Chapter 4). This will include managing the medical needs of children with long-term conditions such as asthma, diabetes and epilepsy as well as sometimes making arrangements to include children with more complex medical needs such as tube-feeding. Children who have a complex medical need may come under the rulings of the DDA (OPSI 1995) and later amendments (OPSI 2001). This broadly means that schools and early years settings are required to make 'reasonable adjustments' (OPSI 1995, 2001) in order for them to be able to attend the setting (see Chapter 4 for further information).

Key worker systems can be helpful in establishing information about a child's condition and working with parents or carers to provide a routine. It is important that parents or carers are reassured about their child's care and are not made to feel that special arrangements are a burden on the setting. In the case of children with long-term medical needs key workers can also be involved in additional training with health professionals such as community nurses to ensure that they are well prepared to meet children's needs. They should not, however, be given sole responsibility as other members of staff will need to be able to carry out these duties in an emergency or in case of staff absences.

Case study

Jade (18 months) was due to attend a children's centre while her mother returned to work. The staff would usually help toddlers on to a changing table using a small step but Jade was not yet mobile and was too heavy to be lifted regularly. Jade also needed tube-feeding. The children's centre manager arranged to meet with Jade's mum and the community nurse who had supported Jade's arrangements at home. The nurse agreed to give staff training in using the tube-feeding equipment so that enough members of staff were trained to cover any pattern of attendance, although one member of staff would normally be Jade's key person. The centre also purchased a sturdier changing table and hoist so that Jade could be lifted more easily.

Safety and well-being

Each setting must have a specific policy and procedure for managing medicines. Certain staff will be asked to administer medication as an additional responsibility and this should be part of their contract, not an informal addition. A policy for managing medicines should include:

- daily procedures;
- emergency arrangements;
- procedures for trips and outings;
- information about parental responsibility and permissions;
- information about staff training, roles and responsibilities;
- storage of medicines;
- record keeping; and
- disposal of medicines.

Parents should be encouraged to administer medicines outside the time that the child is in the setting. If this is not possible parents should attempt to provide an additional supply to be kept at the setting as providers are not allowed to administer medicine from a relabelled container (DfES 2005b). With regard to unforeseen events, all settings should maintain an accident book, which is completed in ink, undertake risk assessment in the setting and when travelling beyond it and ensure that staff are trained in emergency procedures and first aid. Parents, staff and carers must be informed about any bumps to the head that individual children have sustained so they can monitor for signs of concussion.

Children are vulnerable to accidents and the responsibility for avoiding as many as possible is that of all adults in an EYFS setting (PLA 2008). However, practitioners, parents and carers need to be aware that even with careful health and safety procedures children will still occasionally injure themselves. They also need opportunities to experience low-level physical risks, such as running on a hard surface or climbing on a low bench in order to develop their own judgement of situations for the future. Research suggests that children's own understanding of risk may be limited and adults can improve this through the experiences that are available to children (RoSPA 2008). Practitioners should aim to strike a balance between meeting the legislative requirements and limiting children's freedom to learn from experience. The safety aspect of the welfare requirements also covers the EYFS provider's responsibility for healthy food and drink; the implications of this are discussed in more detail in Chapter 4.

The welfare requirements overall also uphold the principle of appropriate expectations. For example, positive and supportive relationships between children, staff and families are part of the statutory expectations placed on EYFS providers. This now includes designating a key person to build a special rapport with particular children and families and act as a point of contact for a setting. Another part of this responsibility is responding to children's individual needs and prior experiences in the home. Children's behaviour should be managed in a way appropriate to their age and understanding and EYFS practitioners should work with parents and carers to develop routines and arrangements appropriate for their child by reflecting home language, continuing with an existing sleep routine, or providing for their dietary needs. In a school environment teachers or teaching assistants will be expected to fulfil this role for the children in their care. Policy, procedure and staff training can help to ensure that all members of staff are well informed about things they can do to maintain health and safety. The arrangements for risk assessment, accidents, emergencies and maintenance of premises and equipment should be clearly laid out. Parents and carers will also need to be informed about the measures that are in place and consulted about their children's individual needs. Individual staff members and managers should work together to ensure that children's welfare is fundamental to everyday practice.

Part 5

Areas of Learning and Development

17 Personal, social and emotional development

This chapter covers some ways in which practitioners can help children to develop self-esteem and social and emotional skills, including a positive self-image and care for others. It outlines some links between emotional literacy and learning.

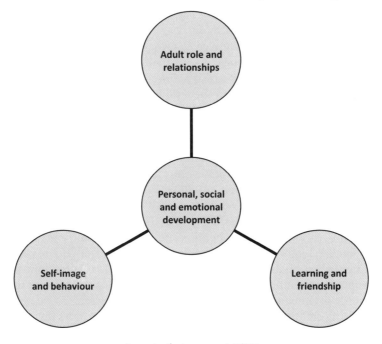

Aspects that support PSED

The Early Years Foundation Stage (EYFS) document (DfES 2007a) divides *personal, social and emotional development* (PSED) into the following headings: *Dispositions and attitudes, Self-confidence and Self-esteem, Relationships, Behaviour and self-control, Self-care* and *Sense of community*. The link between the development of skills and understanding in PSED is highlighted by the EYFS as key to underpinning successful learning in all other areas. In order to help children to become confident, secure and keen to learn, EYFS providers will need to find ways to foster a sense of belonging and to give children the opportunity to express their views and feelings. With very young children and babies, adults will need to be especially skilled at noticing the individual ways in which they communicate needs and emotions. EYFS practitioners are expected to support this area of learning through adult role models, relationships with key adults and working with parents. Other practical strategies will be considered in this chapter.

Recent guidance from the DCSF (2008a) sets out specific recommendations for the support of children's personal, social and emotional development between 0 and 3 years. This has been produced as an attempt to provide a precursor to the commonly used **Social and Emotional Aspects of Learning** materials in the Early Years Foundation Stage of primary and infant schools. While this is likely to be useful for those practitioners working with children in other EYFS settings it may suggest a divide that does not really exist. Babies, children and indeed adults have strong similarities in the way that they sustain successful relationships and remain emotionally healthy. EYFS practitioners need to understand how they can meet these needs for themselves and for babies and children of all ages in their care.

The starting point for all aspects of PSED needs to be children's understanding of themselves. This encompasses ideas such as self-awareness, self-esteem and self-confidence. Essentially, children first need to recognize and value their own individuality. For babies this begins with playing with their hands and feet and realizing that they have control over their own body as well as having their messages understood and responded to by the adults around them (Roberts 2002; Broadhead 2004; Dowling 2005; Lawrence 2006; DCSF 2008a). Babies quickly learn that crying will summon an adult and that smiling may produce a smile in return. Practitioners who work with the youngest children need to learn each baby's individual language of cries, gurgles and body movements, just as their family would do, and respond accordingly. This is an important undertaking which necessitates the close relationship provided by a dedicated key worker (Dowling 2005; Lindon 2005; DCFS 2008a). EYFS providers should enable children of all ages to develop positive feelings about themselves by including photographs of themselves, friends and family in the setting. They should provide mirrors for babies and children to see themselves and others together. Practitioners should also include familiar words, routines and objects of comfort from home particularly to soothe children when tired, ill or anxious (Dowling 2005), as this allows children to use their experience from home to cope with their emotions and enables them to feel that they belong in the setting.

Encouraging children to accept and know themselves includes reflecting positive images of their lives and families through a thoughtful choice of resources, images and stories that practitioners incorporate in everyday learning. It also includes helping children to recognize and express their own emotions and offering adult support when managing difficult feelings. This aspect of PSED is often called emotional intelligence or emotional literacy. Children need to develop this understanding in order to form successful relationships with others. It is very important that children are not inadvertently given the message that some emotions are unacceptable. EYFS practitioners must make sure that children realize that certain types of behaviour may be unacceptable but it is normal to feel very angry or very sad from time to time. Older children can be taught strategies to cope with feeling very angry such as running, stamping, or punching a cushion, or having a special area to go to when they feel sad, perhaps including soft toys or a dark place in which to hide (Dowling 2005). All children need physical comfort from time to time and practitioners should not feel concerned about hugging children or holding their hand if they are anxious and seeking reassurance; these gestures are how children learn to calm themselves and help others (Lindon 2005).

Case study

When Ben's grandfather died he decided to explain his feelings to his Reception class. He believed that it was important for them to understand that he, a significant adult in their lives, had feelings and to raise the subject of grief. In carpet time he explained that he had been away from school for a day because his grandfather died. He said that he felt very sad and he was glad to see everyone because being at school helped him to feel a bit better. He reassured the children that his grandfather was very old (so they were not worrying about their grandparents) and said that his body had just worn out like a very old machine. He explained that he would feel sad for a while. He allowed them to see that he was upset. The children were very quiet and showed concern on their faces; they then spontaneously offered their own experiences of sadness and death.

It is worth remembering that at times children may be overwhelmed by intense feelings particularly as they are frequently coping with new situations, people and places (Dowling 2005). This may mean that they are unable to cope with the normal expectations of the setting let alone be relaxed enough to learn. Having clear routines, explanations and adult support can help children to adjust to a new setting or experience, or help them through difficult times at home. Key workers have a vital role to play in this for individual children as they should be aware of family changes and know children well enough to notice that they are emotionally vulnerable. They are also a reassuring point of contact and support for children who are new in a setting. In Reception classes the class teacher and teaching assistant can fulfil the role of key worker if they make time for conversation and play with the children in their care (DCSF 2008a). They should do everything possible to avoid becoming so overwhelmed by the demands of a school timetable that they are unable to really get to know each child individually.

Case study

Dalmar had recently arrived in England with his family. He was born in Somalia but had already attended kindergarten in Denmark. He did not speak English. The class teacher took responsibility for ensuring that Dalmar understood the routines in the setting. She used pictures on all equipment and a visual timetable, as well as a photo to show him his peg. She spent time taking him to different areas of the room and showing him what was available. He liked to hold her hand and follow her during the day at first, copying words, phrases and songs that she used, but after a few weeks played happily with others although still seeking her out to show her things, or lead her over to what he had done. One day he was busily involved connecting straws. His face lit up and he shouted across to her where she was with some other children, 'Mrs Smith, a flower!' After the teacher had confirmed that it was indeed a beautiful flower Dalmar skipped around the room showing his creation and calling out 'A flower' to everyone. He was able to use her support to build his confidence and self-esteem enough to use new language and share it with everyone else.

Children are more able to cope with day-to-day challenges if they have high self-esteem (Mortimer 2003; Dowling 2005; Lindon 2005; DCFS 2008a). This does not mean that they should be reliant on adult praise but that they should be able to recognize their own strengths and have realistic expectations for themselves. Practitioners can support children to develop self-esteem by giving specific praise based on particular achievements and also personal qualities. If adults praise children for helping others, being cheerful, trying something new or taking pride in their appearance, children will learn that their self-worth is not only based on getting things 'right' or on academic success (Mountford and Hunt 2001; Lawrence 2006). These are important life lessons that will enable children to be aware of their own individual qualities and make them more resilient when things go wrong.

The EYFS encourages practitioners to help children to become independent in both learning and self-care; children will need to persevere and attempt new challenges in order to do this (see Figure 17.1). Understanding health and managing personal hygiene is discussed to some extent in Chapter 4 but the principles of independence in this area and in learning are the same. In order to become independent, children need to think and work through areas of interest without being disturbed and to attempt new activities, such as doing up buttons or their own shoes, even if this takes a long time. Children need planning time for the next steps in their own activities; this should be supported by an adult and may follow the **High/scope** method of plan, do, and review (Lindon 2005). In both learning and self-care, children of all ages need to be allowed to make choices. The skills of decision making should not be thrust upon children as a bewildering open-ended range of possibilities, but should be introduced through limited and manageable choices such as choosing between an apple and an orange at snack time, choosing to play in the sand or the water, or selecting from different sizes of paper for painting (Dowling 2005). These can all be incorporated into normal routines and can include children who do not communicate verbally by offering practical objects or picture cards to choose from.

Adults can also spend time observing children's social play and noticing where children are working together and interacting well. Pat Broadhead (2004) offers a way of assessing the level of social interaction called the social play continuum. When using this in classroom research she found that children's social play was not most developed in the role-play area, as some practitioners had supposed, but was very effective in unstructured imaginative play when open-ended equipment was available in an area

Figure 17.1 Children should learn to help each other, through simple routines, as well as managing their own self-care.

called the 'whatever you want it to be place'. Providing a box of cardboard containers, blankets and cushions or carpet squares for this kind of open-ended play may be one way to stimulate social relationships in the EYFS (Figure 17.2). Some children may find it difficult to make friends with others and this is also part of PSED that practitioners can help to develop. In a setting where children are helped to value their own and others' identity, gender, ethnicity, religion or appearance, children are less likely to be left out because of these differences. This ethos can be supported by resources and the messages given by adults in the setting (see Chapter 5) but children may also need specific intervention. This can range from suggesting to a rejected child that he or she tries to join in by watching and then copying what others are doing or by playing alongside others, to regular use of PSED approaches such as circle time, persona dolls or puppets and role play, particularly for the 3 to 5 age group.

Many EYFS practitioners will already be familiar with using persona dolls and circle time approaches for PSED. If used consistently these can be powerful ways to support children's development in this area of learning and when linked to a carefully

Figure 17.2 Children using open-ended materials are able to negotiate and create imaginative play situations together.

planned system of rewards and sanctions they will make a valuable contribution to improving behaviour. Children will be able to learn why they should behave sensitively towards others and understand the impact of their actions rather than simply responding to the extrinsic methods of punishment and reward (Mosley 1998; Brown 2001; Lawrence 2006). A persona doll is introduced to the group as a doll with its own life story; children are told about the doll's likes and dislikes and also a particular problem or difference that practitioners want to discuss (often something that children in the setting are experiencing). Different dolls and stories can be used over the children's time in the setting to encourage children to develop empathy with the doll and suggest how it can be helped with a particular problem. Brown (2001) suggests involving parents in offering guidance about culturally appropriate life stories for dolls and using the dolls to tackle children's understanding of racism, disability, gender stereotyping and family breakdown. Circle time can be very valuable but should not be associated with show and tell or used as a vehicle for highlighting individual misdemeanours. It is likely to be most effective when used with small groups in the EYFS and it may be less threatening for children to start by sitting in a group rather than a circle (Collins 2001). Specific themes should be discussed, such as feeling angry or left out, as well as the positive aspects of friendship and family. These can be enacted by a puppet role play or started by each completing a statement such as 'a friend is...' Circle time authors agree that including fun games and songs is an important aspect of regular circle time slots (Mosley 1998; Collins 2001; Mountford and Hunt 2001).

Successful development of personal, social and emotional skills cannot be left to chance. Children will need adult help to recognize their own strengths, encouragement to try new challenges and support to empathize with and relate to their peers. Where this is a consistent feature of EYFS provision most children will display appropriate behaviour. EYFS practitioners can help this to occur by noticing their own emotions and supporting one another when stressed or anxious. They can model empathy and caring relationships with children, staff and parents and carers. They can ensure that they have appropriate expectations for children in their care and find out about individual circumstances that may affect children's behaviour as well as planning for learning experiences that will help children to consider one another's needs and feelings.

Reflections

- How can we support the emotional needs of the adults in the setting?
- How do we encourage children to view themselves and their families positively?
- What do we do to help children to develop empathy?
- Is there anything else we can do to help children to recognize and manage their emotions?

18 Communication, Language and Literacy Development

This chapter outlines the acquisition of the key skills of speaking, listening, reading and writing in the EYFS (DfES 2007a).

By the end of the chapter practitioners should be aware of the importance of oracy skills in the development of communication, language and literacy skills.

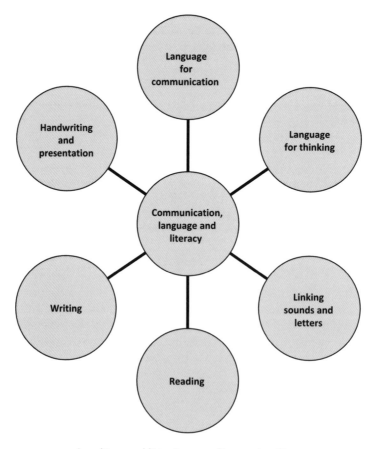

Speaking and listening, reading and writing

This area of the curriculum is underpinned by the principles of the EYFS and is key to learning in the Early Years Foundation Stage as it includes the programmes of study for speaking and listening and phonemic awareness which are the foundations of **dialogic learning and teaching** for young children, developing **oracy** skills and reading and writing, which are **literacy skills**. This means that practitioners have a responsibility to provide opportunities and **authentic activities** in a social context that will support babies and young children in developing the disposition and confidence to acquire oracy and literacy skills in a range of situations and for a variety of purposes.

Language for Communication

The development of oracy skills is important as the foundation of communication. From the earliest stages of development, most babies learn to communicate in their first language and some learn more than one language simultaneously when each adult consistently speaks one language. Fitzpatrick's (2002) research identifies that even in the womb babies kick or have a reduced heart rate in response to external stimuli such as their mother's voice or classical music. Some mothers choose to read to their babies before they are born and research shows that these children are born with an enthusiasm for certain kinds of music or books. Most young babies read the facial expressions and body language of their main carers, parents and the key individuals with whom they build warm and trusting relationships. The exceptions include children with **autistic spectrum disorder**, **Asperger's syndrome** and **attention deficit hyperactivity disorder (ADHD)**. Most babies continue to develop speech by crying and making noises. Adults who respond to these early sounds with interactions encourage babies to experiment with making more sounds by babbling. For example, in the western culture, most fathers respond enthusiastically to the early sounds of 'dad . . . dad' and encourage the baby to repeat the sound, imbuing the sound with meaning and encouraging repetition. This social interaction is an important part of early speech and should also be encouraged by practitioners who work with babies. It is therefore essential to identify a key person who is proactive in supporting each individual child. This key person needs to become aware of the child's personal interests and needs to empower the child to develop a positive self-image in order to access learning effectively. Always be aware of the lighting conditions when modelling language for children. All children will find it hard to watch a practitioner who is standing in front of a window with his or her back to the sun. Children with visual or hearing impairments will find this particularly challenging. Most babies recognize the subtle differences of a raised eyebrow or compressed lips. Also notice how young babies reward eye contact with chuckles and smiles and therefore how important eye contact and non-verbal communication is to young children. Voices are used to express a variety of emotions long before the child can form words, phrases and sentences. Key carers can distinguish between happy sounds and signals that the infant has needs that are not being met. King and Park (2003) emphasize the importance of early response to these early communications, which enable babies to forge a personal identity. Long before they utter their first words, babies are learning about tone, inflection and rhythm of speech from listening to the people around them.

From birth, most babies listen and turn towards familiar sounds and show a star-tle response to sudden loud noises. All children develop at different rates but there are average milestones such as adding single consonants to early 'oh' and 'ah' at between four and six months of age. By seven to nine months of age babies often have a reper-toire of sounds and silences that mimic words and phrases. By the first birthday, most children can understand familiar phrases and produce single words, nods, waves or gestures that have meaning.

By 2 years of age, most babies have developed their language and the foundations for literacy into two-word phrases such as 'Mummy gone.' They will have an average of fifty words in their personal vocabulary. Fitzpatrick (2002) suggests that many babies find adjacent consonants tricky, particularly with r, l, fs, sh, zh, th, and either omit a consonant or substitute a simpler solution. This is not a delay in need of therapy. As the child matures, these adjacent consonants will be pronounced correctly.

Watch the toddler climb into a chair and practise conversations of babble with empty chairs on either side, recognizing the 'sounds and intonations' of spoken lan-guage Fitzpatrick (2002), mimicking the model seen in social situations. It is therefore essential to realize that the quality of these early communications is vitally important for the effective development of social and interpersonal skills. Children need both one-to-one conversations and practice with taking turns in small-group situations. They also need to initiate conversations and have times of silence and thinking time in order to develop their knowledge and understanding of shared conversations. Carers need to talk to children in grammatically correct English phrases, encouraging early vocaliza-tions by sharing picture books, visual stories, poetry, talking and singing. In order for speech to develop, children need to speak to adults and to other children. So speech de-velops from making sounds, to making sounds appropriately, developing recognizable words to echolalia, to short phrases, then longer phrases, to sentences. Children can quickly develop indoor voices and outdoor voices to experiment with the repertoire of sounds that they can make, provided that they understand the difference between the two and that carers model the volume of talking that they want from the children.

Where a child has a home language other than English, the child will quickly pick up English from a native speaker provided that the home language is continued. Where there are two languages at home, research shows that children pick up both languages if each language is spoken by a different speaker. Statistically, children with more than one language develop language acquisition skills for other languages and often excel in reading and writing. Sometimes, bilingual children are slower in producing spoken language and sometimes there is a short period of confusion between the two languages. Parents benefit from reassurance that this will be overcome quickly. Where possible, it is helpful and reassuring for children to speak in their home language from time to time. Where this is not possible, practitioners should develop a visual timetable and visual prompts with parents and if possible with the ethnic minority advisory service. See www.sparklebox.co.uk for a free example.

Children have an innate ability to develop new vocabulary based upon what they hear in a social context. They will also repeat phrases and sentences with the exact inflection heard. It is never appropriate for staff to discuss the intimacies of their social life over the heads of the children or to use inappropriate language in the presence of the children. Where children bring inappropriate language into the setting, it is important not to overreact. The child needs a quiet conversation about not using that word in the setting. A loud or shocked reaction will reinforce the repeated use of the word by that child and by others.

Language for Thinking

Children need small-world experiences in order to imagine and recreate familiar experiences, with opportunities to engage in oracy development through conversations with adults and other children. This involves encouraging the children to use social language such as greetings in context. The equipment that is offered is often representational. For example, a length of material can represent the sea or become a sari or bride's veil in different contexts. Much of a child's early life is centred around the home. Therefore, most settings have a home corner in which children can cook, wash up, make cups of tea and feed the dolly in the highchair using and exploring previously heard social interactions in context. Most children revisit familiar experiences. For example, if Mummy taps the pencil on the notepad while answering a telephone call, so will her daughter in the role-play corner. Fisher (2005a,b) cautions adult interventions in these explorations. Very young children will learn about their environment by picking up familiar items and will investigate shape and texture, feeling items with fingers and also experiencing and comparing items by tasting them and sucking them. At this stage it is very important to be aware of safety issues such as parts of toys that can be swallowed, small beads, pen and felt pen tops that can be a choking hazard.

Linking Sounds and Letters

Currently, the 'simple view of reading', (DCSF 2006a) advocates a systematic, time-limited 'phonics first' approach to learning literacy skills and most school-based EYFS settings are accessing the six phases of 'Letters and Sounds' in a discrete daily synthetic phonics session of about twenty minutes, which is comprised of a series of interactive activities that link sounds and letters. Schools are advised to have fidelity to one scheme and to stick to 'Letters and Sounds' where possible. This will enable children to move from the setting into a variety of mainstream schools. Having a drawstring bag for each phoneme, containing words that start with that phoneme or contain e.g. digraphs, minimizes time wasted in collecting resources for learning. A bag for letter 'C' could contain a car, a candle, a crayon and a picture of a caterpillar. Each item also has a matching laminated card showing the word. Highlight the difference in the length of the word, comparing 'car' with 'caterpillar'. Make up alliterative stories using the resources or play a game in which the children look at the items for several seconds then have to remember as many as possible.

Each activity to link sounds and letters is clearly described in 'Letters and Sounds'. And free resources for use with the children are available from www.standards.dfes.gov.uk/local/clld/las.html.

The various phases teach the children to segment words into chunks that aid reading and writing so that these can be blended back together as reading and writing. As segmenting and blending skills develop, the children are able to manipulate larger chunks of words and known prefixes and suffixes with confidence.

Teachers have found this resource useful and are predicting an improvement in children's ability to read and spell by the end of Key Stage 1, because the system is set within a broad and rich language curriculum with plenty of opportunities to practise both language for communication and language for thinking. It is too soon to measure how successful this will be. Schools are aiming for children to learn to read by Y2 so that they can read to learn in Key Stage 2. As children develop phonological awareness through rhyme and **alliteration**, they begin to gain an understanding of the alphabet. In the early stages of reading they will need to associate letter shapes or graphemes with corresponding phonemes or sounds (**grapheme phoneme correspondences or gpcs**) rather than letter names. Most children progress through the developmental phases of 'Letters and Sounds' without major problems. By 3 years of age children can often pick out local signs within the community. For example, most children can recognize the Post Office logo or their favourite chocolate bar in the supermarket. Where there are children from other cultures, include some dual language labels and positive images of a variety of cultures, avoiding stereotypes. Encourage an awareness of print within the environment by using familiar logos and numerals in the role-play area. Offer children the opportunity to find their name card by looking for the initial sound or outline shape of their name and then post their label in a box on arrival at the setting.

All practitioners are encouraged to audit their provision and review current practice in preparing children for learning to read.

Reading

Reading is a complex process in which a child needs to develop a range of the skills necessary both to decode and comprehend or understand print. Daily opportunities are needed to share and talk about a variety of books including poetry books, nursery rhyme books, board books, pop-up and interactive books, story books and non-fiction information books. Children need to learn that books are special and should be treated with respect. It is the practitioners' enjoyment of stories and enthusiasm in delivering them that will motivate children to want to read books.

Many children do not have books at home and the setting may be their first experience of the joy of a story. There should be shared expectations of how to share a story, for example turning the pages to face the children and sharing enjoyment from the illustrations. Always prepare the book before sharing a story with a child. Find a warm and comfortable spot, possibly on floor cushions. Choose one illustration that is going to be special. Keep the children in suspense with an awareness that they are going to come to the special page. Vary the volume, pace and pitch of your voice to bring out the excitement of the story and ask the children open questions so that they begin to infer meaning from the story or illustrations.

> ## Reflections
> Ask a member of the staff team to video you sharing a book with a child or children.
> Do you use the full range of colours and tones in your voice? Do the different characters in the story have different voices that show their personalities?
> Did you share repeated language with the children – for example huffing and puffing before attempting to blow the house down?
> Is there a sense of suspense waiting for the next page?
> Are some pages passed over quickly and some held on to for as long as possible?

Be aware of individual needs. There will be some children with visual impairments who need to access texts in alternative ways including through ICT using a talking programme.

For very good reasons, most adults wait until a child is asleep to read a personal book or magazine of their own choice and therefore it is unusual for children to see adults engaged in reading for pleasure. Consider opportunities to sit with children, engaged in your own book as they choose books to enjoy and, if possible, take them to a library to choose books to read and take home.

Most settings display an alphabet on the wall. Check that the children walk past this in the reading direction from left to right. Sing an alphabet song and encourage the children to recognize where the letters appear in relation to the quartiles or quarters of the alphabet. For example, point out A at the beginning, M in the middle, Z at the end. Check that your alphabet does not contain miscues. For example, there are very few words in English that start with Y. Most young children have never seen a yacht! Many children enter school saying Y is for boat. Similarly, how many children have seen bottles of ink?

Writing

As with reading, writing develops in recognizable phases. Making sounds equates to making marks on paper. Making sounds appropriately equates to writing culturally specific recognizable letter shapes rather than random symbols. Developing recognizable words equates to beginning to write words that contain the phonemic sounds known so far to communicate in text. Echolalia equates to producing recognizable words. Short phrases are similar to using and then producing correct **high-frequency words**, then longer phrases, then sentences. Young children should begin to understand that writing is a form of communication on paper or on screen and should be encouraged to look at and become aware of print in their environment. Think about what writing looks like from the children's perspective. It is something that they see practitioners doing every day: making lists, taking registers, assessing learning and passing notes to other members of the staff team, or sending letters home. Writing is a real or authentic activity. The practitioner models this as an adult task in front of the child.

Just as children learn to speak by speaking, they learn to read by reading and learn to write by writing. Early writing is a tricky job and is often stressful. Practitioners need to promote enjoyment in making marks on paper and motivate the children to want to write by promoting it as a fun activity. Hand bones and muscles need to be developed through fine motor activities such as picking up seeds with tweezers and placing marbles into inverted flowerpots.

Reflections

- Sign your name on a piece of scrap paper.
- Put the pencil in your non-preferred hand and attempt to copy your signature.
- A number of points to notice are that the process is slower, often there is a marked difference in the pressure of the pencil on the page, and control is less steady and less confident.
- Concentration is required to make the hand achieve what the eye sees.

This is the experience of the beginner writer.

Early marks on paper are often circles and straight lines and by 3 years of age there is usually a connection between writing and drawing. As these early marks develop, there is an awareness of culturally specific marks. Writing is comprised of two separate skills. One is called composition, which involves devising written language to communicate meaning, and the other is called transcription or handwriting, which is the process of forming the letters and words and arranging them on the page or screen. This section concentrates on composition skills.

Children also need to express themselves physically and need opportunities to access big paper on walls, tables and easels, **sky write** with a variety of body parts and respond to music, art, dance and drama by making marks. They need to experiment with a variety of mark makers such as chalk, felt pens, chubby crayons and paint brushes. At an early stage, children will want to write the letters of their own name. Names start with capital letters. The other letters should be **lower case.** These will appear in a jumbled order in shopping lists in the home corner then progress into strings of letters on the page, sometimes with breaks between groups of these. It is usual to find the capital letter from the beginning of the child's name inserted into the strings of letters. As children learn the correct formation of letters and learn the GPCs, the initial and end sounds appear in the writing. Vowels appear at a later stage when the child begins building words by blending sounds together in phonic sessions. At this stage the child has to concentrate on word building and creating sentences that make sense. It is vitally important to prepare the progress of what is to be written and rehearse sentences in the child's head before trying to write these down. By the end of the foundation stage, many children are able to read aloud to the practitioner what they have written. To support further this desire to communicate in writing, practitioners should talk with the child about what has been written. They should also create a conversation on paper, responding to the child's attempts. This should be read back to the child enthusiastically. Sometimes the child will respond by writing additional words.

The child communicates that her gerbil is furry. The practitioner replies 'My cat is furry too.' The child is motivated by this personal response. Alternatively, the child writes for a purpose to her puppet's Mummy. The puppet's Mummy must reply to each letter, motivating the child to write again. Models from appropriate texts such as *Each Peach Pear Plum* and *The Jolly Postman* help to shape stories, poems and non-fiction writing from the child's life-world experience and help to create a real purpose for writing.

Case study

A drawstring bag containing four or five items, for example a teddy bear, sunglasses, a car, a torch and a bunch of keys, can be the starting point for writing. The practitioner reveals each item and places them on the table. The children in the group decide on the sequence of the story using all of the resources. They discuss the various possibilities and rehearse the story sequence. This is recorded on big paper from left to right using a **story hand** to remind the children to decide: who is in the story? Where does it happen? What is the main event (the conflict)? How is this resolved (resolution)? What did they think about it?

The children might decide that the bear wanted to go out in his open top car because it was a lovely sunny day. He took his sunglasses with him because the sunshine was very bright and bears must not look straight at the sun because this is dangerous. It is such a lovely day that the bear stays out very late until it gets dark. He drops his keys in the dark. He remembers the torch in his glove box and searches until he finds his keys. Then he goes home for tea. He thinks it was a good job that he had taken his torch with him.

Notice that the children initially work in pairs or a group and enhance their own vocabulary by sharing ideas, which they capture in drawings. Ideas are clarified through talk but each child retains ownership of his or her own writing. The children choose what to include in their writing. Each element of the story is rehearsed and recorded as an aide memoire *before* the children try to transcribe the words. The adult role is as an observer who assesses the child's written communication, deciding when to mediate with support. He or she is also the facilitator of learning that is appropriate and sets the next learning steps in the child's learning journey to becoming a writer. As an enabler, the adult comments positively about the content, acting as an expert, supporting the novice's early attempts at writing in an ethos where risk taking is encouraged. The children are praised for their attempts and all attempts are valued. Suggestions for improvement are given carefully, discussing what has been written in positive terms, so that children want to write again in the future. Sometimes the adult acts as the scribe, translating ideas into written communication. Smallwood (1990) importantly stated that 'Language is not only a tool for communication but must also be a pleasure in its own right.'

In every setting there should be a writing corner or opportunity within the role-play area to write on paper of various shapes, sizes and colours, using mark makers, postcards, old greetings cards, envelopes, labels and forms.

Handwriting/Presentation

Strand 12 of the CLLD framework introduces key skills to be taught in the later foundation stage. These include pencil grip, controlled lines and forming letters correctly using the correct sequence of movements. Pencils are useful writing tools because there is friction between the lead and the page, which allows the child to control the marks made on paper. Most school policies prescribe black beauties, or fat pencils with a soft lead for children in the foundation stage. These make marks on paper without excessive pressure. Pencils should be free of tassels, toys or distractions. Triangular pencils and triangular pencil grips are helpful in supporting correct grip and letter formation from the beginning of teaching handwriting skills. If working in a school, read through the school's handwriting policy, which may state that children are not allowed to use pencils from home.

Good posture is very important for writing. Children should be encouraged to write at a table, sitting with their back to the back of the chair. Feet should be flat on the floor. Some children with special educational needs, such as children with cerebral palsy, may benefit from tilting the writing surface by working on a wedge surface.

The chair should be pulled in until the child's tummy touches the table. Check that the child's head is at least 30 cm from the paper.

The tripod grip is the preferred grip. The pencil is pinched between the thumb and forefinger. The long, middle finger is used as a support. The wood of the pencil rests in the V formed by the thumb and forefinger. Drawing back the hand, the end of the pencil points towards the child's shoulder. To help with the pincer grip, practise picking up peas with the thumb, forefinger and middle finger. Correct grip is important. Many children develop tension headaches in later life from holding their pencil incorrectly. Many practitioners will notice that they do not hold a pencil correctly and have poor handwriting habits as a result. Some commercially produced handwriting schemes offer early opportunities to practise controlling a pencil. Children need opportunities to practise writing from left to right. Right handed children should have their paper parallel to the edge of the table. Turn the top right corner of the paper for left handed children so that they are discouraged from developing a hook grip to avoid smudging their writing. A mix of custard powder and water in a plastic drawer or large receptacle creates a resistant material that is very tactile for letter formation.

Handwriting can be taught using families of letters that are formed similarly:

a c d g o q s f (e)
i l t u y j
k v w x y z
b h n m p r k

A cat looks like a cat whichever way we look at it, but this is not true of letter shapes, which form different letters if they are reversed or inverted. Notice the similarities between the following:

b and **d**
p and **q**
numbers **6** and **9**.

These are the letters and numbers that cause confusion for children and should not be taught at the same time. Once the similarity from the learner's perspective is identified, change of practice will follow.

s and **z**
numbers **5** and **2**.

Try to avoid early miscues by teaching these at different times and by keeping them apart.

Use letter patterns as sky writing, warm-up exercises for writing. Particularly practise 'o' and 'c' with left handed children.

Make links between the letters that are written and the sounds that these make in words which are called gpcs or grapheme phoneme correspondences.

Note the three definable spaces related to the horizontal line of writing. Some letters have ascenders or lines going up and some have descenders or lines going down, which should become consistent in size.

Letter zones can be taught by the following groupings:

a c e i m n o r s u v w x z
d f h k l t b
g y p q y

A table showing how to form each letter can be downloaded from www.standards. dfes.gov.uk/primary/publications/literacy/63337/nls_dew00501app.pdf.

Reflections

- Is the first impression neat or grubby?
- Has the child started at the correct place? Note: Always go down the stick of a letter, never up.
- Are the letter closures complete?

19 Problem solving, reasoning and numeracy

This chapter covers each of the areas of learning identified in the Early Years Foundation Stage document (DfES 2007a) with suggestions for practice and a discussion of the development of progress as well as consideration of effective practice for implementation. The interrelatedness of the areas is emphasized, using examples of successful cross-curricular themes such as Starting with a Story.

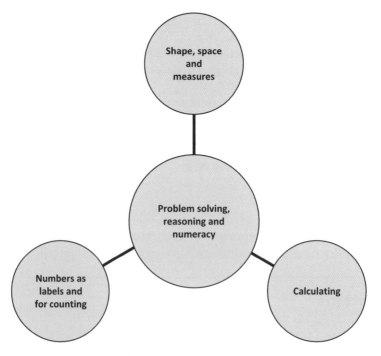

Aspects of problem solving, reasoning and numeracy

Problem solving, reasoning and numeracy

Problem solving, reasoning and numeracy forms part of the Learning and Development area of the EYFS framework. The vocabulary of the title suggests the process children will be using and it is in three parts: numbers for labels and for counting, calculating and shape, space and measures. The EYFS framework states that

> Children must be supported in developing their understanding of problem solving, reasoning and numeracy in a broad range of contexts in which they can explore, enjoy, learn, practise and talk about their developing understanding. They must be provided with opportunities to practise these skills and to gain confidence and competence in their use.

Concepts associated with this area of learning can develop as part of a child's everyday life. These will be integrated into the understanding acquired through the three strands of the EYFS *problem solving, reasoning and numeracy* area of the framework. The vocabulary used in the framework identifies the emphasis placed on the process of the learning to develop understanding. There are a wide variety of assessments available to identify where a child is in the *learning, development and care* area of the framework. Following this framework enables children to have a smooth transition both between providers and when they enter Key Stage 1. Children can access activities at an appropriate level for their development in both limited age and mixed aged groups frequently found in early years provision.

Positive relationships

Good relationships will encourage the development of concepts and careful support of children's learning based on children's desire to explore problems in the real-life contexts of their daily routines and play. They develop a growing awareness of mathematical dimensions in the world around them. Adults can help to foster positive attitudes to mathematical learning, creating an enthusiastic enquiry approach to investigations concerning mathematical knowledge and vocabulary through first-hand experiences. They can guide and support children's developing knowledge through questioning, sharing, consolidating and confirming their explorations. High expectations of children's abilities should be evident regardless of age, ability, gender or ethnicity. More able children should be sufficiently challenged to promote their learning.

Enabling environments

Mathematical understanding can be incorporated into the enabling environment to ensure that children have access to a range of learning styles and exciting opportunities to explore ideas and concepts. This can be achieved through adult-led and children's independent activities. They can form part of the daily routines of the setting. Awareness of aspects of the area can be explored both indoors and outdoors. The natural environment can be used to promote the understanding of mathematical vocabulary and concepts. Buildings, trees, flowers and so on can be used as a focus for enquiry.

Opportunities should be given for children to record their findings in their play. A range of surfaces, including coloured paper or card, flip charts, clip boards and whiteboards with various type of mark – making equipment should be readily available to enable children to practise their emergent marks as part of their play activities. Books incorporating mathematical concepts, both fiction and non-fiction, should be displayed as a source of reference for the children to use.

Case study

In Autumn a setting based work on leaves: sorting, counting, using non-standard measures and comparing differently shaped leaves to heighten awareness of key mathematical points. Harvest fruit was estimated and counted. Children used clip boards to record the shapes observed and the numbers counted.

Interactive displays focusing on the area of learning can enhance understanding, for example matching shapes, counting children on a bus or car ride or making patterns. Children can take responsibility for changing the achievements on display as their growing knowledge of certain aspects develops and progresses. Number lines can incorporate written and mathematical numbers, pictures to aid correspondence and 3D apparatus to provide kinaesthetic support.

Opportunities for children's independent, active and practical learning can be fostered throughout the setting in a cross-curricular manner. Activities based on making dens can incorporate designing and using shapes, counting pathways to the den, counting the number in the den and sorting equipment needed.

Numbers as labels for counting

Numbers are all around us and can be utilized in the recognition of numerical values, for example buttons on coats, numbers of children in groups, numbers who choose various fruits/snacks, prices of items or door numbers.

Gelman and Gallister (1978) identified principles of counting which included one-to-one correspondence, stable order principle, cardinal principle, abstraction principle and order-irrelevance principle. Children gradually begin to understand and recognize numerical values and incorporate them into their play. Work on the theme can produce a plethora of activities based on number and size, for example comparing the size of shoes; height charts; clothes lines of numbers; sock matching; counting toes and fingers; making patterned bracelets; necklaces; counting clothes and sorting clothes for different members of the family. It can incorporate discussions of night and day and the passing of time, linking with the *knowledge and understanding of the world* strand of the framework.

Case study

Activities based on the theme 'Growing Things' could include work around the story of 'Jack and the Beanstalk' with a comparison of articles from Jack and the giant, counting during activities such as caring for plants and visiting animals, or describing pets, as well as counting rhymes such as 'Five Little Ducks' or 'Five Speckled Frogs'. Number games can be incorporated into play, for example ladybird dominoes or counting pathways.

Calculating

Calculations can begin with objects and articles around the child to enable interest in the enquiry. These can be discussed to identify features of the objects, for example how many are there? What shape are they? How many are there altogether? Children can record their findings through the available materials in the setting. From these emergent beginnings numerals can be observed as a means of labelling items. Children can start to gain awareness of forms of recording. 'It is important to encourage children to see the connections between the ways in which they represent their own ideas and the ways in which other people choose to do so' (Worthington and Carruthers 2003:105).

Children will develop their own methods of calculating numbers of items and explore the possibilities of recording. Children gain understanding of the value of numbers and how they correspond to the amount, for example using number lines with a range of learning styles including through songs, stories, role play, objects, games, matching and sorting.

Counting will continue as children consolidate their understanding of the numerical system but it then develops into a visualization of separate sets of objects which can be added together and experiment with small numbers to use symbolic representation. Children begin to appreciate that numbers can be 'added together' or 'taken away'. Numbers can be compared, for example how many choose milk and how many choose fruit juice at break time?

Shape, space and measures

Shapes can be introduced through discussions of items, such as a favourite toy, to describe basic properties of the shape. Children can be encouraged to notice shapes in the environment including door handles, windows or bricks. Play equipment, for example balls, cylinders and large construction equipment can be used as an ongoing reminder of properties of shapes. 3D materials can be used as part of creative development to consolidate learning and provide a range of learning styles for children. Games, shape pictures and barrier games can be accessed as the children play. Appropriate mark-making tools should be provided to allow children to experiment with the resources. Construction equipment and a variety of materials can be organized to support children's independent learning in the environment of the setting. Activities can be devised to collaborate with parents or carers, for example making houses while identifying the shapes used. The model houses can then be used to design a model area of the town, village or street in the city to support children's awareness of where they live and the community around them. Positional language can be enhanced through everyday activities and structured ones, for example setting a table, organizing and playing with toys, or negotiating places for objects in a game.

According to Pound (2003:38), 'The measurement of length, mass, volume, capacity and even time is part of many day-to-day conversations'. Recipes are an enjoyable way to develop and consolidate knowledge and understanding in all areas of the framework. Children can devise their own recipes, for example making sandwiches, and follow made recipes. These can be written to enable young children to follow the instructions, such as washing hands. Ingredients could be measured using cups or spoons to enhance children's ability to access the recipes. A visit to the shops provides an understanding of exchanging money and how food is sorted. In a role-play area table cutlery can be organized by colour, sorting items and shapes to match. Three-dimensional shapes can be created from construction equipment or made by the children themselves to support learning. Resources and materials could be accessible for making articles such as a toy box for the setting, homes, dens, shops, garages and smaller items, for example a container for a gift.

Reflections

- Does the provision in your setting include a mathematically rich environment where children can explore mathematical books, record their findings, display their work and independently access a range of materials to sort, count, assemble and create?
- Are the facilities accessible to all children including those with English as an additional language?

Children are fascinated by symmetrical patterns, which can be introduced at an early age through practical activities such as painting symmetrical wings for a butterfly model. They enjoy making their own patterns, which can be displayed to support discussions and help children attempt different ones. Patterns can be displayed around the setting to reinforce the concept, such as the use of soles of boots printed to identify an alternate differently coloured pattern, or any relevant object to link with a medium-term theme, for example prints of circles when thinking about wheels. Awareness of space can be developed through discussions based on children's experiences, for example of the locality of areas within the setting.

Formative assessments should be maintained throughout the child's attendance at the setting in collaboration with colleagues and parents/carers. They follow the framework in the six broad areas of development culminating in the Early Learning Goals. Children will be summatively assessed at the end of the Reception year as part of the Early Years Foundation Stage Profile.

20 Knowledge and understanding of the world

Knowledge and understanding of the world is part of the Learning and Development area of the EYFS framework. It covers exploration and investigation, designing and making, ICT, time, place and communities. The EYFS framework states that

> Children must be supported in developing the knowledge, skills and understanding that help them to make sense of the world. Their learning must be supported through offering opportunities for them to use a range of tools safely; encounter creatures, people, plants and objects in their natural environments and in real-life situations; undertake practical 'experiments'; and work with a range of materials.

> (DfES 2007b)

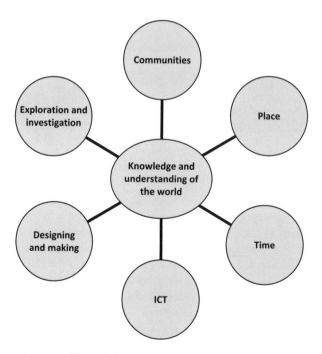

Aspects of knowledge and understanding of the World

Children bring their own diverse understandings and experiences to this aspect of the framework. This might be influenced by the opportunities to interact with strands of learning and the development of this learning at home, in the setting and in the wider community. Children could have practised skills of investigation and exploration as they develop awareness of their surroundings in their home; outdoors in such areas as parks, gardens, community spaces; in their journeys with parents and carers such as going shopping, visiting relatives and places of interest. Collaborative activities, for example signing cards, baking, tidying the home, extend children's understanding of the world in which they live.

Positive relationships

Positive relationships support children's explorations and questioning about their world. Building from a child's earliest experiences, the world can be explored through a range of learning experiences. Recent research on babies has demonstrated that newborn infants are capable of assimilating and responding to input around them. Behaviour is modelled and the senses are used to learn about their world. Babies distinguish those close to them through sound, smell or sight and develop their understanding. As children get older this can be developed through sensitive questioning and encouragement of their thinking skills, helping them to develop a conceptual awareness of their surroundings. Questions can develop in complexity from straightforward questions requiring a simple response to those requiring further thought. Such questions might begin, for example, 'How can we...?' 'Why does this...?' or 'What will happen if...?' Activities should be designed to promote children's thinking skills, incorporating communicating, social skills, problem solving, empathy, processing information, enquiry, prediction, decision making, discovery and investigations. These should be first-hand experiences to build on what children know and can do.

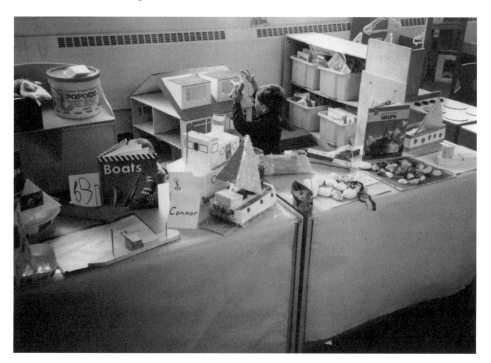

Enabling environments

Stimulating environments can promote a child's interest and motivation to explore. A range of learning styles could be used to develop children's enthusiasm for their surroundings. The environment should include a variety of everyday items, for example a bread board with writing engraved in it, baking ingredients, a wide selection of toys and the outdoors. These ongoing events and experiences can be used to the full as children delight in the newness of the events, such as falling leaves in Autumn.

Exploration and investigation

Exploration and investigation are skills that cover the whole of the curriculum but for the purposes of the Knowledge and Understanding of the World strand the strategies include development towards the Early Learning Goals concerned with objects and materials, the use of the senses, finding out about, identifying features and of living things, objects and events they observe, while noting similarities, differences and patterns and developing the ability to ask questions about why things happen and how things work. Children with sensory impairment should be given the facilities to explore and investigate their surroundings.

Objects and materials from the wider world can be used, such as wooden offcuts, plastic items and equipment used in the setting. The outdoor environment can provide a wealth of experiences for the children including those based on the weather and such themes as growing things, where minibeasts can be observed in their natural habitat. Children can design and create their own gardens and observe the changes taking place to the seeds and plants they are growing, or to frogs, caterpillars or butterflies as they progress through their life cycles. Children delight in being able to use the correct terminology for their findings. Incubators could be hired to hatch eggs, following safety procedures regarding hygiene. Visits to farms provide a range of learning experiences including following plans and maps, observing the growth and change of animals and how they are cared for and designing and making models of farm buildings. Links can be made to healthy eating, for example in the observation of food production as well as following recipes and baking. Activities concerning pets or plants can relate to strategies for promoting the understanding of caring for others. In all the activities in the early years stereotypes should be challenged.

Designing and making

This aspect includes planned activities and those to incorporate into the enabling environment for learning and teaching. Planned activities could be included throughout the curriculum, woven into themes to promote children's enquiry, problem solving, visualization and information processing skills, among others. Children can use design to support their planned ideas and develop their creativity, for example by designing a structure such as a bridge or den to support their role play or making a puppet to use as part of the play. Puppets are an excellent resource for the children to use, especially those that they have designed and made themselves. A range of materials could be used and the size and design should be chosen by the child, depending on the available resources and the requirements of the play. Finger puppets are an easy resource to make: they cost little but will allow children creativity in choosing their own design for the product. Mark-making materials should be readily available in each area of the setting to enable children to express their ideas as a design for further activities or as a record of possible imaginative thoughts. Appropriate materials should be easily accessible for children to explore, helping them to develop a knowledge and understanding of the properties of the available resources and how they can be used. Containers should be labelled with writing and pictures to help children locate and choose suitable materials, returning them later to maintain a stimulating and safe environment.

Case study

Activities based on 'Goldilocks and the Three Bears' included designing and making models of the home the bears lived in, remaking Baby Bear's chair, and organizing the areas where the bears lived. Children were able to use equipment and materials available in the setting to complete the tasks both independently and with adult support when needed. Weatherproof homes were designed and tested for strengths and weaknesses including waterproofing, strength and design of the walls and the ability to withstand wind power. Parents/carers were invited to make a model home with their child in their own homes. Materials for children's favourite toy bears were explored when they were brought to the setting as part of the 'Teddy Bears' Picnic'. Dens were made outdoors and indoors for the bears and food prepared such as oat and honey biscuits and sandwiches for the picnic. Children had access to a teddy program on the computer.

Information and communication technologies (ICT)

Children can be exposed to a range of ICT facilities and will respond to them readily. Music can be played, enjoyed and incorporated into routines for children to respond

to by dancing, singing, making musical instruments, learning rhymes and songs such as traditional nursery rhymes, and experimenting with sound. It can enhance areas in the enabling environment, for example providing a backing atmosphere for a role-play area, such as 'Sounds of the Sea' in a seaside theme.

There are many software packages available for young children to use. Children can be supported in their use of computers as they learn to incorporate IT successfully into their repertoire of skills. Cameras can be used to help children focus on their observations and awareness.

Time

Opportunities for children to develop an awareness of time can be taken as they happen and also incorporated into their planned activities. Routine examples might include pointing out the time at the beginning of the day, lunch time and when a parent or carer returns at the end of a session. This can promote understanding of vocabulary linked to time such as yesterday, today, tomorrow. Examples of time passing can be discussed through occurrences such as a new baby, or the death of a pet. Work on babies could include a visit by a parent to show a baby and aid discussion of a baby's development, such as what a baby eats and why, clothes, toileting and a baby's need for care and reassurance. Timelines of the child's development provide an enlightening focal source for discussion of key events that the child has experienced so far and can be happily reflected upon as occurrences in the past. Family members and friends can be included to further an awareness of age, for example through the consideration of visits to grandparents or older members of the community and questioning of older members of a settings team. Stories are a rich source of stimulus for discussion about time, with inclusion of those that are set in a different time or have characters who are in differing age phases. Cross-curricular links could be forged with *personal, social and emotional development* when reflecting on aspects such as caring for others, while being interlinked with other areas of the curriculum.

> **Case study**
>
> Activities based on 'Little Red Riding Hood' included pathways to the den, through woods made to the children's design, sewing leaves, making play dough fruit and wooden boxes. Children's own versions of the story were written and there were discussions about not talking to strangers. Older members of the community received harvest produce and consideration was given to caring for others. Discussions about taking produce to 'Grandma' incorporated a visit to the shops, shopping lists, recipes, routes to the shops and food from other countries.

Place

Learning and teaching associated with place explore children's own experiences and their own relationship to the spaces they occupy, developing into contexts in the setting and in the wider community. Activities including map making of routes to the setting, discussion of journeys to visit relatives or have a holiday and small-world play to consolidate notions of space can help to support children's concepts of place. These can be developed through planned activities and independent play in the environment. Stories can enhance the concept of space and incorporate routes taken by the characters involved, enabling children to make links between the various areas described in the story. Links can also be sought in the wider world with collaboration of settings in appropriate networks in different countries.

> **Case study**
>
> A role-play area based on the theme of travel changed the focus of the medium-term planning of the theme to incorporate children's large models of a boat, a bus and an aeroplane. Children brought photographs of journeys they had been on and designed maps of places they would like to visit. Cross-curricular links included making boats strong enough to carry a number of toys to explore floating and sinking, discussion of feelings and writing postcards and books about the journeys experienced. Partnerships with parents/carers can be strengthened with discussions of visits taken and people met.

Communities

Each setting has a unique association with the surrounding community and influence on it. Partnerships with the community can enhance the learning and teaching in the setting and add to the diversity of the provisions within it. Children can develop their

understanding of the diverse nature of their surroundings through such links, which can be fostered as part of the curriculum through visits undertaken, using appropriate risk assessments, or inviting visitors to the setting. For example, a lollipop lady might enhance awareness of road safety; a visit by firemen could demonstrate aspects of a theme based on 'People Who Help Us'. Partnerships could also be forged through events including open days or fayres.

Reflections

- Are discovery, investigative and exploration opportunities available for all the children in your setting, including those with sensory impairment?

This aspect of the Learning and Development framework should be formatively assessed on an ongoing basis as part of a cycle of observations, assessments and planning within the six broad areas of development in the *knowledge and understanding of the world* strand. These areas of development lead to the Early Learning Goals. Summative assessments will be made at the end of the Reception year in the Early Years Foundation Stage Profile.

21 Creative Development

This chapter explores creativity within the EYFS setting.

On completion of the chapter, practitioners should have an increased awareness of the challenges and developmental opportunities offered through this important area of learning.

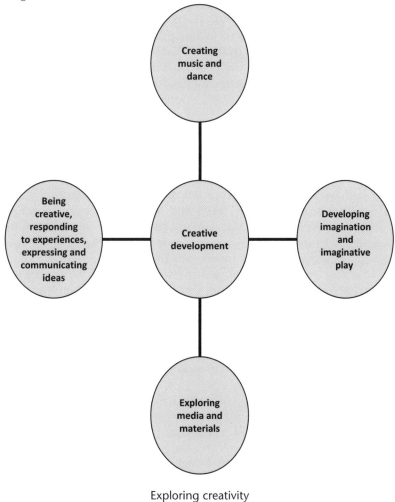

Exploring creativity

Being Creative – responding to experiences, expressing and communicating ideas

All Our Futures: Creativity, Culture and Education (NACCE 1999:29) offers a definition of creativity as: 'Imaginative activity fashioned so as to produce outcomes that are original and of value.'

This was an important milestone in the elevation of the status of creativity in the Early Years Curriculum. *Creative development* was outlined as an important area of learning for 3- to 5-year-olds in the original *Curriculum Guidance for the Foundation Stage* (QCA/DfEE 2000) and was highlighted as important in strengthening 'resilience and resourcefulness' (Craft 2005) in *Every Child Matters* (DfES 2003).

As a starting point for discussion, it suggests that a child is entitled to a blank canvas approach to problem solving and to communicating a response to stimuli based on prior knowledge and sensory exploration that is considered by those around the child to be of high value. Creativity could also be defined as 'Applied imagination that includes action and purpose as a process to investigate understanding' (Craft 2002). It is about children starting with an idea related to what they already know and moving their thinking forward into the possibilities of 'what could be'. Craft argues that creativity is about 'possibility thinking'. Therefore all children are capable of being creative in order to share intellectual and emotional responses. What is important is the idea of process rather than product.

From birth children naturally use all five senses to explore their surroundings and make sense of the world. It is therefore essential to make use of this natural curiosity, providing a variety of opportunities first to experience and then to express and communicate a response in order to develop children's important decision-making ability and problem-solving skills. Bruce (2004a) emphasizes the important role of adults in engaging sensitively with babies and toddlers, 'emergent possibilities for creativity that are in every child'. She cautions that 'without sensitivity, without listening to children's ideas and taking them seriously, creativity does not develop or can be quickly extinguished'. This means that the most important resource in any setting is you! First you need to provide the stimulus and then to enthuse about what may appear to be a limited response, deferring judgement about the outcome or product.

Research shows that core features of good practice include:

- encouraging children to ask questions and to seek answers;
- offering imaginative play experiences that encounter and solve problems;
- offering a caring environment in which independent learning and risk taking is encouraged and supported and where the curriculum is flexible enough to allow the children to dwell on engrossing tasks.

Craft (2002) distinguishes between 'high' and 'low' creativity. High creativity bears a similarity to Vygotsky's 'social constructs', Harlen's disequilibrium theory and

Rummelhart and Norman's (1978) 'accretion', altering the previous perception through engaging with the learning opportunity and testing out the new understanding in new situations.

The practitioner has both the indoor and outdoor environments from which to draw a variety of experiences. The natural world provides changing seasons and colours, plants and creatures and the man-made world provides the media through which thoughts and ideas can be expressed. For example, collecting conkers in a bucket provides opportunities for filling and emptying, for exploring rough and smooth and for scrunching through a dry carpet of leaves which might be described as absorbing knowledge and understanding of the world. The creativity begins when the children remove the collected treasure from the bucket and roll the conkers through their fingers or down their legs, rattle the conkers, listening for a sound, roll it over their lips and marvel at its design.

The enthusiasm for a conker comes from you, diligently fixed on an important task, pronouncing in the whispery voice that expresses amazement at finding treasure, in the way that the precious item is held, in carefully placing the conker in the bucket. From this modelling, children are inspired to look carefully and focus on what they see through the practitioner's eyes.

Some children like to order their collection in size, others to make a pattern, with several conkers of various sizes. It is important that children are aware that their personal response is valuable and valued.

Practitioners need to think through the activities that are offered to children to identify the learning possibilities so that the learning potential is planned for and exploited where possible. Setting learning challenges allows children to think through a problem and solve it in their own way. This process takes time. It is important to plan for sufficient time to enable a child to gain maximum learning from challenges set.

Exploring Media and Materials

Practitioners need to prepare the work space to allow children to work independently, with opportunities to explore and play with colour, texture, shape, space and form in two and three dimensions and using ICT. It is important for practitioners to understand that a house can be rainbow coloured and does not have to have a door in the middle and a window at each corner.

In order for this discovery learning to be successful, to allow children to take risks and make connections, there needs to be a high level of organization. Paint brushes need to be stored with the brush end upwards in a tin or plastic pot; round ended, left-handed and right-handed scissors need to be kept in a block so that missing pairs are quickly retrieved. Paste needs to be free from fungicides and PVA glue needs to be kept in small containers with lids to prevent it from drying out.

A creative development area is usually a messy area. Never store tins of powder paint under the sink. When a pipe leaks or bursts, the cascade of water through the powder paint creates a disaster! Most practitioners and parents soon become aware of the magenta and black paints that are very hard to remove from clothing and quickly learn that both adults and children need to dress in washable clothing to work in the messy area.

Most EYFS settings have a messy area close to a sink at child height that has a wipe-clean floor rather than a carpeted floor. From eighteen months to two years, the average height of work tops is 40cm compared with 50 or 55cm for children in a later foundation stage class. A large table with a wipe-clean surface is useful for most activities. Children do not need to sit at the table. Most settings also have brightly covered wipe-clean table coverings. Near to the working space, aprons or old shirts need to be readily available as cover-ups and children need to be trained to roll up their sleeves when working in the messy area.

In a group setting, it is sensible to consider the size of the area available and therefore the number of children who will be able to make use of the space at any time. Some settings provide team bands for this. If a team band is available, a child can choose to work in the messy area. If none are available, the child needs to wait for a turn.

When paint is involved, there needs to be either a storage dryer for wet paintings or a washing line with pegs to peg out the paintings while they dry. This area of a setting can quickly become very untidy unless systems are in place to keep equipment organized. To encourage the children to manage the space for themselves, decide where every item should be kept and draw round and visually label the outline of each container so that children return items to their correct place. This has two strengths. First, the working area stays tidy without daily organization by adults and secondly, children can manage tools and equipment independently.

The practitioner needs to be aware of the wealth of possibilities from which to choose to be creative.

Planning should ensure that a variety of options are offered at different times during the week. There should be enough flexibility to allow children to continue an activity they have enjoyed.

Case study

The practitioner sets up shoe boxes lined with art paper and children add small amounts of paint. A marble is rolled round within the shoe box to make a picture. The children have all had one opportunity to try this idea. Some would like to try again. The practitioner extends the activity to allow for this.

The practitioner initiates and models an activity that a group of children try out under supervision. Having tried the activity unaided, the children subsequently revisit the activity independently without the need for close supervision.

Reflections

- Does your planning respond to the interest level of the children?
- Do you keep assessment notes of what they have enjoyed so that you can use the idea again in another context?
- Is the equipment organized to promote and enable independent learning?

Children respond to starting point stimuli and work well when an adult works next to them, involved in his or her own creativity. This allows the child to talk to the adult about the shared experience rather than the adult hovering over the child with the temptation to 'help' the child to achieve an outcome rather than to experience the process of a learning opportunity. Choosing crayons, paints or other media can be part of the process of creativity. Working with real painters, illustrators, poets and musicians from the wider community is very powerful in generating enthusiasm for the task. Children need to have their on-task activity acknowledged and receive praise for work that they feel is significant. For most children, creativity is set up as an experiential opportunity rather than to achieve an outcome.

In order to create a culture where it is safe to try new ideas, the practitioner must move away from a notion of correctness. Young children may not choose to paint a red ladybird or a brown cow, instead opting for a purple ladybird with brown eyes or a blue cow. Crace (2003) comments that these are the first steps to representational drawings and that many adults, both parents and practitioners, hurry the child through these important steps towards a notion of correctness in shape and colour. Templates also limit the children's creativity.

Many adults describe themselves as 'no good' at painting because someone has commented negatively on their artistry at a formative age. Notice that some children do not value the product of their painting and may even paint over a picture.

Reflections

- Am I happy to paint or draw in front of other adults? Why?
- Is there a point at which I stop painting because I am satisfied that the work is complete?
- How do I know?

In the early stages, children develop from daubs on paper to representations of ideas that communicate meaning. Some marks will be culturally specific. It is important to consider the child's unique life-world experience when offering suggestions of what to paint from memory.

The art curriculum suggests that the child is encouraged to make marks with anything and everything. A few examples are chocolate, coffee, fruits, soil, feathers, marbles, sponges, leaves, brushes of differing thicknesses and cotton wool buds, but there are many others.

Creating Music and Dance

Practitioners should learn from watching children develop from diverse cultural backgrounds.

> ### Case study
>
> Desmond was from Trinidad. From a very young age he was encouraged to beat out rhythms with a variety of tools. At the lunch table he would drum with his spoon on the table; in the home corner he enjoyed the sound of a wooden spoon on a metal saucepan. Because of the time spent on task, he excelled at drumming. This was culturally important to his parents who wanted him to aspire to play in a steel band like his grandfather. His sense of a regular beat was far in advance of his pre-school friends and even at such an early age he was able to use a beater in both hands at once.

The practitioner is challenged to consider whether to encourage Desmond's creative talent or to insist he conforms to pre-conceived notions of correctness. In consultation with his parents, his talent and needs are discussed by the whole team.

Children can be encouraged to feel the beat of music by dancing, moving and swaying and by making marks on paper in time to the music and in response to either crescendos in the music or changes of pitch. Dancing on paper with feet covered in paint similarly helps the child to associate the movement with the music. However, forward planning ensures that this is done outside with bowls of warm water ready to wash feet at the end of the activity.

- Offer touchy/feely experiences to children with visual impairments.
- Encourage children with communication differences to respond to, for example, music with gestures.

Developing Imagination and Imaginative Play

Practitioners need to retain their fairy godmother within their soul, so that the children's ideas gain a 'Yes, let's' response. Children happily work with representational objects and resources, quickly slipping into complex stories and dramas in which anything can happen and probably does.

Creativity does not need to be limited to independent work.

Case study

A foundation stage class collectively decided that the role-play corner needed to become a castle. They needed to recreate the rough texture of the castle walls that they had touched in an outing on the previous day. They suggested adding oats to the exterior paint to create an uneven texture. This was mixed and tested and was considered to be too beige. They suggested adding chocolate to make the paint browner. The children were really pleased with their 'paint', because the castle smelled of chocolate and was rough.

Notice that the ideas were from the children, who were encouraged to take risks to try out their ideas. They were in charge of the creative element of making the castle; the adult simply enabled them by gathering the necessary resources.

22 Physical development

This chapter covers the links between *physical development* and other aspects of learning. It suggests appropriate activities and flexible resources for a range of ages and environments. It highlights the need for thoughtful planning and provision for progression in the development of fine and gross motor skills, balance and coordination.

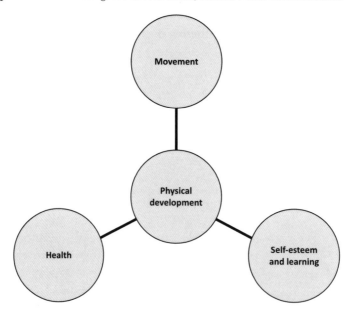

The impact of physical development

The Early Years Foundation Stage (EYFS) (DfES 2007a) outlines expectations for physical development experiences, skills and understanding within the birth to 5 age range. The key aspects include what could be traditionally thought of as physical education or exercise under *movement and space*, fine movement development needed for *using equipment and materials*, and education for healthy lifestyles under *health and bodily awareness*. This chapter will mostly focus on the first two aspects as health and bodily awareness has already been considered in Chapter 4. The EYFS document emphasizes the links between confidence, self-esteem and physical health and movement. It also points out the importance of physical development in all aspects of learning within the EYFS.

Children are naturally physical beings even before birth and, once born, babies can be observed testing out their bodies through spontaneous kicking, arm waving and movements of toes and fingers (Davies 2003; Doherty and Bailey 2003; Lindon 2005; Doherty and Brennan 2008). It would be easy to assume that because of this children will develop all the physical skills they need naturally, with little input from the adults around them. Charts of expected chronological development may also suggest that children between certain ages will automatically move on to the next level of coordination and movement. While there are clearly some general patterns in the way that babies and children develop physically, the impact of their environment, genetic inheritance, personality and experience all influence the way in which physical proficiency is acquired (Davies 2003; Doherty and Bailey 2003; Doherty and Brennan 2008). Therefore, the responsibility of the early years educator to provide appropriate support and learning opportunities, whether working with small babies or 5-year-olds, is a crucial factor. The EYFS sets out some broad suggestions for resources and expectations within possible age ranges. The intention is to highlight experiences that practitioners can provide and skills they can identify and promote. This chapter aims to discuss some aspects of this in more detail.

Promoting movement

Between 0 and 2 years of age stability, locomotion and manipulation are the key features that need to be developed (Doherty and Bailey 2003). These will continue to be essential elements that are refined throughout primary school but at this early stage they include those expectations sometimes described as developmental milestones, such as rolling over, sitting unaided, standing, walking and self-feeding. These developments can be encouraged by the intervention and provision available for babies in EYFS settings. It is important in busy day care settings or in a childminder's home, with the possible demands of a mixed age group, that babies get sufficient opportunities to kick freely without a nappy, to be placed on their front with toys to reach out for and to be given an increasing range of objects to grip and manipulate. Even moving the position of furniture when a child has become familiar with walking around the room by holding onto it can present a new physical challenge (Davies 2003; Doherty and Bailey 2003). Providing for babies to have physical opportunities will enable them to make cognitive connections as well as building bone density and strength for later life (Lindon 2005). Later, other challenges for EYFS providers in small-scale or home-based settings might be finding sufficient space away from immobile babies for children to use sit-on and ride or push-along toys or experiment with equipment for throwing and catching. As seen in Chapter 11, inside space and community areas can be used inventively for this purpose.

Lack of movement development or motor skills and body awareness can affect children's self-esteem as they experience failure and social difficulties when unable to join in with the physical play of their peers (Piotrowski 2000; Davies 2003; Doherty and Bailey 2003; Macintyre and McVitty 2004; Doherty and Brennan 2008), while increased physical activity and challenge can improve mood and raise self-esteem, as well as enabling children to maintain a healthy weight (Biddle 2000; Fox 2000; Doherty and Brennan 2008). There are also connections between underdeveloped motor skills and difficulties in other areas such as speech and language, toileting, and early reading and writing skills (Macintyre and McVitty 2004; Lindon 2005). Practitioners can address some of these areas of difficulty by including play activities and games that encourage children to: cross the **midline** of their body, for example by touching opposite hands to opposite knees; crawl, in order to use cross-body coordination and strengthen shoulders; strengthen their hands and fingers by pressing bubble wrap, manipulating clay or pegging out the washing; develop **oro-motor skills** by blowing bubbles, or playing blow football with a straw and ping pong ball and encouraging children to make shapes with their mouth and tongue while looking in the mirror (Blythe 2000; Macintyre and McVitty 2004). They should aim to help children to develop body awareness (**proprioception**) to aid balance and coordination, perhaps playing games where the children close their eyes or use feely bags so they cannot rely on visual information and have to use touch instead, or asking children to make different shapes and balances with their bodies (Macintyre and McVitty 2004; Doherty and Brennan 2008). Babies can develop some of this bodily awareness when they are able to explore everyday objects of different shape, size and texture from a 'treasure basket', or a selection of resources placed within their reach (Goldschmied and Jackson 1994; Lindon 2005).

Traditionally, physical education has been seen as part of the school curriculum based around gymnastics, dance and games. In childcare, pre-school and nursery environments structured lessons targeting these areas of movement are uncommon. The EYFS does not suggest that we should impose the structure of a school-based curriculum on the birth to 5 age range but find ways to stimulate and support this range of learning in appropriate ways for the children in our care. Doherty and Bailey (2003) and Davies (2003) suggest that children from birth to 5 can, and often naturally choose to, engage in experiences that are the early steps towards these different types of movement. For example, grasping and releasing an object from a high chair is the starting point for the skills of throwing used in ball games, while bouncing along to music while seated or holding onto furniture may be the early response starting point for dancing. What early educators must do is combine a range of approaches to ensure that children's physical impulses are encouraged and extended by:

- observing individuals and planning for next steps;
- identifying and capitalizing on spontaneous opportunities;
- planning for guided physical learning opportunities with adults;
- planning for resources and stimuli that may be used in child-initiated play.

Practitioners should consider how the full range of movement is being promoted in these ways to include whole-body and limb movement (gross motor) as well as manipulation using fingers and hands (fine motor).

All types of movements develop along a continuum of refinement including changes in pressure, speed, shape and awareness of space, such as: strong stamping to light tiptoeing, slow crawling to fast running, rolling freely with arms flailing to remaining contained in a small area (Davies 2003; Doherty and Bailey 2003; Doherty and Brennan 2008). Babies learn the difference between light and strong pressure, fast and slow movement and concepts such as up and down, through their experience of being handled by adults as they are swooped through the air or jogged on someone's knee (Davies 2003). This close physical contact is vital between practitioners and babies, accompanied by eye contact, facial expression and the noises of play. The baby learns about interaction, communication and movement simultaneously. Older children can learn to distinguish between finer elements of movement during play, through adult intervention, modelling and verbalizing.

Case study

When using plastic cutters with the play dough to make animal shapes Iona (3) was frustrated as the play dough remained stuck to the outer edges of the cutter.

Adult: Shall I help you?
Iona gives the cutter to the adult.
Adult: Let's do it together. Put your hand on the cutter. Puuush down and tuuurn.

Putting her hand gently over Iona's hand the practitioner pressed down and turned the cutter from left to right. She repeated this action and then said 'Now you try.' As Iona tried again the adult used the same word, emphasis and rhythm. 'That's it, puuush down . . . and tuuurn.'

In this example Iona is able to feel the correct amount of pressure and the sliding sideways movement used to free the cutter from the dough. This is reinforced both by what the adult says and the way it is said.

Environment and further adult support

EYFS providers are not expected to have extensive and expensive equipment to promote physical development. Children will often make inventive use of what is available. However, in order to progress physically children need a number of different opportunities to consolidate and generalize skills (Davies 2003; Doherty and Bailey 2003). This may be achieved by changes in the equipment the children use, where they use it, or who they use it with. So, the new skill of bouncing a ball may be extended and developed by moving from using a large rubber ball to a small rubber ball to a plastic airflow ball, from bouncing on an even flat surface to a textured one, from controlling the ball with two hands to one handed, from bouncing by oneself to bouncing to a partner or from using hands to using a bat to bounce the ball. From the time that they are mobile, children need at different points: space to run; something to climb on and through; opportunities for balancing and rolling on a comfortable surface using different body parts; wheeled toys for pushing and pedalling; and the chance to respond to music in

Figure 22.1 Using reclaimed materials, balance and coordination for 'ski-ing'!

a safe open space. This range of play allows children to strengthen core muscle groups and improves balance and coordination (see Figure 22.1). They need a variety of different apparatus to manipulate such as bats, balls, hoops, scarves, bean bags, as well as construction, threading, mark making, scissors and puzzles to develop fine motor coordination. Adults can ensure that children engage with these resources in a high-quality way by showing encouragement and interest in the children's achievement. They can also help children to develop specific skills through guiding tasks and questioning.

Good outdoor provision can enable much physical practice and exploration to take place but physical development also needs to be planned for inside and outside in a way that develops progression over a series of experiences. Practitioners can use a range of approaches in order to achieve this, following a sequence moving through exploration, discovery, combination, selection and refinement (Gallahue 1982; Davies 2003; Doherty and Bailey 2003; Pickup and Price 2007). A possible way of interpreting the range needed between adult prescription and child-led discovery that enables children gradually to develop more complex skills and understanding is through the suggestions below:

- **Suggest a specific action for children to try out**
  Can you move like a butterfly?
  How many different ways can you dig in the sand?
- **Ask them to find out how a particular part of the body moves during this action**
  What are your arms doing? And your feet? And your hands?
  What shape did your back make when you were digging?
- **Set a task which involves combining the new action with another skill**
  Can you move like a butterfly flying up and down?
  Can you dig down and then lift up the sand and put it into my bucket?
- **Children choose which action would be most useful for a particular purpose (e.g. as part of a game)**
  What can you do with your body to show that you are landing on a flower?
  What can we do to make a big hill out of the sand?

Such a sequence of learning could take place on one occasion or be applied to individual or group learning on a number of occasions. It enables practitioners to see physical development over a longer period and not just as a one-off event. In order to intervene and assess appropriately practitioners will need to observe and record but also be aware of the possible areas of refining skills: time, weight, space, flow, relationships, body actions and body shapes (Davies 2003; Pickup and Price 2007) mentioned earlier. They will also need to teach skills explicitly and give age-appropriate feedback.

Safety and risk

Obviously, when engaging children in physical activity, safety is very important. Providers will need to have clear rules and procedures for managing accidents, checking outside areas and indoor and outdoor equipment for potential hazards and risk assessment where appropriate. However, it is equally important that adult fear of accidents does not prevent children from experiencing some physical activities that have low-level risk such as jumping down from the low rungs of a climbing frame, cutting fruit for snack time, or joining materials with a stapler, or even hammer and nails (Edgington 2004; May *et al.* 2006). The appropriateness of these activities will depend on children's understanding of how to use equipment safely and this will depend on the preparation time taken by the practitioners. Rather than discounting an activity as unsafe it would be better to ask how we can minimize the risks or enable children to cope with the risks involved. Children with disabilities or sensory impairments may also be over-protected by well-intentioned adults. Extra consideration must be given to ensure that they are able to access a wide range of physical development activities, which may only require small adaptations to use of space, resources or additional adult support. Equality of opportunity is not expecting all children to be able to do the same thing but ensuring that they have appropriate experiences and choices that are right for them.

Case study

Maisy wanted to join in with sports day. She was much smaller than the other children and had difficulty with balance because her legs were not aligned. The practitioner planned for adapted races to take place for the class, including a slow obstacle course and dressing-up race. These all enabled Maisy to join in, with adult support. Maisy loved the day and her mother was so happy to see Maisy able to take part that she wrote an emotional letter of thanks to the practitioner.

Joined-up learning

Although this chapter has considered provision for some specific aspects of movement and coordination it is important to remember that children do not develop physical skills in isolation. Each learning experience is likely to have a physical element and the physical aspect is often helping the child to develop a particular understanding or schema. In a short observation of outside play in a local EYFS setting the following links were being made.

Case study

Ben rolled a hoop down a slope and through the lower levels of the climbing frame. He retrieved the hoop and returned to the same spot on the slope, then rolled the hoop between the climbing frame and the garage. He continued with this action until the play seemed to develop into rolling the hoop further and further each time.

A group of children experimented with cardboard boxes. Several different children climbed into a box and pulled the lid shut. One intentionally tipped the box over on its side by shifting their weight from side to side while in the box. Another rolled herself up in a long piece of cardboard, unrolled herself and rolled up again. Lastly, one child balanced a cardboard box on his back and bottom and crept along the ground being a 'snail'.

Kirsty played alone with a doll in a pram, pushing it around the garden. She pushed it into the house and then out through the second door. She pushed it around the climbing frame and in between various activities. She pushed it through the play tunnel, bending over so that she could fit herself and the pram through together.

One group were playing in a cardboard box 'boat' but one side of the boat kept flapping down. The practitioner suggested using some string to hold it together and several of the group worked on tying up the outside of the 'boat' and attaching it to a post for security.

The rich nature of this exploratory learning about space, body shape and movement, manipulating materials, controlling apparatus and judging speed, size and distance can all be seen in this natural play. However, this development was not left to chance. The EYFS provider had ensured that there was an interesting range of safe resources – although many were simple and inexpensive. The environment offered ample space even for a large group of children to move safely. She allowed children sufficient time to extend their physical development in a number of ways. She extended physical learning by offering new materials to work with and letting the children try a tricky task for themselves. She intervened when children needed help and observed in order to plan for future experiences inside and out. She even engaged a group of children in a spontaneous discussion about the changes in their heartbeat and breathing as they came to see her after a strenuous game. Knowing what children need to learn next and planning and intervening to make sure that this happens are the skills that the EYFS practitioner needs in all areas of learning. It is important then that this is given equal priority in the area of physical development.

Reflections

- What are our aims for physical development?
- Have we focused on its contribution to health?
- What else do we want children to gain from it?
- How do we make sure that children of all ages are developing stability, locomotion and manipulation?
- What can we do to encourage children to refine these skills in their activities?
- How do we support progression in these areas?
- How are children with movement or sensory needs included and challenged?

Conclusions

Holistic Learning

The Early Years Foundation Stage provides a basis for children's earliest experiences and a framework for their learning and development. Practitioners can support a holistic approach to the child and have a vital role in listening, responding to and supporting the children in their care, to enable them to enjoy their childhood to the utmost and use their experiences to meet future challenges confidently and creatively.

International perspectives

The effects of internationalization and events in the world such as the 'credit crunch' have implications for everyone that have become increasingly apparent. How could international considerations affect early years provision?

   Historically, international systems have been influenced by trade, negotiations between countries and the sharing of ideas. The speed of these networks has intensified through faster transport links and internet access; many organizations and companies now work on a global scale. International factors could have an impact on early years issues.

   According to Woodhead (Lauder *et al.* 2008:7), 'Early education is now part of the process of globalization'. Thus it is possible that 'Current crises . . . are related to profound changes in a now globalized modernity in which the child was previously located' (Stephens 1995:8). These political considerations could affect early years provision through international collaboration and debate, yet internationalization can be both economic and cultural, affecting many areas including trade, resources, employment, population growth, transport and technology. There are also growing concerns about climate change on a global scale, which affect whole populations, cross national boundaries and are reflected in early years provision.

Economic

Growing world trade and cheaper transport, with improved communication through the internet and mobile phones, interlink international networks. Competition for jobs requires people to respond to employment needs, possibly having to relocate to an area where conditions are more favourable. Parental need and desire to obtain employment could result in increased pressure for early years provision. The cost of this provision could be a concern, particularly in an increasingly challenging economic climate. Resources, sustainability, climate change and food production add to pressures to sustain a 'shrinking world'. In this dynamic framework traditional industries are changing, spawning new skills for a workforce involved in a knowledge or creative economy.

Cultural

The interdependent nature of the global networks fosters a sharing of ideas. The growth of pre-school provision, while providing valuable provision for children, also supports parents who are working and require good quality care for their children. Diversity can be celebrated as children become 'world citizens'.

Political

Some issues now have global importance and are discussed at an international level. The 'credit crisis' has accentuated the notion of uncertainty and questioning of existing structures to meet the needs of the future. These generalizations have a specific basis in international legislation. The international concerns which could affect early years provision can also be put in the context of legislation that influences policies.

The United Nations Convention on the Rights of the Child in 1989 stated 'Individuals, including children, and communities have actively voiced their views and called for change' and is described in the *Every Child Matters: Change for Children* website. Children's voices can be heard, listened to, valued and respected.

> **Article 2** Guiding principles: The Convention applies to all children . . . No child should be treated unfairly on any basis.
> **Article 4** Survival and development: Governments have a responsibility to take all available measures to make sure children's rights are respected, protected and fulfilled. This involves assessing their social services, legal, health and educational systems. In some instances this may involve changing existing laws or creating new ones.
> **Article 29** Goals for education: Children's education should develop each child's personality, talents and abilities to the fullest.

The European Commission Quality Targets in Services for Young Children 1996–2006 contained 40 targets which included the following:

> **Target 1** Governments should provide a published and coherent statement of intent for care and education services to young children aged birth to 6 years and explain how such initiatives will be coordinated between services.
> **Target 14** All services should positively assert the value of diversity.
> **Target 18** The educational philosophy should be broad.

The Organization for Economic Cooperation and Development (OECD) in 2006 gave guidelines for practice incorporating the targets identified in the European Commission report. The policy areas proposed for consideration by governments included consideration of children's 'social context' for development, family and community involvement and systems that support 'broad learning, participation and democracy' (OECD 2006:4).

A *World Education For All Monitoring Report* (2009) by the United Nations Educational, Scientific and Cultural Organization (UNESCO) highlighted policy recommendations for Early Childhood Education and Care:

- Prioritize early childhood education and care in planning for all children.
- Strengthen the links between education planning and health provision.

Looking to the future

Ideas regarding quality in early years provision have changed with experience, research and the sharing of notions of what constitutes good quality. Professional practice will need to assess the best way to implement the Early Years Foundation Stage framework in order to meet the needs of all children.

Practitioners can respond to the requirements of the early years provision by providing opportunities for the children in their care to be creative and flexible in their learning and development, in order to help them gain the confidence they need to enjoy their childhood and positively meet the challenges of the future.

Appendices

Appendix A List of records required

The following records are mandatory:

- The certificate of registration must be either displayed or shown to parents and carers on request.
- The name, home address and telephone number of the provider and anyone else living on the premises.
- The name, home address and telephone number of anyone else in regular unsupervised contact with the children attending the setting.
- A daily record of the names of children looked after on the premises, their hours of attendance and their named key worker.
- A record of all risk assessments clearly stating when these were carried out, by whom, the date of review and any action taken following a review or incident.

All settings must keep proper records of the children in their care. These records include:

- Full name
- Date of birth
- The name, address and contact details of all parents and carers known to the setting including other settings attended by the child, highlighting the home setting and emergency contact details. It is advisable to find out whether there are any legal injunctions preventing any family members from having access to the child.

All settings will be required to submit the following information to their local authority as part of the Early Years Census:

- Names, dates of birth
- Home addresses
- Gender
- Ethnicity (where the parent has pre-identified the ethnicity of the child)
- Special educational needs status, the number of funded hours taken up during the census week, and the total number of hours taken up at the setting, both funded and unfunded.

Appendix B Sharing activities between home and setting

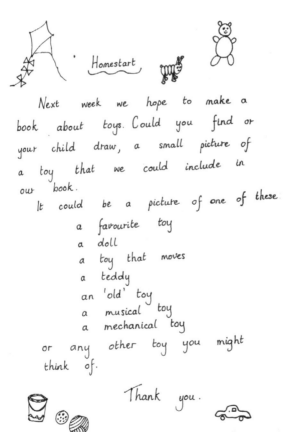

Homestart

Next week we hope to make a book about toys. Could you find or your child draw, a small picture of a toy that we could include in our book.

It could be a picture of one of these

    a favourite toy
    a doll
    a toy that moves
    a teddy
    an 'old' toy
    a musical toy
    a mechanical toy

or any other toy you might think of.

Thank you.

Appendix C   Sharing information about a child

Child's name _____

Date of birth _____

Address _____

_____

Telephone _____ Contact 'phone no. _____

Parent/Guardian's name _____

Position in family (e.g. first child, second, etc) _____

Birth certificate seen – YES/NO

Name & address of Doctor _____

_____

Health visitor (if known) _____

Immunisation _____

1. Does your child have eyesight problems?   YES/NO
2. Does your child have speech problems?   YES/NO
3. Has s/he ever attended a speech therapist?   YES/NO
4. Has your child ever had hearing problems?   YES/NO
5. Has your child ever had any of the listed conditions?   YES/NO
6. Is your child having any special treatment or medicine
   from your doctor?   YES/NO

Appendix D Medium-term planning grid for the EYFS

Theme: _____

	Week 1	Week 2	Week 3	Week 4	Week 5
Personal, Social and Emotional Development					
Communication, Language and Literacy					
Problem Solving, Reasoning and Numeracy					
Knowledge and Understanding of the World					
Physical Development					
Creative Development					

Appendix E   Planning grid

Plan the specific activities for each week

	Monday	Tuesday	Wednesday	Thursday	Friday
Graphics area					
Mathematics					
Role-play area					
Science investigations					
Craft					
Malleable					
Art					
Large construction					
Small-world					

	Monday	Tuesday	Wednesday	Thursday	Friday
Outdoors					
Sand					
Water					
Songs/ rhymes					

Appendix F   Observation format

Name **Age**	
Date	**Time**
Links with EYFS areas of learning and development	
Observer	

Appendix G   Observation format

Name		
Age		
Date	**Time**	
Personal, Social and Emotional Development	Communication, Language and Literacy	Problem Solving, Reasoning and Numeracy
Knowledge and Understanding of the World	Physical Development	Creative Development
Observer		

Appendix H   Observation format

Focus   Area of the enabling environment – The role-play area
Date   Time
Observer

Appendix I   Risk assessment checklist

Include risk assessment of the following:

- Boundaries and gates – check security and repair fences. Lock gates and secure perimeters.
- Water hazards – ponds, drains, pools, baths, sinks.
- Hazardous substances – medicines, cleaning products.
- Hazardous equipment.
- Hazardous plants – laburnum, deadly nightshade, toadstools, thorns, berries.
- Pets and excrement including covering sandpits.
- Electricity and gas – socket covers.
- Doors and widows – safety glass and intrusion-free perimeters.
- Floors and stairs – wet floors, trip hazard.
- Stacked furniture.
- Kitchen hazards including heat, steam and sharp equipment.
- Hygiene – cleanliness and minimizing infection.
- Outings and trips.
- Fire safety – guards, matches.
- The condition of toys and equipment.
- Monitoring sleeping children.

Appendix J   Information booklet from an early years setting – for sharing with children, parents, carers and colleagues

Welcome to our Early Years setting!

[The first page could contain a list of the practitioners with photographs to help parents/carers to identify them.]

The staff would like to extend a warm welcome to you and your child as you begin your time in our setting. Starting early years is an exciting new step and we hope you will enjoy your time with us.

Working together

Provided children are given a stimulating and caring environment they learn more, and at a faster rate than perhaps at any other time. With parents and staff working together we hope to provide the best possible quality of life for our children and continue a sound foundation for the future.

Starting in the early years

We have a staggered entry of not more than three new children per session. This means that the staff have time to devote to your child when he/she first starts.

Organization of the day

Our routine of the day is carefully organized to provide a secure environment for the children and develop their confidence and independence.

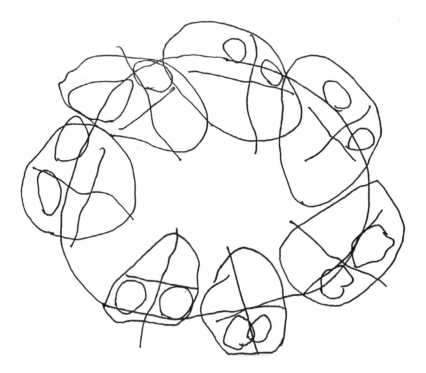

Timings of our day: 9 am–11.30 am   12.30 pm–3 pm

A possible routine could be:

> Meeting and greeting children and parents/carers. Registration
> Activities – independent learning indoors and outdoors
> Recall/tidy time
> Songs
> Outdoors
> Snack time/practise skills
> Story

These activities will reflect the ethos of the setting; for example, snacks could be available on an ongoing basis along with provision for an indoor and outdoor learning environment.

The first part of the session is taken up with greeting the children and talking to parents/carers. Please do not hesitate to discuss with the staff anything which is worrying your child or you. Children will be allocated to a small group with an adult who will ensure that your child is happy and suitably occupied. The children can choose what they would like to play with from a selection of activities for part of the session. The whole area of the setting may be used during the session. There is a break for fruit and drinks in the middle of the session. Please would you let the staff know when you fill in the entry form whether your child is allergic to any foods. We also have groups during the week who experience baking a range of food, such as pizza, buns, biscuits, vegetable soup etc.

The children share songs, poems and rhymes. They also work in their pastoral groups for skills activities, for example language games or discussing observations.

Our activities

Each term there is a general topic around which our activities centre. This is divided into weekly themes. Our planning sheet is available for you to see on the parents' noticeboard. Looking at this will help you to talk to your child about the things that are taking place in the setting. Individual records are kept, which are updated each term. These begin with a home/setting record discussed with parents on the child's entry to the setting. Programmes are formulated for children's special needs.

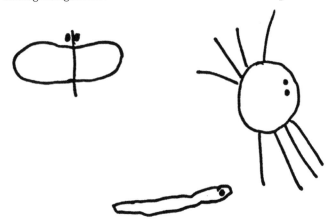

The setting

The setting has three main areas.

The painting area contains a craft table, sand tray, water trough, chalk boards, a painting table and easels, a small-world area and a large construction area.

The quiet area contains a reading corner, a graphics table, a mathematics area, a jigsaw table, science investigations, a shop and a role-play area. Computers, walkmans for stories and songs etc. and calculators are housed in this area. The outdoor area is used as part of the learning environment. Bikes, scooters, slides and large construction equipment are stored here. Full use is made of the covered area and sloping grassed area for imaginative and creative activities. A planting area is used to grow flowers and plants for the setting environment and to observe vegetables growing.

We believe it is important that the children learn to care for each other and their environment so we encourage them to tidy away their own activities and behave politely to each other and to staff. The setting aims to promote good behaviour with a 'positive behaviour' approach.

Can you help?

Parents/carers could be invited to help in the setting. Care should be taken to ensure the child could cope with sharing the parent with other children. Requests for further items to broaden resources could be given when attempting certain activities such as collecting shiny articles. Parents/carers would need to satisfy appropriate safety checks for security and children's welfare while working in the settings. However, working together in this way strengthens the trust and respect developed during the delivery of the activities.

Home time

It is useful to explain procedures at the end of a session so that confusion does not occur. It is important to know the faces of those collecting their child and information given if it is not the usual person to avoid embarrassing or difficult incidents. It could be wise to include the insistence that adults collect children rather than slightly older siblings.

Health and safety

The staff try to ensure that all reasonable steps are taken to establish and maintain a safe and healthy environment throughout the nursery. The children participate in fire drills. They are encouraged to follow safe procedures, for example walking in certain areas. If your child is ill we will contact you using the telephone number given in the contact form filled in at the initial visit. Visitors are asked to sign in the Visitor's Book and badges are to be worn and returned on departure.

If your child is ill please contact us to let us know.

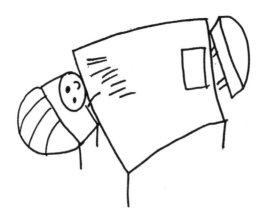

We take pride in providing a happy, caring atmosphere and look forward to sharing it with you.

Glossary

'A' frame: A steeply sided metal frame with two sides that meet to form an A. It usually has one or more rungs on either side, which can be used to balance benches or planks in between for climbing.

Accommodate: See Assimilation.

Alliteration: Using a series of words that have the same first letter or initial sound. Big, bad bears or cowardly, creeping caterpillars.

Anaphylaxis: A severe allergic reaction that requires immediate medical attention after contact with the food or substance. Can be triggered by eggs, nuts, stings, fruit, latex, milk, fish.

Appraisal: A programmed opportunity to reflect on previous practice, to celebrate what has been achieved successfully, to listen to any difficulties that need to be addressed or suggestions of alternative practice and to set targets for the next six or twelve months.

Asperger's syndrome: A condition which is similar to autistic spectrum disorder in that there are often repeated patterns of behaviour and social interaction is affected. This syndrome tends to be associated with higher order abilities. Adults with this condition are often poor communicators with an interest that takes over their life. Where work and hobby merge, the individual leads a contented existence, for example if the adult's interest is in cars and he or she works as a car salesperson.

Assessment of prior learning: Observations of children as they are learning are recorded and used to inform the next steps in learning.

Assimilation: Piaget's term describes a child taking in a new experience and linking it to an existing understanding or schema, for example a young child might use a familiar word to describe new similar objects such as car for bus, lorry, van etc. Understanding of the differences between the new objects is known as **Accommodation**.

Asthma: A common condition causing shortness of breath, wheezing and coughing. Children will have an inhaler to aid breathing when necessary.

Attention deficit hyperactivity disorder (ADHD): A condition in which the mind processes too quickly to concentrate on a task for any length of time. Adults with the condition describe it as being like a television that constantly flicks through the channels.

Doctors sometimes prescribe the drug Ritalin. This sometimes helps to overcome the problem but also has many unpleasant side effects like hallucinatory night terrors. Children are sometimes described as 'spacey'.

Authentic activities: Activities set in a real context to practise a skill, for example working as a builder to build a wall that is strong.

Autistic spectrum disorder (ASD): A whole spectrum of disabilities that become more apparent by the end of the Early Years Foundation Stage. Children with ASD may function perfectly well in mainstream provision. There remain a few children who will benefit from special provision because of their inability to socialize with other children of a similar age.

Beebots: See www.beebot.org.uk. Beebots and constructabots are programmable devices that are simple enough to be used independently by children in the 40- to 60-month age phase.

Cerebral palsy (hemiplegic): A disorder from birth causing difficulties with muscle control and coordination. Varies widely in extent of the muscle groups affected. Hemiplegic cerebral palsy is on one side of the body.

Cluster group: A group of schools or settings that are linked geographically. Practitioners meet to share training and good practice or to access SEN support.

Common Assessment Framework (CAF): A process of assessment with a standard form that is completed by a professional working with a child and family. This assists with identification of support needs in order to plan work with other agencies.

Community cohesion: A society where all groups of people feel that they belong, diversity is appreciated and everyone has equal life chances. Different cultural, ethnic, religious, linguistic or social groups relate positively to one another.

ContactPoint: An online directory that is available to authorized staff. This holds basic information about a child such as date of birth and which professionals are involved with that child.

Coomber listening sets: A set, available from www.coomber.co.uk, comprising six sets of headphones attached to a cassette or CD player that is also a recording device. It can be used to share a story between six children who follow the illustrations and text independently and it can be used to record group responses to a variety of stimuli.

Corporal Punishment: The use of unreasonable violence or physical punishment (including humiliation) to change or control behaviour. This has been banned by law in 23 countries.

Creative Partnerships: An organization that works with schools using experts to lead projects in art, music and dance.

Criminal Records Bureau (CRB): The Criminal Records Bureau maintains a list of the names of people who are considered unfit to work with vulnerable people, including children. All applicants for employment with children are asked to disclose any reasons why they may be unsuitable for employment with children. Names are then checked against the list and suitable applicants may then be employed.

Detachment: A child entering a setting and confidently allowing a parent or carer to leave with an understanding that the parent or carer will return at a predetermined time.

Diabetes: Diabetes is a medical condition where children have fluctuating sugar levels in the blood, caused by insufficient or ineffective insulin. In children this is usually controlled by daily injections (Type 1 diabetes) but can sometimes be managed through diet and exercise (Type 2).

Dialogic learning and teaching: This is a highly disciplined approach to learning which uses talk to stimulate, scaffold and extend children's thinking. It is not the same as question–answer or show and tell. The practitioner is a listener rather than a talker, learning from the social interactions of the children.

Digi blue: A digital still and movie camera that is robust and is designed to be used independently by small children. In many school-based EYFS settings, the digi blue camera is attached to an interactive whiteboard via a docking station so that images can be quickly uploaded to the board or stored for EYFS profile evidence.

Early Support Family File: This file is often given to families of children with complex medical needs who are working with a range of health professionals and professionals from other agencies. It is a record of personal information about the child, family and involved services. The family may bring this to meetings in order to avoid having to retell their story several times and to make sure that everyone is well informed.

Early Years Foundation Stage Profile: A summative assessment at the end of the Early Years Foundation Stage, usually undertaken when a child is in a Reception class.

ECEC: Early Childhood Education and Care.

Echolalia: A phrase spoken by the practitioner is repeated back by the child who may or may not respond with an appropriate action. For example, the practitioner says 'Sit down.' The child replies 'Sit down.' The practitioner says: 'Sit on the chair.' The child says: 'Chair.'

Educational psychology: A branch of psychology that focuses on children's learning and behaviour. Educational psychologists may assess children's needs and give advice to early years staff and parents.

Emotional health: How emotions affect our well-being. Being emotionally healthy is a state of balance, where difficult emotions and stress are not unmanageable.

Emotional intelligence: An aptitude for managing emotional situations, coping with your own and others' emotion. A way of viewing concepts and ideas from an emotionally sensitive standpoint.

Emotional literacy: An awareness of your own and others' emotions and the ability to behave in a way that is sensitive to these.

Empathy: The ability to imagine how some one else is feeling.

Enabling environment: See the appropriate chapter

English as an additional language: When a child or adult is learning or has learned English at the same time as, or after, another language or languages that are mainly used in his or her home.

Epilepsy: Epilepsy causes seizures but these vary very widely in terms of effect and frequency. They may be whole-body seizures or confined to a small area of face or vision. Practitioners will need to find out about individual needs and treatment.

EPPE: Effective Provision of Pre-School Education Project.

Extended schools: By 2010 schools will offer care including breakfast clubs and after-school activities to extend the school day in support of the working hours of parents.

Fine motor skills: Control of small objects using hands fingers and thumbs.

Firewall: A computer software package that helps to prevent predators from accessing images of children and young people and prevents unwanted and unsuitable files being accessed by children. Protection levels can be adjusted to suit the needs of the setting. All settings should ensure that a firewall is in place before allowing the children to access the internet.

Forest schools: A movement for educating children about caring for the environment, independence and self-care in an outdoor setting. Children will spend part of the day or a series of days involved in activities such as building shelters, making camp fires, exploring nature.

Gardiner's Multiple Intelligence Theory: Dr Gardiner proposed different intelligences to account for a broad range of human potential.

Grapheme phoneme correspondences (GPCs): The child associates the written letter shape with the phonic sound of the letter.

Gross motor skills: Control of a range of movements involving whole body and limbs, e.g. pedalling, throwing.

Gypsy Roma Traveller: This minority group includes Gypsies whose name is a derivative of Egypt, their place of origin. Gypsies traditionally were nomadic but many are now in settled housing and regular work. Travellers is a loose term describing Irish travellers, circus people and horse travellers and there is an additional group of new age travellers who choose a nomadic lifestyle but do not follow the mores and traditions associated with the Gypsy community.

Heuristic play: Young children explore a collection of interesting everyday objects of different shapes, sizes and textures in a quiet environment with their peers. The play is open-ended and supported by an adult presence but not intervention.

High-frequency words: These are the words which appear most often in the English language. A list of the first 45 words that children need to learn to read, write and spell are available in 'Letters' and 'Sounds' and online at 'Sparklebox'.

High scope: An approach to early education that focuses on active learning through hands-on experience and fostering children's independence and initiative.

Hypotheses: Suggestions for solving problems.

Individual Education Plan (IEP): A written plan that records areas of support and development for children with any special educational needs or possible difficulties with an aspect of learning. It suggests manageable targets and support strategies and is composed by the early years staff with advice from parents and other agencies.

Induction training: Training prior to working in a setting or on the first day of working in a setting that is specific to the setting, outlining expectations of time keeping, the dress code, the setting's policies and everything that will be required as part of the setting's team.

Integrated Children's System: A system that professionals may use, when assessing and planning for children's needs. This includes using the CAF and a database that records how different agencies will work together to plan for a child and family. This will be used for children and families who require additional support from more than one team.

KEEP: Key Elements of Effective Practice.

Learning challenges: Children are set opportunities to learn in which they are challenged to solve problems and in the process they learn the key skill set as an objective.

Literacy skills: Foundations of reading and writing.

Locomotion: Coordinated travelling movement, walking, running.

Looked after children: Children who are in public care, cared for by foster carers or other family members or friends in this role, or in children's homes.

Lower case letters: Letters that are not capital letters.

Makaton: A sign language with associated visual symbols that is widely used with children with communication needs.

Manipulation: Fine motor skills, pincer movement of thumb and finger, grasp.

Mantle of the expert: A way of working with children using drama/role play. Children are given a scenario to work through or problem to solve. They adopt different roles and work through the problem posed, responding as they imagine their character would do. New elements will be introduced by the adult to develop this further over time.

Medical deficit model of disability: Defining children's needs by labelling them as damaged goods, for example children with ADHD or cerebral palsy.

Midline: An imaginary line running through the centre of the body from the head to the foot. Activities involving moving arms or legs across this line enable the right- and left-hand side of the brain to work together.

Multi-agency working: Police, social services, health professionals, schools, Sure Start centres, EYFS settings and local authority representatives working together and sharing information in order to share information and protect children.

Occupational therapist: An occupational therapist gives advice and support to children with physical needs and helps them with seating and appropriate resources for writing or communication.

OECD: Organisation for Economic Cooperation and Development.

Open questions: Questions that are worded in such a way that they cannot be answered by yes or no or a one-word response.

Oracy skills: Speaking and listening.

Oro-motor skills: Control over lips, tongue and jaw, needed for blowing, sucking, chewing and clear speech.

Peripheral devices: An external attachment that connects to a computer such as a scanner, printer, copier, or camera.

Personal education plans: An individual education plan for looked after children that focuses on supporting their educational attainment, not only for children with special educational needs. This should be drawn up by a social worker with the early years staff.

Philosophy for children: A way of working that encourages children to formulate abstract questions and wonder. This can be in response to stories or music. Adults do not give answers but encourage children to discuss their own explanations.

Picture exchange system: A system of pictures instead of words (PECS) that help adults to communicate with children.

Plan, do, review: A High scope way of working where children are encouraged to plan what tasks or activities they will use in the session and what they want to achieve. After the activity is complete they will then review their progress, through discussion with an adult, and suggest what they may do next time as well as identifying their achievements.

Point and click software: Programs designed to be simple to use. The child simply controls the mouse, which is moved until the cursor is located over an item of choice on the screen. The child is able to left click on the mouse.

Portage: A home-visiting system of educational support for families and children who have an additional support need identified from birth or soon after.

Positive discipline: Using praise, clear expectations and boundaries, rules, rewards and sanctions to promote good behaviour.

Proprioception: Unconscious awareness of your own body and its place in relation to other objects. This is needed for balance and coordination, even sitting upright.

Reggio Emilia: A region in Northern Italy where a particular philosophy and practice of early education is in place. Artists are part of every early years setting. The environment is planned to be aesthetically pleasing and children follow creative projects based on their individual interests.

Representative play: Children use one object, sometimes with slightly similar visual characteristics, to represent another, such as a banana for a telephone.

Reptilian brain: An area of the brain that monitors physical well-being.

Safeguarding Children: 'The process of protecting children from abuse or neglect, preventing impairment of their health and development, and ensuring they are growing up in circumstances consistent with the provision of safe and effective care that enables children to have optimum life chances and enter adulthood successfully' www.dfes.gov.uk (December 2008).

Schema: Piaget's term describes a concept or understanding that children explore in a range of different contexts, often through movement, such as travelling over and under.

Self-awareness: Understanding of your own emotions and how you react or feel in certain situations.

Self-esteem: Your feeling of self-worth including recognition of your own strengths and weaknesses and acceptance of these.

Silent period: A period of time in which children who are new to an English-speaking setting and use another language or languages at home often choose not to speak.

Sky write: Many children find it hard to write small, neat letters on paper. When letters the size of the child are formed in the air they disappear as quickly as they are formed but the process of forming the letters physically helps to imprint the correct formation into long-term memory.

Small-world play: Play using small representations of real-world items such as farmyards, cars and houses.

Social constructivism: Learning is made up of social constructs or ideas that are modelled by the expert to the novice learner. The novice learner develops an idea or a skill in response to engaging in a learning challenge to solve a particular problem using the construct modelled by the expert.

Social and emotional aspects of learning: A set of DFES materials, resources and suggested lessons used in primary schools to develop social and emotional skills. These cover themes that are revisited annually in different age-appropriate ways.

Socio-dramatic play: Role play based on a real-life experience or theme.

Stability: The ability to balance and reach out unaided begins with babies rolling over and pulling up to sitting. This is needed as a basis for all movement combinations such as throwing, kicking and dance skills.

Starting point stimuli: A picture, visual or auditory prompt, role-play corner or initial story that sets the scene and encourages the child to engage in the learning opportunity.

Statutory Assessment Procedure: Professionals and parents gather information about a child with additional needs in order to request additional funding for support and resources in an educational setting.

Story hand: An aide memoire for the children to begin to understand story structure. This is important for story development in Key Stage 2. Spread out your right hand and encourage the children to do the same. Touch your little finger (Baby Small) with your left hand and say to the children, 'Who is in the story?' Touch your ring finger. 'Where does it take place?' Touch the middle finger (Toby Tall) What is the main event (the conflict)? Touch your index finger (Peter Pointer) How is the story resolved (conflict resolution)? Touch the thumb. What did they think about it?

Sustained shared thinking: A process of adult and child interaction where the adult tunes into the child's interests. The adult listens, watches attentively and may join in with the child's chosen activity. The adult helps to develop the child's thinking with suggestions or open questions over an extended period of time.

Treasure basket: A basket or open container, that babies can reach into.

Tube-feeding: A procedure where children, often those who have difficulty with swallowing and are at risk of choking, are fed liquid food from a special machine attached to an external 'button' on the child's body that connects with the stomach internally.

Tuffcam and scope: www.Tuffcam.co.uk. The tuffcam is a digital movie and stills camera designed for small hands. It has a 'scope' which connects to the camera to be able to see e.g. magnified minibeasts.

VAK or **visual, auditory and kinaesthetic approach to learning:** A multi-sensory approach incorporates visual literacy, the spoken word and a kinaesthetic or physical movement opportunity.

Visual timetables: A pictorial representation of the events or activities that will happen during the day or session.

Wrap-around care: As part of the extended care, multi-agency working will offer, for example, visits from the educational psychologist or social services on or near to the school premises to enable all children to access services.

Zone of proximal development (ZPD): a phrase developed by Vygotsky to describe the next step in learning that the child could not achieve independently but can achieve with structured questioning.

Reference List and Bibliography

Abbott, L. (2001) Perceptions of play: a question of priorities, in L. Abbott, C. Nutbrown and P. Moss (eds) *Experiencing Reggio Emilia: Implications in Pre-school Provision*. Buckingham: Open University Press.

Alexander, R.J. (2005) *Towards Dialogic Teaching: Rethinking Classroom Talk*. London: Routledge.

Alexander, R. (2008a) *Essays on Pedagogy*. London: Routledge.

Alexander, R. (2008b) *Towards Dialogic Teaching: Rethinking Classroom Talk*, 4th edn. Cambridge: Dialogos.

Andrews, J. and Yee, W.C. (2006) Professional researcher or a 'good guest'? Ethical dilemmas involved in researching children and families in the home setting, *Educational Review*, 58 (4): 397–413.

Anning, A. (1991) *The First Years at School*. Milton Keynes: Open University Press.

Anning, A. and Ball, M. (2008) *Improving Services for Young Children: From Sure Start to Children's Centres*. London: Sage Publications.

Ashley, J. and Tomasello, M. (1998) Cooperative problem solving and teaching in pre-schoolers, *Social Development*, 1 (2): 143–63.

Athey, C. (1990) *Extending Thought in Young Children: A Parent–Teacher Partnership*. London: Chapman.

Austin, R. (2007) *Letting the Outside In: Developing Teaching and Learning Beyond the Early Years Classroom*. Stoke on Trent: Trentham Books.

Barrow, G., Bradshaw, E. and Newton, T. (2001) *Improving Behaviour and Raising Self-Esteem in the Classroom*. London: David Fulton.

Bennett, N., Wood, E. and Rogers, S. (1997) *Teaching Through Play: Teachers' Thinking and Classroom Practice*. Buckingham: Open University Press.

Biddle, S.J.H. (2000) Emotion, mood and physical activity, in S.J.H. Biddle, K.R. Fox and S.H. Boutcher (eds) *Physical Activity and Psychological Well-Being*. Abingdon: Routledge.

Biddle, S.J.H., Fox, K.R. and Boutcher, S.H. (eds) *Physical Activity and Psychological Well-Being*. Abingdon: Routledge.

Bilton, H. (2004) *Playing Outside*. London: David Fulton.

Bilton, H., James, K., Marsh, J. *et al.* (2005) *Learning Outdoors: Improving the Quality of Young Children's Play Outdoors*. London: David Fulton.

Blatchford, I., Clarke, K. and Needham, M. (eds) *The Team Around the Child*. Stoke on Trent: Trentham Books.

Blythe, S.G. (2000) Early learning in the balance: priming the first ABC, *Support for Learning*, 15 (4): 154–9.

Bourne, J. (ed.) (1994) *Thinking Through Primary Practice*. London: Routledge.

Bowlby, J. (1953) *Child Care and the Growth of Love*. London: Pelican Books.

Bray, M., Adamson, B. and Mason, M. (eds) (2007) *Comparative Education Research*. Hong Kong: Springer.

British Nutrition Foundation (2004a) *Diet Through Life*. www.nutrition.org.uk/home.asp?siteId=43&sectionId=315&parentSection=299&which=1 (accessed 10 August 2008).

British Nutrition Foundation (2004b) *Dental Health*. www.nutrition.org.uk/home.asp?siteId=43&sectionId=649&subSectionId=321&parentSection=299&which=1#1119 (accessed 8 December 2008).

Broadhead, P. (2004) *Early Years Play and Learning: Developing Social Skills and Cooperation*. Abingdon: Routledge Falmer.

Bronfenbrenner, U. (1979) *The Ecology of Human Development: Experiments by Nature and Design*. Cambridge, MA: Harvard University Press.

Brooker, L. (2002) *Starting School: Young Children Learning Cultures*. Buckingham: Open University Press.

Brown, B. (2001) *Combating Discrimination: Persona Dolls in Action*. Stoke on Trent: Trentham Books.

Brownell, C.A and Carriger, M.S. (1991) Collaborations among toddler peers, in M. Woodhead, D. Faulkner and K. Littleton (eds) *Cultural Worlds of Early Childhood*. London: Routledge.

Bruce, T. (2004a) *Cultivating Creativity in Babies, Toddlers and Young Children*. London: Hodder and Stoughton Educational.

Bruce, T. (2004b) *Developing Learning in Early Childhood*. London: PCP.

Bruner, J. (1966) *Toward a Theory of Instruction*. Cambridge MA: Harvard University Press.

Bullock, A. (1975) *A Language for Life* (Bullock Report). London: HMSO.

Burnett, G. (2003) *Learning to Learn*. Carmarthen: Crown House Publishing Ltd.

CACE (Central Advisory Council for Education) (1967) *Children and their Primary Schools* (Plowden Report). London: HMSO.

Carlin, J. (2005) *Including Me. Managing Complex Health Needs in Schools and Early Years Settings*. London: DfES and Council for Disabled Children.

Cerny, P.G. (2007) Neoliberalism and Place: Deconstructing and Reconstructing Borders. Paper presented at University of Warwick conference.

Children's Society (2007) *The Good Childhood. Evidence Summary 1*. www.childrenssociety.org.uk/resources/documents/good%20childhood/Friends%20evidence%20summary_2721_full.pdf (accessed 9 December 2008).

Clark, A., Kjorholt, A.T. and Moss, P. (2005) *Beyond Listening: Children's Perspectives on Early Childhood Services*. Bristol: The Policy Press.

Clarke, C. (2007) Parent involvement in the transition to school, in A.W. Dunlop and H. Fabian (eds) *Informing Transitions in the Early Years: Research Policy and Practice*. Maidenhead: Open University Press.

Clarke, M.M. and Waller, T. (2007) *Early Childhood Education and Care*. London: Sage Publications.

Cleave, S., Jowett, S. and Bate, M. (1982) *And So To School*. Windsor: NFER Publishing Company.

Cole, R. (2006) *The Creative Imperative: Unravel the Mystery of Creativity*. Lichfield: Primary First.

Collins, M. (2001) *Circle Time for the Very Young*. Bristol: Lucky Duck.

Conteh, J. (2003) *Succeeding in Diversity: Culture, Language and Learning in Primary Classrooms*. Stoke on Trent: Trentham Books.

Costello, P.J.M. (2000) *Thinking Skills and Early Childhood Education*. London: David Fulton.

Crace, J. (2003) The Guardian 15 July in Rogers, S. (2004) *Early Childhood Studies*. Exeter: Learning Matters.

Craft, A. (2002) *Creativity and Early Years Education: A Life-wide Foundation*. London: Continuum.

Craft, A. (2005) *Creativity in Schools: Tensions and Dilemmas*. Abingdon: Routledge.

Craft, A. and Jeffrey, B. (2004) Creative practice and practice which fosters creativity, in L. Miller and J. Devreux (eds) *Supporting Children's Learning in the Early Years*. London: David Fulton.

Croghan, E. (2007) *Promoting Health in Schools. A Practical Guide for Teachers and School Nurses Working with Children aged 3 to 11*. London: PCP.

Dahlberg, G. and Moss, P. (2005) *Ethics and Politics in Early Childhood Education*. Abingdon: Routledge Falmer.

Dalli, C. (2002) From home to childcare: challenges for mothers, teachers and children, in H. Fabian and A.W. Dunlop (eds) *Transitions in the Early Years: Debating Continuity and Progression for Children in Early Education*. Abingdon: Routledge Falmer.

Datta, M. (2000) *Bilinguality and Literacy: Principles and Practice*. London: Continuum.

Davies, M. (2003) *Movement and Dance in Early Childhood 0–8*, 2nd edn. London: PCP.

DCSF (Department for Children, Schools and Families) (2006a) *Rose Review*. www.standards.dcsf.gov.uk/phonics/rosereview/ (accessed 3 January 2009).

DCSF (2006b) *Excellence and Enjoyment: Learning and Teaching for Bilingual Children in the Primary Years*. London: The Stationery Office.

DCSF (2007a) *Supporting Children Learning English as an Additional Language: Guidance for Practitioners in the EYFS*. London: DCSF.

DCSF (2007b) *New Arrivals Excellence Programme Guidance*. London: DCSF.

DCSF (2007c) *Children's Plan: Building a Brighter Future*. London: The Stationery Office.

DCSF (2007d) KEEP: Key Elements of Effective Practice. London: The Stationery Office.

DCSF (2008a) *Social and Emotional Aspects of Development*. Nottingham: DCSF Publications.

DCSF (2008b) *Setting the Standards for Learning, Development and Care for Children from Birth to Five*. www.teachernet.gov.uk/teachingandlearning/eyfs/ (accessed 17 March 2009).

DCSF and NHS (2008a) *National Healthy Schools Programme*. www.healthyschools.gov.uk/Default.aspx (accessed 6 December 2008).

DCSF and NHS (2008b) *National Healthy Schools Programme. Sneezesafe and Catch it Bin it Kill it*. www.healthyschools.gov.uk/Resources/Detail.aspx?ResID=38 (accessed 6 December 2008.

Dehart, G.B., Sroufe, L.A. and Cooper, R.G. (2004) *Child Development: Its Nature and Course*. New York: McGraw-Hill.

Devereux, J. and Millar, L. (2003) *Working with Children in the Early Years*. London: David Fulton.

DfES (Department for Education and Schools) (2001) SEN Code of Practice. Norwich: The Stationery Office. www.publications.teachernet.gov.uk/eOrderingDownload/DfES%200581%20200MIG2228.pdf (accessed 17 March 2009).

DfES (2003) *Every Child Matters*. Green Paper. London: The Stationery Office. www.everychildmatters.org.uk (accessed 9 September 2008).

DfES (2004a) Children Act. London: DfES.

DfES (2004b) *The Effective Provision of Pre-school Education Project: Findings from Pre-school to End of Key Stage 1. Final Report.* London: DfES/Sure Start.

DfES (2005a) *What To Do if you're Worried a Child is Being Abused*. London: The Stationery Office.

DfES (2005b) *Managing Medicines in Schools and Early Years Settings*. London: DfES.

DfES (2006a) *Statutory Guidance on the Duty on Local Authorities to Promote the Educational Achievement of Looked After Children under Section 52 of the Children Act (2004).* Nottingham: DfES.

DfES (2006b) *Seamless Transitions: Supporting Continuity in Young Children's Learning.* London: DfES/Sure Start.

DfES (2006c) *Working Together to Safeguard Children*. London: The Stationery Office. http://publications.teachernet.gov.uk/eOrderingDownload/DfES%200581%20200MIG2228.pdf (accessed 17 March 2009)

DfES (2007a) *Practice Guidance for the Early Years Foundation Stage*. Nottingham: DfES.

DfES (2007b) *Early Years Foundation Stage Framework*. London: DfES.

Dockett, S. and Perry, B. (2007) Children's transition to school: changing expectations, in H. Fabian and A.W. Dunlop (eds)*Transitions in the Early Years: Debating Continuity and Progression for Children in Early Education*. Abingdon: Routledge Falmer.

DoH (Department of Health) (2003) *The Victoria Climbie Inquiry. Report of an Inquiry by Lord Laming*. London: The Stationery Office. www.victoria-climbie-inquiry.org.uk/finreport/finreport.htm (accessed 18 December 2008).

DoH (2006) *Forecasting Obesity to 2010*. www.dh.gov.uk/en/Publicationsandstatistics/Publications/PublicationsStatistics/DH_4138630 (accessed 17 August 2008).

DoH (2008) *Healthy Weight, Healthy Lives. A Cross-government Strategy for England*. www.dh.gov.uk/en/Publichealth/Healthimprovement/Obesity/DH_082383 (accessed 10 August 2008).

Doherty, J. and Bailey, R. (2003) *Supporting Physical Development and Physical Education in the Early Years*. Buckingham: Open University Press.

Doherty, J. and Brennan, P. (2008) *Physical Education and Development 3–11: A Guide for Teachers*. London: David Fulton.

Dowling, M. (2005) *Young Children's Personal, Social and Emotional Development,* 2nd edn. London: PCP.

Dowling (2005:89) in O Hara Teaching Children 3–8 Great Britain Biddles Ltd.

Drake, J. (2003) *Organising Play in the Early Years: Practical Ideas and Activities for All Practitioners*. London: David Fulton.

Drury, R. (2007) *Young Bilingual Learners at Home and School: Researching Multilingual Voices*. Stoke on Trent: Trentham Books.

Duffy, B. (2006) *Supporting Creativity and Imagination in the Early Years*, 2nd edn. Maidenhead: Open University Press.

Duffy, B. and Stillaway, J. (2004) Creativity: working in partnership with parents, in. L. Miller and J. Devreux (eds) *Supporting Children's Learning in the Early Years*. London: David Fulton.

Dunlop, A.W. (2002) Perspectives on children as learners in the transition to school, in H. Fabian and A.W. Dunlop (eds) *Transitions in the Early Years: Debating Continuity and Progression for Children in Early Education*. Abingdon: Routledge Falmer.

Dunn, J. (1993) *Young Children's Close Relationships: Beyond Attachment*. Newbury Park, CA: Sage Publications.

Dunn, J. (1998) Young children's understanding of other people: evidence from observations within the family, in M. Woodhead, D. Faulkner and K. Littleton (eds) *Cultural Worlds of Early Childhood*. London: Routledge.

Early Support (2008) *The Family File*. www.earlysupport.org.uk/decMaterialsZone/modResourcesLibrary/HtmlRenderer/Family%20file.html (accessed 11 December 2008).

Edgington, M. (2002) *The Great Outdoors: Developing Children's Learning through Outdoor Provision*, 3rd edition. London: British Association for Early Childhood Education.

Edgington, M. (2004) *The Foundation Stage Teacher in Action. Teaching 3, 4 and 5 year olds*, 3rd edition. London: PCP.

Every Child Matters (2006) *Integrated Working*, www.everychildmatters.gov.uk/deliveringservices/integratedworking/ (accessed 11 Dec. 2008).

Every Child Matters (2007) *ICS, CAF and Contact Point an Overview*, www.everychildmatters.gov.uk/_files/ICS%20CAF%20and%20ContactPoint%20overview%20Nov%202007.pdf (accessed 11 December 2008).

Fabian, H. (2002) Empowering children for transitions, in H. Fabian and A.W. Dunlop (eds) *Transitions in the Early Years: Debating Continuity and Progression for Children in Early Education*. Abingdon: Routledge Falmer.

Fisher, R.J. (2005a) *Teaching Children to Think*, 2nd edition. Cheltenham: Nelson Thornes.

Fisher, R.J. (2005b) *Teaching Children to Learn*, 2nd edition. Cheltenham: Nelson Thornes.

Fitzgerald, D. (2004) *Parent Partnership in the Early Years*. London: Continuum.

Fitzpatrick, M. (2002) *Theories of Child Language Acquisition*. www.babyparenting.about.com/od/childdevelopment/a/babytalk.htm, accessed 12 November 2008.

Fogarty, F. (1997) I listened carefully to the way children were spoken to. Equality and the under threes, in L. Abbott and H. Moylett (eds) *Working with the Under-3s: Responding to Children's Needs*. Maidenhead: Open University Press.

Fox, K.R. (2000) The effects of exercise on self-perceptions and self-esteem, in S.J.H. Biddle, K.R. Fox and S.H. Boutcher (eds) *Physical Activity and Psychological Well-Being*. Abingdon: Routledge.

French, J. (2007) Multi-agency working: the historical background, in I. Siraj-Blatchford, K. Clarke and M. Needham (eds) *The Team Around the Child: Multi-agency Working in the Early Years*. Stoke on Trent: Trentham Books.

Gallahue, D. (1982) *Understanding Motor Development in Young Children*. New York: John Wiley.

Garrick, R. (2004) *Playing Outdoors in the Early Years*. London: Continuum.

Glaxton, G. and Carr, M. (2004) *A Framework For Teaching Learning: The Dynamics of Disposition*. Early Years 24(1) 53:1 in Basford J and Hodson E *Teaching Early Years Foundation Stage* (2008) Exeter: Learning Matters.

Goldschmied, E. and Jackson, S. (1994) People Under Three: Young Children in Day Care. London: Routledge.

Goleman, D. (1996) *Emotional Intelligence. Why It Can Matter More Than IQ*. London: Bloomsbury.

Hadow, W.H. (1931) *The Primary School* (Hadow Report). London: HMSO.

Hall, N. and Robinson, A. (2003) *Exploring Writing and Play in the Early Years*, 2nd edn. London: David Fulton.

Harlen, W. (2000) *The Teaching of Science in Primary Schools*. London: David Fulton.

Heathcote, D. (2002) *Contexts for Active Learning*. www.moeplanning.co.uk/wp-content/uploads/2008/05/dh-contexts-for-active-learning.pdf (accessed 23 November 2008).

Holland, R. (1997) What's it all about? How introducing heuristic play has affected provision for the under-threes in one day nursery, in L. Abbott and H. Moylett (eds) *Working with the Under-3s: Responding to Children's Needs*. Maidenhead: Open University Press.

Holt, N. (2007) *Bringing the High/Scope Approach to your Early Years Practice*. London: David Fulton.

Home Office (2000) Race Relations (Amendment) Act 2000. London: HMSO.

Hurst, V. and Joseph, J. (1998) *Supporting Early Learning: The Way Forward*. Buckingham: Open University Press.

Hutchin, V. (2003) *Observing and Assessing for the Foundation Stage Profile*. London: Hodder and Stoughton Educational.

Hutchin, V. (2007) *Supporting Every Child's Learning Across the Early Years Foundation Stage*. London: Hodder Education.

IAPC (Institute for the Advancement of Philosophy for Children) (2008) *What is Philosophy for Children?* www.cehs.montclair.edu/academic/iapc (accessed 23 November 2008).

IC (Information Centre for Health and Social Care) (2007) *Statistics on Obesity, Physical Activity and Diet, England 2006*. www.ic.nhs.uk/statistics-and-data-collections/health-and-lifestyles/obesity/statistics-on-obesity-physical-and-diet-england2006 (accessed 9 September2008).

Isaacs, B. (2007) *Bringing the Montessori Approach to Your Early Years Practice*. Abingdon: Routledge.

Jarvis, P. (2008) *Democracy, Lifelong Learning and the Learning Society*. London: Routledge.

Johansson, I. (2007) Horizontal transitions: what can it mean for children in the early school years?, in A.W. Dunlop and H. Fabian (eds) *Informing Transitions in the Early Years. Research Policy and Practice*. Maidenhead: Open University Press.

Jones, P. (2005) *Inclusion in the Early Years: Stories of Good Practice*. Abingdon: David Fulton.

Kantor, R., Elgas, P. and Fernie, D.E. (1998) Cultural knowledge and social competence within a pre-school peer-culture group, in M. Woodhead, D. Faulkner and K. Littleton (eds) *Cultural Worlds of Early Childhood*. London: Routledge.

Keenan, T. (2002) *An Introduction to Child Development*. London: Sage Publications.

Kiddle, C. (1999) *Traveller Children: A Voice for Themselves*. London: Jessica Kingsley.

King, K. and Park, E. (2003) *Cultural Diversity and Language Socialization. The Early Years* Accessed 12.11.2008.

Klein, M.D. and Chen, D. (2001) *Working with Children from Culturally Diverse Backgrounds*. Albany, NY: Delmar.

Klugman, E. and Smilansky, S. (eds) (1990) *Children's Play and Learning*. New York/London: Teachers' College Press.

Knight, C. (2001) Quality and the Role of the Pedagogista, in L. Abbott, C. Nutbrown and P. Moss (eds) *Experiencing Reggio Emilia: Implications in Pre-school Provision*. Buckingham: Open University Press.

Knowles, E. and Riley, W. (2005) *Another Spanner in the Works: Challenging Prejudice and Racism in Mainly White Schools*. Stoke on Trent: Trentham Books.

Lancaster, Y.P. (2003) *Promoting Listening to Young Children: The Reader*. Maidenhead: Open University Press.

Lauder, H., Lowe, J. and Chawla-Duggan, R. (2008) *Primary Review Interim Report. Aims for Primary Education: Changing Global Contexts*. Cambridge: University of Cambridge.

Lawrence, D. (2006) *Enhancing Self-Esteem in the Classroom*, 3rd edn. London: PCP.

Leavers (1996) in J. Basford and E. Hodson (2008:21–22) *Teaching Early Years Foundation Stage*. Exeter: Learning Matters.

Lindon, J. (2005) *Understanding Child Development: Linking Theory and Practice*. London: Hodder Arnold.

Lipman, M. (2003) *Thinking in Education*, 2nd edn. Cambridge: Cambridge University Press.

McGregor, D. (2007) *Developing Thinking, Developing Learning. A Guide to Thinking Skills in Education*. Maidenhead: Open University Press.

Macintyre, C. (2001) *Enhancing Learning Through Play*. London: David Fulton.

Macintyre, C. and McVitty, K. (2004) *Movement and Learning in the Early Years*. London: PCP.

MacNaughton, G. (2003) *Shaping Early Childhood: Learners, Curriculum and Contexts*. Maidenhead: Open University Press.

Margetts, K. (2002) Planning transition programmes, in H. Fabian and A.W. Dunlop (eds) *Transitions in the Early Years: Debating Continuity and Progression for Children in Early Education*. Abingdon: Routledge Falmer.

Margetts, K. (2007) Understanding and supporting children: shaping transition practices, in A.W. Dunlop and H. Fabian (eds) *Informing Transitions in the Early Years: Research Policy and Practice*. Maidenhead: Open University Press.

Maslow, A. (1968) *Toward a Psychology of Being*, 2nd edn. London: Litton Educational Publishing.

May, M., Ashford, E. and Bottle, G. (2006) *Sound Beginnings: Learning and Development in the Early Years*. London: David Fulton.

Mercer, N. and Littleton, K. (2007) *Dialogue and the Development of Children's Thinking: A Socio-cultural Approach*. Oxford: Routledge.

Mortimer, H. (2003) *Emotional Literacy and Mental Health in the Early Years*. Lichfield: QED.

Mosley, J. (1998) *More Quality Circle Time*. Wisbech: LDA.

Moss, P. (2001) The otherness of Reggio, in L. Abbott, C. Nutbrown and P. Moss (eds) *Experiencing Reggio Emilia: Implications in Pre-school Provision*. Buckingham: Open University Press.

Mountford, A. and Hunt, C. (2001) *Family Links Nurturing Programme: Trainer's Handbook*. Oxford: Family Links.

Moyles, J. and Adams, S. (2001) *StEPs: Statements of Entitlement to Pay: A Framework for Playful Teaching*. Bury St Edmonds: St Edmundsbury Press.

Moyles, J., Adams, S. and Musgrove, A. (2002) *SPEEL: Study of Pedagogical Effectiveness in Early Learning*. London: DfES.

Myhill, D., Jones, S. and Hopper, R. (2006) *Talking, Listening and Learning: Effective Talk in the Primary Classroom*. Maidenhead: Open University Press.

NACCE (National Advisory Committee for Creative and Cultural Education) (1999) *All Our Futures: Creativity, Culture and Education*. www.tactyc.org.uk (accessed 10 October 2008).

Neaum, S. and Tallack, J. (1997) *Good Practice in Implementing the Pre-school Curriculum*. Cheltenham: Stanley Thornes.

Neuman, M. (2002) The wider context: an international view of transition issues, in H. Fabian and A.W. Dunlop (eds) *Transitions in the Early Years: Debating Continuity and Progression for Children in Early Education*. Abingdon: Routledge Falmer.

NICE (National Institute for Health and Clinical Excellence) (2007) *Play Sector Briefing 5*. www.playengland.org.uk/play/free-play-improving-physical-health-nov2007.pdf (accessed 16 August 2008).

Nutbrown, C. (2006) *Key Concepts in Early Childhood Education and Care*. London: Sage Publications.

Nutbrown, C. (2007) *Threads of Thinking: Young Children Learning and the Role of Early Education*, 3rd edn. London: Sage Publications.

Nutbrown, C. and Clough, P. (2006) *Inclusion in the Early Years: Critical Analyses and Enabling Narratives*. London: Sage Publications.

Nutbrown, C. and Page, J. (2008) *Working with Babies and Young Children*. London: Sage Publications.

OECD (Organization for Economic Co-operation and Development) (2006) *Starting Strong 11*. Paris: OECD.

Ofsted (Office for Standards in Education) (2005) *Early Years Firm Foundations: Outcomes for Children*. www.live.ofsted.gov.uk/publications/firmfoundations/chapter1.htm (accessed 16 August 2008).

Ofsted (2008) *Annexe C: Typical Actions Needed to Meet the Standards and Regulations*. www.ofsted.gov.uk/Ofsted-home/Leading-to-excellence/Annexes/Annex-C-Typical-actions-needed-to-meet-standards-and-regulations/(language)/eng-GB (accessed 15 November 2008).

O'Hara (2003) *Teaching 3–8* Great Britain, Biddles Ltd.

Oliver, J. (2008) *School Dinners: Facts and Figures*. www.jamieoliver.com/school-dinners/facts-and-figures (accessed 6 December 2008).

OPSI (Office of Public Sector Information) (1995) Disability Discrimination Act (DDA) 1995. London: HMSO. www.opsi.gov.uk/acts/acts1995/ukpga_19950050_en_1 (accessed 16 November 2008).

OPSI (2000) Race Relations (Amendment) Act 2000. London: HMSO.

OPSI (2001) Special Educational Needs and Disability Act (SENDA) 2001. www.opsi.gov.uk/ACTS/acts2001/ukpga_20010010_en_1 (accessed 16 November 2008) www.opsi.gov.uk/ACT/acts2000/20000034htm. 2008).

Osborn, A.F. and Milbank, J.E. (1987) *The Effects of Early Years Education*. Oxford: Clarendon Press.

Ouseley, H. and Lane, J. (2006) We've got to start somewhere: what role can early years services and settings play in helping society to be more at ease with itself?, *Race Equality Teaching*, 24(2) Spring: 39–43.

Palmer, S. (2006) *Toxic Childhood: How the Modern World Is Damaging Our Children and What We Can Do About It*. London: Orion.

Panju, M. (2008) *Seven Successful Strategies to Promote Emotional Intelligence in the Classroom*. London: Continuum.

Peters, S. (2002) Teachers' perspectives of transitions, in H. Fabian and A.W. Dunlop (eds) *Transitions in the Early Years: Debating Continuity and Progression for Children in Early Education*. Abingdon: Routledge Falmer.

Piaget, J. (1954) *The Construction of Reality in the Child*. London: Routledge and Kegan Paul.

Pickup, I. and Price, L. (2007) *Teaching Physical Education in the Primary School*. London: Continuum.

Piotrowski, S. (2000) Physical education and health-promoting primary schools, in A. Williams (ed.) *Primary School Physical Education: Research into Practice*. London: Routledge Falmer.

PLA (Pre-school Learning Alliance) (2001) *Equal Chances: Eliminating Discrimination and Ensuring Equality in Pre-school Settings*. London: Pre-school Learning Alliance.

PLA (2008a) *Survey Results*. www.pre-school.org.uk/food/survey-results.php (accessed 16 September 2008).

PLA (2008b) *Safe Early Years Environments*. www.seye.pre-school.org.uk/ (accessed 15 November 2008).

Pollard, A. (2005) *Reflective Teaching: Evidence-informed Professional Practice*, 2nd edition. London: Continuum.

Porter, L. (2005) *Gifted Young Children: A Guide for Parents and Teachers*, 2nd edn. Maidenhead: Open University Press.

Pound, L. (1999) *Supporting Mathematical Development in the Early Years*. Buckingham: Open University Press.

Pryke, R. (2006) *Weight Matters for Children. A Complete Guide to Weight, Eating and Fitness*. Oxford: Radcliffe.

Pugh, G. (ed.) (2001) *Contemporary Issues in the Early Years*. London: Paul Chapman Publishing.

Qualifications and Curriculum Authority (QCA)/Department for Education and Employment (DfEE) (2000) *Curriculum Guidance for the Foundation Stage*. London: QCA/DfEE.

QCA on cultural identity accessed 2.01.09 curriculum.qca.org.uk/key-stages-3-and-4/cross-curriculum-dimensions/culturaldiversityidentity/index.aspx?return=/search/index.aspx%3FfldSiteSearch%3Dequal+opportunities%26page%3D1

Renowden, H. (1997) 'It's a princess': fostering creative and aesthetic development in young children, in L. Abbott and H. Moylett (eds) *Working with the Under-3s: Responding to Children's Needs*. Maidenhead: Open University Press.

Rinaldi, C., Dahlberg, C. and Moss, P. (2005) *In Dialogue with Reggio Emilia: Listening, Researching, Learning*. Abingdon: Routledge Falmer.

Roberts, R. (2002) *Self-Esteem and Early Learning*. London: PCP.

Robinson, S. (2006) *Healthy Eating in Primary Schools*. London: PCP.

Robson, S. (2004) The physical environment, in L. Miller and J. Devreux (eds) *Supporting Children's Learning in the Early Years*. London: David Fulton.

RoSPA (Royal Society for the Prevention of Accidents) (2008) *It's a bit Risky Is This*. www.rospa.com/safetyeducation/index.htm (accessed 15 November 2008).

Rumboldt, A. (1990) *Starting With Quality* (Rumboldt Report). London: HMSO.

Rumelhart, D. and Norman, D. (1978) Accretion, tuning and restructuring: three modes of learning, in J.W. Cotton and R. Klatzky (eds) *Semantic Factors in Cognition*. Hillsdale, NJ: Erlbaum.

Rumelhart, D. and Norman, D. (1981) Analogical processes in learning, in J.R. Anderson (ed.) *Cognitive Skills and their Acquisition*. Hillsdale, NJ: Erlbaum.

Sammons, P. , Taggart, B., Samms, R. *et al.* (2003) *The Early Years Transition and Special Educational Needs (EYSEN) Project*. London/Oxford: Institute of Education, University of London; University of Oxford; Birkbeck College, University of London.

Santrock, J.W. (2004) *Child Development*. New York: McGraw-Hill.

Schaffer, H.R. (1996) *Social Development*. Oxford: Blackwell.

SCAA (School Curriculum Assessment Authority) (1996) *Nursery Education: Desirable Outcomes for Children's Learning on Entering Compulsory Education*. London: SCAA and Department for Education and Employment.

School Food Trust (2008) *Why the New Standards?* www.schoolfoodtrust.org.uk/content.asp?ContentId=409 (accessed 6 December 2008).

Scottish Office (2006) *Public Inquiry into the Shootings at Dunblane Primary School*. London: The Stationery Office.

Sedgwick, F. (2008) *100 Ideas for Developing Thinking in the Primary School*. London: Continuum.

Shaw, S. and Hawes, T. (1998) *Effective Teaching and Learning in the Primary Classroom: A Practical Guide to Brain-compatible Learning*. Leicester: Optimal Learning.

Siraj-Blatchford, I. (1999) Early childhood pedagogy: practices, principles and research, in P. Mortimore (ed.) *Understanding Pedagogy and its Impact on Learning*. London: Paul Chapman.

Siraj-Blatchford, I. (2008) *The Case for Integrating Education with Care in the Early Years*, in I. Siraj-Blatchford, K. Clarke and M. Needham (eds) *The Team Around the Child: Multi-agency Working in the Early Years*. Stoke on Trent: Trentham Books.

Siraj-Blatchford, I. and Clarke, P. (2000) *Supporting Identity, Diversity and Language in the Early Years*. Maidenhead: Open University Press.

Siraj-Blatchford, I., Sylva, K., Muttock, S., Gilden, R. and Bell, D. (2002) *Researching Effective Pedagogy in the Early Years*. Research Report 356. London: HMSO.

Sleap, M., Warbuton, P. and Waring, M. (2000) Couch potato kids and lazy layabouts: the role of primary schools in relation to physical activity, in A. Williams (ed.) *Primary School Physical Education. Research into Practice*. London: Taylor Francis.

Smallwood, H. (1990) speaking at the national 'Letterland' Conference, Cambridge.

Smidt, S. (2005) *Observing, Assessing and Planning for Children in the Early Years*. London: Routledge.

South, H. (1999) *Working Paper 5: The Distinctiveness of EAL: A Cross-Curriculum Discipline*. Watford: NALDIC.

SPEEL Study of Pedagogical Effectiveness in Early Learning Moyles J., Adams S., Musgrove A. (2002) Accessed 03.01.2009 www.dcsf.gov.uk/research/data/uploadfiles/RR363.pdf www.standards.dfes.gov.uk/eyfs/resources/downloads/pns_seal135405_gd2bme

Stephens, S. (1995) *Children and the Politics of Culture*. Chichester: Princeton University Press.

Sure Start (2003) *Birth to Three Matters*. London: Sure Start.

Sutherland, M. (2005) *Gifted and Talented in the Early Years: Practical Activities for Children aged 3 to 5*. London: PCP.

Sutherland, R., Claxton, G. and Pollard, A. (eds) (2003) *Learning and Teaching Where World Views Meet*. Stoke on Trent: Trentham Books.

Sylva, K., Melhuish, E., Sammons, P., Siraj-Blatchford, I., Taggart, B. and Elliot, K. (2003) *The Effective Provision of Pre-School Education Project: Findings from the Pre-School Period*. www.ioe.ac.uk/schools/ecpe/eppe/eppe/eppefindings.htm (accessed 10 October 2008).

Sylva, K., Melhuish, E.C., Sammons, P., Siraj-Blatchford, I. and Taggart, B. (2004) *The Final Report. Effective Pre-school Education*. London: DfES/Institute of Education University of London. www.surestart.gov.uk/_doc/P0001378.pdf (accessed 17 March 2009).

Taggart, G., Ridley, K., Rudd, P. and Benefield, P. (2005) *Thinking Skills in the Early Years: A Literature Review*. Slough: NFER.

UNESCO (2009) *World Education for All Monitoring Report*. Paris: United Nations Educational, Scientific and Cultural Organization. www.unesco.org.en.education (accessed xxxxx).

Vygotsky, L. (1978) *Mind in Society: The Development of Higher Psychological Processes*. Cambridge, MA : Harvard University Press.

Wallace, B. (2002) *Teaching Thinking Skills Across the Early Years*. London: David Fulton.

Waller, T. (2005) *An Introduction to Early Childhood: A Multidisciplinary Approach*. London: Paul Chapman Publishing.

Watson, J. and Wilcox, S. (2000) Reading for understanding: methods of reflecting on practice, *Reflective Practice*,1: 57–67.

Whitebread, D. and Coltman, P. (1996) *Teaching And Learning in the Early Years*. London: Routledge.

Whitmarsh, J. (2008) Negotiating the moral maze: developing ethical literacy in multi-agency settings, in I. Siraj-Blatchford, K. Clarke and M. Needham (eds) *The Team Around the Child: Multi-agency Working in the Early Years*. Stoke on Trent: Trentham Books.

Wigfall, V. and Moss, P. (2001) *More than the Sum of its Parts? A Study of a Multi-agency Child Care Network*. London: National Children's Bureau and Joseph Rowntree Foundation.

Wikipedia (2008) Poisonous plant list. www.en.wikipedia.org/wiki/List_of_poisonous_plants (accessed 23 December 2008).

Wood, E. and Attfield, J. (2005) *Play, Learning and the Early Childhood Curriculum*, 2nd edition. London: PCP.

Worthington, M. and Carruthers, E. (2003) *Children's Mathematics. Making Marks, Making Meaning*. London: Sage Publications.

ICT Recommendations from EYFS settings and schools

All Day To Play Suite (accessed 23 December 2008) www.boardworks.co.uk/all-day-to-play-suite_212/noscript

Facebook (accessed 23 December 2008) www.en-gb.facebook.com/

'Flying colours' (accessed 23 December 2008) www.magicmouse.com/h_flyingc.html

'Izzy's numbers, Izzy's Island' (accessed 23 December 2008) www.shop.sherston.com/products/details.aspx?p=1&prodId=106

Learning and Teaching Scotland (accessed 3 June 2008) www.ltsscotland.org.uk/earlyyears/images/benign_addition_tcm-122419.pdf

Letters and Sounds www.standards.dfes.gov.uk/local/clld/las.html (accessed 4 January 2008).

Literacy Trust www.literacytrust.org.uk (accessed 26 November 2008).

MAPE: Foundation Stage and ICT (accessed 3 June 2008) http://www.mape.org.uk/curriculum/earlyyears/foundation_ict.htm

Monterey Bay Aquarium (accessed 23 December 2008) www.mbayaq.org/efc/cam_menu.asp

Mouse Music (accessed 23 December 2008) www.themouseclub.co.uk/Shop/Mouse_Music/

Multiverse www.multiverse.ac.uk/ViewArticle2.aspx?anchorId=17844&selectedId=301&menu=17875&ContentId=13113 (accessed 3 December 2008) www.multiverse.ac.uk (accessed 3 January 2009).

'Natural Art' www.logo.com/rna/presentation.html

Partnership for Children www.partnershipforchildren.org.uk (accessed 27 December 2008).

PolkaDot Park Habitats (accessed 23 December 2008) www.shop.sherston.com/news.aspx?newsId=42&p=0&c=0

Promethean Interactive Whiteboards www.prometheanworld.com/index.php

SEN toolkit www.teachernet.gov.uk/wholeschool/sen/sentoolkit/ (accessed 2 January 2009).

Small size mouse for computer www.tts-group.co.uk/Product.aspx?cref=TTSPR595009
&rid=198&cid=4

SMART Interactive Whiteboard (accessed 23 December 2008) www.smarttech.com/

Sparklebox www.sparklebox.co.uk/.

TTS (accessed 23 December 2008).

One of several sites offering a range of ICT products suitable for use with children in
the EYFS www.tts-group.co.uk

RM Colourmagic (accessed 23 December 2008) www.rm.com/shops/rmshop/product.
aspx?cref=PD1105

2simple titles including 2 animate, 2 create a story, 2 calculate (accessed 23 December
2008) http://www.2simpleshop.com/

Wii (accessed 23 December 2008) www.nintendo.com/wii/

X-box (accessed 23 December 2008) www.xbox.com/en-GB/

Index

RETHINKING LEARNING IN EARLY CHILDHOOD EDUCATION

Nicola Yelland, Libby Lee, Maureen O'Rourke and Cathie Harrison

"I think a real strength of the book is the use of the case studies to ground the points made and to offer in-depth insights into practice."
Jackie Marsh, University of Sheffield, UK

This exciting book considers the nature of young children's lives and how this can, and should, inform early childhood education in practical ways. It examines:

- What is it like for young children to learn in the 21st century?
- How can we link this to new and innovative ways of providing relevant and engaging learning contexts for young children?
- What it means to be multiliterate in the 21st century

The book explores how learning and engagement with ideas can be extended through the use of new technologies, describing how information and communications technologies enable young people to extend the boundaries of their learning and social interactions.

These experiences have important implications for formal learning environments and the nature of the curriculum, including bold new approaches to teaching and learning which offer opportunities for children to investigate in new ways. This book provides examples of the ways in which early childhood teachers have extended opportunities for new types of learning for children by creating contexts in which they are able to explore and represent their ideas and thinking in multimodal formats using new technologies.

This book represents a research-based discussion for rethinking learning in the 21st century and includes various case studies and scenarios to enable students and practising teachers to try out new ideas. Finally, it considers new ways of thinking about children's learning by creating a multiliteracies portrait, pedagogies and pathways profile that enables teachers to build on their strengths to plan for effective learning outcomes.

Rethinking Learning in Early Childhood Education is key reading for students on Early Years courses or Primary Education pre-service teacher education programmes.

Contents: *Acknowledgements - About the authors - New millennium learners - Collective inquiry and a partnerships approach to change in education - Becoming multiliterate in contemporary times - Multimodality - Connecting with identities for enhanced learning - Engaging with diversity - Portraits, pedagogies and pathways - Pathways to the future - Appendices - References - Index.*

2008   184pp
978-0-335-22882-9 (Paperback)   978-0-335-22881-2 (Hardback)

UNDERSTANDING EARLY CHILDHOOD 2e
Issues and Controversies

Helen Penn

Review of the first edition:

"This book should be essential reading for every student of Early Childhood. Helen Penn is a highly regarded academic who has the rare ability to write simply and lucidly about complex issues. This eagerly awaited new edition provides a lively critical overview of the field. Highly recommended."

Professor Trisha Maynard, Head of the Department of Childhood Studies,
Swansea University, UK

Understanding Early Childhood provides students with a clear, user-friendly introduction to a number of difficult concepts and theories in early childhood education. Drawing on research evidence from various countries and reviewing studies about children from different disciplines - including anthropology, economics, history, psychology and sociology - it offers broad and insightful perspectives on the ways in which we understand and study young children.

Revised and updated throughout, the second edition covers contemporary theories and debates in a concise and accessible style. Unique features include:

- A critical discussion of child development
- A broad interdisciplinary approach
- A general overview of theoretical approaches and research methodologies
- New coverage of global trends about childhood.
- An important new chapter on the economics of early education and care
- Updates on the relevance of neuroscience and genetic research to early childhood
- 'What to read next' at the end of each chapter
- The ability to be used by varying levels of students

The book concludes with a postscript on the theme of interdisciplinary thinking and a critique of current policy initiatives in the UK.

Understanding Early Childhood is key reading for early childhood students and practitioners working with young children.

Contents: *Preface - Remembering childhood - Researching reality - Not Piaget again - Genes, neurons and ancestors - On the other side of the world - Past, present and future - Children's rights - What it costs and what it is worth: the economics of early childhood - Practice makes no difference - Postscript: an interdisciplinary approach? - References - Index.*

2008 232pp
978-0-335-22550-7 (Paperback)

EARLY YEARS FOUNDATIONS
Meeting the Challenge

Janet Moyles

With so many challenges facing early years professionals, there are continual dilemmas arising between doing what one knows is essentially 'right' for birth-to-five-year-olds from all backgrounds and conforming to the demands made by government and policy makers. This exciting and original book supports practitioners in thinking through their roles to meet some of the many issues they encounter.

Using the new *Early Years Foundation Stage* principles as its framework, the contributors support early years professionals in dealing with issues and challenges in a sensitive and professional manner, with particular emphasis upon the need for practitioners to personalise the requirements for each child in their care and to reflect closely upon their own and children's experiences.

The writers are all experienced and avid early years advocates. Their topics include: the changing landscape of early childhood, culture, identity and diversity, supporting playful learning, outdoor learning, documenting children's experiences, developing independence in learning, the meaning of being creative, play and mark-making in maths, and literacy.

Each section is introduced with some background research and information to provide evidence and guidance upon which practitioners can make their own decisions. Individual chapters include questions for reflection, points for discussion and suggestions for additional reading.

Early Years Foundations: Meeting the Challenge is essential reading for the full range of practitioners working and playing with birth-to-five-year-olds.

Contributors: *Deborah Albon, Pat Broadhead, Liz Brooker, Naima Browne, Elizabeth Carruthers, Tricia David, Dan Davies, Jackie Eyles, Hilary Fabian, Rose Griffiths, Alan Howe, Paulette Luff, Rod Parker-Rees, Theodora Papatheodorou, Emmie Short, David Whitebread, Marian Whitehead and Maulfry Worthington.*

Contents: *Notes on contributors - Introduction - Changing the landscape of early childhood - Section one: A unique child - Introduction - Primary communication: What can adults learn from babies? - Difference, culture and diversity: Challenges, responsibilities and opportunities - Identity and children as learners - Section two: Positive relationships - Introduction - Working together to support playful learning and transition - Somebody else's business: A parent's view of childhood - Coping with bereavement - Vision, mission, method: Challenges and issues in developing the role of the early years mentor teacher - Birth-to-three: The need for a loving and educated workforce - Section three: Enabling Environments - Introduction - The challenges of starting school - Children's outdoor experiences: A sense of adventure? - Written observations or walks in the park? Documenting children's experience - Food for thought: The importance of food and eating in early child-hood practice - Section four: Learning and development - Introduction - Developing independence in learning - What does it mean to be creative? - Multi-modality, play and children's mark-making in maths - 'Hi Granny! I'm writing a novel.' Literacy in early childhood: Joys, issues and challenges - Endpiece - Appendix - Index.*

2007   308pp
978-0-335-22349-7 (Paperback)   978-0-335-22348-0 (Hardback)